WILD PARTNERS

INDIGENOUS WORLDS AND INDUSTRIAL GIANTS IN PAPUA NEW GUINEA

WILD PARTNERS

INDIGENOUS WORLDS AND INDUSTRIAL GIANTS IN PAPUA NEW GUINEA

PATRICK GUINNESS

ANU PRESS

MONOGRAPHS IN
ANTHROPOLOGY SERIES

ANU PRESS

Published by ANU Press
The Australian National University
Canberra ACT 2600, Australia
Email: anupress@anu.edu.au

Available to download for free at press.anu.edu.au

ISBN (print): 9781760467159
ISBN (online): 9781760467166

WorldCat (print): 1548612913
WorldCat (online): 1548601515

DOI: 10.22459/WP.2025

Cover design and layout by ANU Press. Cover photograph: Hunters with forested Mount Ivi in background, 1974. Source: Patrick Guinness.

This book is published under the aegis of the Anthropology in Pacific and Asian Studies editorial board of ANU Press.

Contents

List of illustrations

Figures

Maps

Tables

Acronyms

AMF   Airmen's Memorial Foundation

AMS   Airmen's Memorial School

BOPGA   Bialla Oil Palm Growers Association

BP   Burns Philp

CLUA   Community Land Use Agreement

CRC   Christian Revival Crusade

DASF   Department of Agriculture, Stock and Fisheries

FFB   fresh fruit bunches of oil palm

HOPL   Hargy Oil Palm Ltd

ILG   incorporated land group

LACCA   Lamo Auru Community Conservation Association

LADC   Lamo Auru Development Corporation

LLG   local-level government

LSS   Land Settlement Scheme

MR   Malaysian Ringgit currency

NBPOL   New Britain Palm Oil

NGO   non-government organisation

OPIC   Oil Palm Industry Corporation

OPRA   Oil Palm Research Association

OWW   one-world world

P&C   Parents and Citizens

PNG   Papua New Guinea

RSPO   Roundtable on Sustainable Palm Oil

SABL	Special Agriculture and Business Lease
SDA	Seventh Day Adventist
SPPOD	South Pacific Palm Oil Development Pty Ltd
VOP	village oil palm

Acknowledgements

I have had a long association with the people of Bialla, West New Britain, that began with my recruitment to work for the Airmen's Memorial School (AMS) at Ewasse in 1968. I have Fred Hargesheimer, the founder of the school, and Fred Kaad, former district commissioner and lecturer at the Australian School of Pacific Administration, to thank for that. They eased my entry to Papua New Guinea and my acceptance among the school parents and teachers.

I owe a huge debt to all my kin and friends in the eight Maututu villages. Those in Baikakea and Bubuu provided me with a stable home, but I spent many days and nights across all the villages. I want to acknowledge in particular Tauvere and Koma, who became my 'father' and 'mother' in those initial years, and their children, Adi, Kava, Domc, Makoa, Kautu and Siamate, who, with their children, have been my family over 50 years, accommodating me through the long-term fieldwork and welcoming me back again after an absence of over 30 years. Lydia Gah, whom I first knew as a primary school student in 1968–69, contacted me 'out of the blue' 30 years later and encouraged me to return to see my mother before she died. There are so many others in West New Britain that I would love to name here, whom I recognise as kin and respect as leaders in their communities, but the list would cover several pages. They include the elders who first introduced me to Maututu ways of knowing and being, and their children and grandchildren who continue to teach me all I know of their world. They are the reason for my many return visits over these years.

My early fieldwork resulted in a master's thesis that I wrote at the University of Sydney in the Department of Anthropology under the supervision of Dr Jeremy Beckett. Jeremy was a generous guide in my exploration of Maututu myths and I was fortunate to have Dr Terence

Turner to examine the thesis and provide detailed comparative analysis from his South American material. They inspired me to probe into Maututu ways of knowing and being that are the basis of this account.

My academic colleagues at The Australian National University and La Trobe University have provided the scholarly and collegial support for my research in West New Britain. I have benefited in countless ways from our discussions and from my classes with students debating assumptions of development.

At ANU Press I am particularly grateful to Matt Tomlinson, editor of Anthropology in Pacific and Asian Studies, for his support and patience. This book has gone through a number of iterations and benefited substantially from the comments of three anonymous reviewers. I thank them all for their critical appraisal and their encouragement to complete the writing. I acknowledge the invaluable work of my copyeditor Dr Rani Kerin, and Karina Pelling of ANU CartoGIS Services for her work on the maps.

I began to write this account after that first return visit to Bialla in 2008. I made five further visits after that, incorporating my findings into seminar papers and research proposals, interspersed with the many other engagements of academic teaching. For that reason, it has taken much longer than I intended, and it is my wife Cathy Hales who has had to live with that. Her support and that of my sons, Daniel and Harry, have given me the confidence to document what is, for me, an important part of my life experience. I could not have done it without them.

Structure and terminology of the book

The account is informed by government records, historical accounts, my own observations through two critical decades (1965–75 and 2009–19) and the accounts of local actors. It focuses on four historical periods, two of which reflect my own interactions with West New Britain, at first in the late colonial days of 1968–75, and then more recently between 2009 and 2018. I link these ethnographic accounts with two other historical 'periods', the earlier colonial interface for which I gathered oral accounts in the villages and historical accounts from the archives, and the period 1975–2009 between my two ethnographic encounters when industrialisation came to dominate social and economic relations. Having been a participant in the earlier adoption of cocoa and the subsequent introduction of the new crop of oil palm, I brought my own aspirations and disappointments to the account of these transformations. Now, in looking back to those periods and in looking forward to the ongoing responses of multiple actors in West New Britain, I seek to understand more about those 'actions' and what they portray of the dynamics of such interactions.

Where convenient, I prefer to use Maututu spellings of placenames, though these names may be depicted otherwise on maps and documents. Thus, 'Uase' is often written as 'Ewasse', 'Apupulu' as 'Apupul' and 'Bubuu' as 'Bubu'. Mount Ivi is named Garagarasoilo or Galeseulo on many maps, but that name refers to a village site on its slopes, while the volcanic lake so central to Maututu identity is not Lake Hargy to them, but Lamo Auru. The Barema River is sometimes written Balima on maps. I shall use the name Ewasse when referring to the AMS school and the locus of the Nakanai Council and *kiap*'s headquarters because this was the spelling adopted by the colonial administration.

1

The wild and home

Facts force you to believe in them, perspectives encourage you to
believe out of them.

(Viveiros de Castro, 2012)

The unfortunate tendency of the (PNG) indigene … to cling to the
past, to traditions, to special beliefs that oppose the unknown.

(Bank, 1965, p. 37)

The small village of 100 or so people where I lived in 1968 was surrounded
by forest and mangroves. To reach the sea flats inside the coral reefs, residents
guided their outrigger canoes through vast stretches of mangroves. To reach
their gardens they used narrow, winding tracks through secondary forests.
Their gardens were won from primary and secondary forests and had to be
protected from the ravages of wild pigs, flocks of cockatoos and other birds,
and flying foxes. Beyond the gardens lay the deep forest, where hunters
sought wild game and fruits and where their families only ventured in the
company of others. At night the shadow of the forest seemed to hang over
the settlement and the risk of wild spirits became intense. In the months
of the wet season the rain could be heard approaching in a roar over the
surrounding forest, and the local creeks would swell until it became too
dangerous to bathe or collect drinking water. Residents huddled in their
sleep houses, built on stilts from bush materials, with their pigs and chickens
sheltering below, or retreated to their cook houses, built on the ground, to
sit around the fire and narrate accounts of daily events or ancestral myths.
This remains a vivid memory for me of Maututu life when I first lived in
West New Britain, Papua New Guinea (PNG), in 1968. I have come to
understand that this contrast between cleared settlement and threatening
forest framed how my village hosts understood much else in their lives.

This account posits that the Maututu of coastal West New Britain have their own distinctive view of and way of living with their world. This has not only allowed them to establish a presence within their ecological surrounds but continues to bring a distinctive perspective to the radical transformations they have faced over a century of 'development'. The term ontology refers to how a particular group of people understands things/entities of their world, what they are and how they are ordered. The term suggests something more deep-rooted than culture, particularly the concept of culture that is displayed and performed, as in the cultural performances of a multicultural society. Viveiros de Castro (2004, p. 5) describes ontologies as 'views from different worlds, not different perspectives on the same world'. They are different realities rather than different views of same reality. He suggests:

> The affirmation of alterity … signifies … that ontological questions are political questions insofar as they come into existence only in the context of friction and divergence between concepts, practices and experiences within or without culturally individuated collectives.
>
> (Viveiros de Castro, 2015, p. 9)

In the history of colonial and later independent administrations and so-called 'development' programs, certain ways of worlding are legitimised, while others are marginalised yet sustained. I find this a useful approach in constructing this account of a hundred years of transformation in this once remote part of PNG. This account explores the co-existence of multiple ways of knowing and multiple known worlds as these early residents came into contact with waves of outsiders. According to Arturo Escobar (2016), this produces friction between what he calls the 'one-world world' (OWW) of modernity and the pluriverse of local ontologies around which modernisation is played out. Escobar (2016, p. 15) describes the totalising logic of 'Euro-modernity', or OWW, as arrogating 'for itself the right to be "the" world, subjecting all other worlds to its own terms or, worse, to non-existence'. Such a totalising logic is 'the most effective means for the ontological occupation and ultimate erasure of local relational worlds' because the developments instituted by outsiders have 'effaced the relations maintained by the forest-world' (Escobar, 2016, p. 20). In the forest world that he described in South America, Escobar explored another world of indigenous people, marked by a relational ontology in which 'nothing preexist[s] the relations that constitute it. Said otherwise, things and beings are their relations, they do not exist prior to them' (Escobar, 2016, p. 18). He argued that many indigenous communities are 'advancing ontological struggles. The struggle to maintain multiple worlds—the pluriverse'[1]—that is, to pursue their own priorities and understandings in tandem with their engagement with outsiders (Escobar, 2016, p. 20). West New Britain scholar Andrew Lattas, citing both Foucault (1980) and Sahlins (1981), concludes that:

> Modernity's hegemony has always been mediated through local relations, practices and cultural forms that offer their own technologies of control and their own techniques for capturing and localising external powers.
>
> (Lattas 2011, p. 89)

In West New Britain, the forest world and the relations among humans and non-humans that constitute that reality provide a different perspective that has underlain people's response to 'modernity'.

The Maututu

The Maututu Nakanai live in eight villages strung in a north-south direction along the north coast of West New Britain around the new town of Bialla. Maututu tend to differentiate these into inland, mountain villages (Baikakea, Urumaili, Mataruru), seen as more traditional or authentically Maututu, and coastal villages (Bubuu, Apuupulu, Gomu, Uase and Matililiu). The term *maututu* translates as hamlets or villages (in the plural, the singular being *mautu*). The word *mautu* also refers to a tear in a cloth or in a range of mountains, such as is seen in the Nakanai Ranges around Mount Ivi behind Maututu territory (Figure 1.1). The proper noun 'Maututu' is said to be the name the Bileki Nakanai of the Hoskins Peninsular gave to the scattered hamlets with a distinctive dialect further along the coast of the eastern bay. Nakanai refers to the groups speaking variants of the one Austronesian language along the north coast of West New Britain, from the Barema River in the east to the western edge of the Hoskins Peninsular (Map 1.1).[2]

---

1   The 'pluriverse' is a way of looking at reality that contrasts with the OWW [one-world world] assumption that there is a single reality to which there correspond multiple cultures, perspectives, or subjective representations. For the pluriverse proposal, there are multiple reals, yet it is not intended to 'correct' the view on a single real on the grounds of being a truer account of 'reality'. The pluriverse is a tool to, first, make alternatives to the one world plausible to one-worlders, and, second, provide resonance to those other worlds that interrupt the one-world story.

(Escobar, 2016, p. 22)

2   Early researchers, such as Chowning, Goodenough and Valentine, preferred the term Lakalai to the term Nakanai, as the language spoken by these villagers had no phoneme 'n'. Nakanai was probably the term given to these people by the western Tolai of the Gazelle for whom Nakanai means 'seagull'. Ray Johnston, who worked among the Bileki, insisted that contemporary villagers preferred the term Nakanai. Nakanai is now widely accepted by villagers throughout the area, and by researchers, as the name for the larger language, within which numerous dialects persist.

Figure 1.1: Mount Ivi from down the coast, 1968
Source: Author.

In the 1960s, located through the vast forest between the Hoskins Bileki and the Maututu, lived the Pulabe/Kulabe/Muku Nakanai at the eastern inland end of the Hoskins Peninsular, including the villages of Kerapi and Malalia; the Kukula/Vele Nakanai of the Tarobi Peninsular; the Ouka/Loso Nakanai,[3] the Uase and the Mamusi/Sa (non-Nakanai) speakers of the Central Nakanai Mountains around Uasilau and Silanga; the Masegi/Ubae Nakanai of Ubae and Lavege; and a non-Nakanai group, the Peleata, south of the Tiauru River that bordered Maututu territory. Beyond the Maututu area, along the coast to the north, were the Meramera people of Ubili and Lolobau as far as Nantambu;[4] inland lived the Pelevavu/Mengen/Maenge of Gigipuna and the mountains towards the south coast. Hours of walking through the vast forest or canoeing the coastal waters separated these scattered settlements. While Maututu hamlets were in regular contact and exchange, they rarely associated with their non-Nakanai neighbours whom they saw as *moimosi* (strangers, enemies).

---

3   Van Rijswijck (1966) refers to the Ouka/Loso people as Nakanai speakers living in Silanga in Central Nakanai. Both *ouka* and *loso* mean 'no'.
4   Meramera was seen by some as a Nakanai dialect, but more recently has been determined as a separate language.

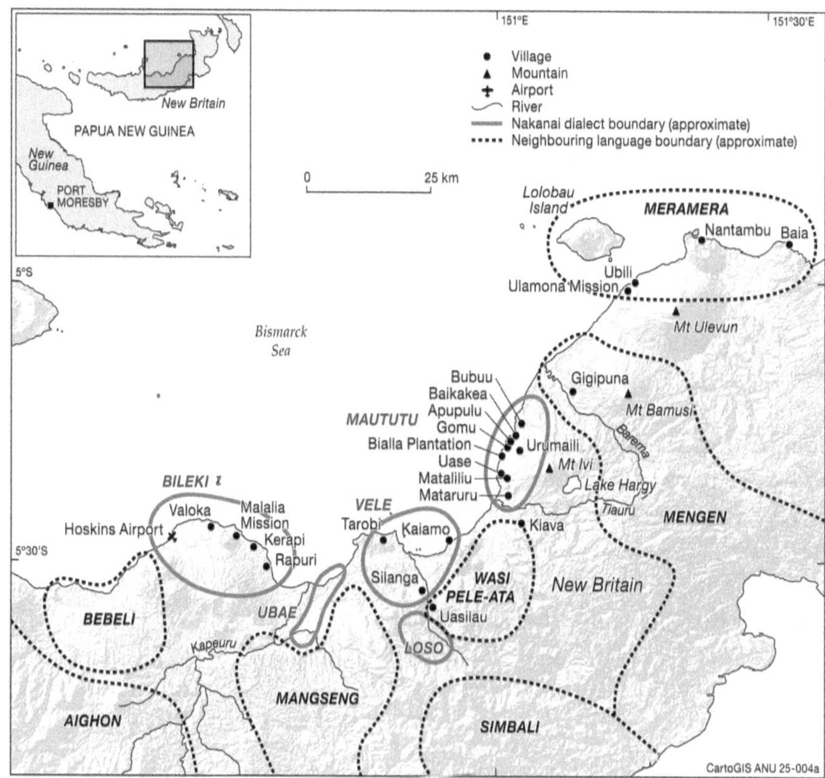

Map 1.1: West New Britain languages
Source: ANU CartoGIS Services.

The wild and home

The perception of Maututu as scattered hamlets within a vast forest on the slopes of Mount Ivi understands such communities as enclosed within formidable areas of 'wildness'. The concept of 'wild' referred to in this account is a perspective I learned from the Maututu, although there is no single Maututu word I would translate as 'wild'. The Maututu refer to the 'wild' domain beyond the settlement and its gardens as *o-gala* or *o-bali* (outside, foreign, strange) or *la hoihoi* (dark forest) or *la moimosi* (hostile agents).[5] It surrounds the settlement and is in constant articulation with residents. Male hunters ventured into the forest as far as the towering

---

5   The prefix *lo-* indicates direction 'from', *so-* and *go-* direction 'towards' while the prefix *o-* indicates presence in a space. Thus *lo-gala*, *so-gala*, *go-gala* and *o-gala*.

cliffs of the Nakanai Ranges in search of pigs, wallabies and cassowaries (Figure 1.2). They waded the streams for eels, fish and crayfish, and groups of men and women journeyed into the forest to harvest the wild almonds when in season. As some acquired shotguns, they hunted flying foxes and birds in the forest canopies. In their cycles of shifting agriculture, they felled the forest for gardens, always leaving fruit trees intact, and, after two or three years, abandoned the gardens to return to forest until 15 or 20 years later when it was reopened. When a hamlet was abandoned, a frequent event in the past, the wild reclaimed it with little but an abandoned stone oven or domestic plant to mark its former existence. In addition to the hamlet names, the forest is dotted with individually named trees of significance, such as almond (*uele*), binuang (*koimu/Octomeles sumatrana*) and breadfruit (*ulu*). Former and current hamlets are often identified with a valued, individually named tree located there. The name 'Baikakea', for example, refers to a jackfruit tree with white seeds and 'Saikoiko' to a *saiogi* (strangler fig) tree. In Urumaili, the hamlets of Popogo, Loko, Teiviria, Sibili, Marapu and Vaele are named for mango trees, and Likiliki, Koioke, Pori, Poposi and Takile te Kosi are named for almond trees.

Figure 1.2: Hunters with forested Mount Ivi in background, 1974
Source: Author.

The Maututu hamlet is seen as *o-luma* (home), a settlement that extended out toward the forest as gardens were created. Maututu do not seek to cut themselves off from the 'wild' but to learn from it and to negotiate a replenishment of their lives with it. In distinction to *go-gala* (go outside, into the strange), they use specific directional terms when visiting neighbouring settlements: *o-muli* (north along the coast) to one neighbouring settlement, *o-ale* (south along the coast) to another, *o-lau* (seawards) or *o-rai* (inland) to others, and *o-talo* (downwards) to more remote settlements west along the coast. The various hamlets of the Maututu world are linked through these directional indicators by well-trod pathways of exchange and ritual. The garden location is indicated as *o-rivo*. This is an intermediate location, on the edge of the settlement, and a space that, in the past, was vulnerable to attack by *la moimosi* (strangers), sorcerers and wild spirits. It is an extension of the 'home' won from the forest and destined to return to the 'wild'. When a person dies, kin and village mates refrain from going to the gardens for three or four days. If they fail to observe this taboo, the spirits of the dead person's clan will consume all the food in the garden, generally through devastation by birds and wild pigs. Beyond the gardens is *la hoihoi* (forest), located *o-ilo* (in the interior of the island) or *o-ata* (above on the mountain slopes). The marine domain beyond the coral reefs that line the coast is also seen as wild and dangerous, and signified as *ogala*.

Maututu elders described to me the past scattering of peoples in small hamlets. They identified many sites of abandoned settlements located inland of present villages, extending high into the mountains. Sometimes these sites were marked by croton plants (its leaves used as dance regalia), or coconut or betel nut palms, or even stone oven remains. But no trace remained of former houses. According to the narrative of one elder, all Maututu originated in the hamlet of Mautu on the inland slope of Mount Ivi, the long-extinct volcano that signals Maututu territory for those travelling by canoe along the coast.[6] In another account, Tubisu was the original settlement.[7] The origin myth narrated below identifies another hamlet, Lamo Auru, later inundated by the 'flood' that filled Ivi caldera; still others listed 25 hamlets that had spread out from the original Tubisu. Another elder informed me that, in the past, there were no Maututu living along the coast; the only hamlets were in the hills. According to this elder, the coastal hamlets were only established when Maututu moved down from the hills to access saltwater and sago palm

---

6   On many maps, Mount Ivi is labelled Galeseulo, a designation derived from Maututu reference to *la gale soilo* (interior region) or Garagarasoilo, a hamlet in the interior. Within its extinct volcanic crater lies the great lake or 'great inland sea' Lamo Auru, designated Lake Hargy on maps.
7   In this account told to me by the Bialla magistrate, people from Tubisu spread to three hamlets, Balive, Garagarasoilo, and Matamaglsi, and from there spread to 20 hamlets that he named for me.

roofing materials. Others suggested that the coastal hamlets were established by Bileki Nakanai fleeing the eruption of the volcano Pago in 1911–18, and by Meramera fleeing the eruption of the volcanoes Ulevun, Bamusi and Lolobau.[8] These histories indicate turbulent times when the wild of the forest world, volcanic eruptions and hamlet hostilities threatened 'home', leading to flight to new locations. This story was repeated during the Second World War.

When households moved residence, they would take the volcanic stones of their ovens with them, because these were difficult to obtain, but the houses themselves would be left to disintegrate. Houses in the past were constructed on the ground from bush timber and pandanus leaf, with sleeping platforms raised above ground adjacent to the stone oven. Maututu told me that they moved residence frequently—to access new garden sites, to link with lineage kin or to escape violence. Each hamlet was centred on the men's house (*la hulumu*) established by the resident *tahalo auru* (big man) who organised the labour of his affiliates, as was the pattern elsewhere in New Britain (Zelenietz & Grant, 1986). Male strangers to the hamlet came directly to the men's house, where they were offered betel nut and where enquiries were made of their intentions. The elders' accounts gave me an overwhelming impression of small groups of people travelling through vast realms of forest, wresting a living in their accommodation with surrounding wild agents. They stressed that such hamlets were cleared spaces within the larger forest (*la hohoi*). Even today, Maututu, and women in particular, painstakingly sweep to the edge of the hamlet weeds and leaf matter, as well as human and animal waste, in an attempt to keep the wild at bay.

Maututu refer to the pre-colonial past as the time of *la gata* (the spear), referring to the fighting between Maututu and intruders from adjacent areas. They tell of their ancestors palisading their hamlets and boarding their house walls against attacks. Persons of different hamlets intermarried but also fought, the relationship with a different hamlet being unpredictable and therefore dangerous. A young man entering a sexual/marital relationship with a partner from another hamlet threatened the relations between settlements, and the couple might be confronted with spears even in the man's own hamlet until an exchange of valuables could be transacted to establish relations with the bride's group. If a man was killed in another hamlet, the dead man's father would reclaim his body, seemingly in acceptance of what had happened, but secretly send ginger to surrounding hamlets to summon

---

8   Pago last erupted in 1933; before then, it erupted in 1920, and it erupted six times in the 500 years prior. The last known eruption of Lolobau was in 1912, while Ulevun (The Father) has erupted 22 times between 1700 and 2019. Nearby Bamusi (South Son) last erupted in 1886, rupturing the cone.

them to war. They would surround the offending hamlet at night and attack it at first light, killing up to five men and/or women, and taking pigs and valuables. But they might also be ambushed in their attack or repulsed by the ginger spells of the hamlet under attack. The feud would only end when the upper arm bone of the original victim was disinterred and attached to a spear that was then used to kill the first stranger to enter the hamlet. Hence, the feud could take several months to resolve. More often, the wounding of one or two on each side by *la gata* would bring the skirmish to an end. Chowning (1969) indicates that, among the Bileki Nakanai, it was common to fight even with those who shared the same culture and language. In these fights, clan mates from either side would ensure they did not attack each other. In 1972, I was told by one hamlet elder that his hamlet used to be much larger, but the residents were killed off by sorcery and in-fighting. Filer and Sekhran (1998, pp. 9–10) observe:

> Melanesian communities have always been on the verge of disintegration, even in pre-colonial times, and it has always taken special qualities of leadership, in each succeeding generation, to prevent them from splitting apart at the seams. In pre-colonial times, such efforts were directed to the pursuit of warfare; the practice of initiation, and the organisation of large-scale gift-exchange, but the rules of these games were no more permanent than the social groups whose continuity depended on the outcome.

Figure 1.3: Singers congregate around the slit-gong for dance rehearsal, 1973

Source: Author.

Figure 1.4: Dance partners perform *e rae*, 2017
Source: Author.

Maututu dance portrays the tension between the home and the wild. At the large feasts called *mage*, men perform *e rae*, a dance that portrays hunters leaving the village *galamo* (slit-gong) to counter the dangers of the forest (Figures 1.3 and 1.4). Slit-gongs are generally considered the property of a particular 'big man' and of his clan or hamlet, and in the past were kept in the men's house as a focus of hamlet song and dance. For performances, the slit-gong is brought to the centre of the hamlet arena and the senior men and women cluster around it to sing the songs that guide the dancers. To prepare for this dance, dancers enter a hideout in the forest environs of the hamlet and emerge dressed in the plants and feathers of the wild. As they emerge the men can chop down saplings and even betel nut palms and damage houses in the vicinity of their preparation area without reproach from their fellow residents. The dancers take their places, squatting in two long lines in front of the slit-gong and its singers; as the song gathers volume, they rise, moving back and away in particular formations. Dancers impress their audience with their energy, the ground shaking with their stamping, but at the end of each dance sequence they return to squat before the slit-gong and its singers. The dance thus vividly portrays the contrast between their calmness at the base of the slit-gong and the energy and wildness with which they move away from it. In some sequences, each pair of dancers attack one another with the motion of throwing spears before reuniting and returning to the slit-gong.

Paradoxically, the wild is portrayed as the source of new life. New songs and dances, cures and spells all derive from the forest where ancestral and spirit beings or stranger populations roam. The song language is said to be that of *la moimosi* Mengen people of Gigipuna. I return to this paradox in the next chapter. The domain beyond the hamlet is rich in material and spirit resources, but unpredictable and dangerous for communities seeking a relationship with its wild inhabitants. Maututu villagers are keenly aware of the spirits who live in the forest and engage with villagers. Over the years people narrated matter-of-factly to me their encounters with such spirits in their travels to gardens or through the forest. Valentine (1961) provided vivid accounts of masked dancers among the Bileki in the 1950s who became spirits or were possessed by spirits during their performance. The spirits within the masks could be petitioned to keep the community safe during the galip nut season, when malevolent spirits, attracted by the rich harvests, might invade the village.[9] The main spirit threat for the Bileki Nakanai was *tamala Gaike* (father of Gaike) who came from the dangerous volcano Mount Pago and who was reported to have brought sickness and death to Maututu villagers after ravaging Bileki villages.[10]

The Maututu world of spirits is diverse. Foremost are the spirits of the ancestors who are most feared in the immediate period after death when they are thought to be wandering near the hamlet before settling in forest spaces beyond. In mortuary rituals, a dance *siloa* was performed in which two men were hoisted onto a platform carried on the shoulders of their comrades and there conducted a fight with spears, one of the dancers said to be facing *soluma* (towards the village settlement) and the other facing *sorivo* (towards the gardens and forest). The dance thus represented the radical divide between human settlement and the spirit abode that was brought to prominence by any death.

Savei (Bileki *hitu*) describes a general category of human-like spirits 'with arms'; the term is also used for ancestral spirits. *Savei* (plural *saveivei*) are thought to accompany, invisibly, human performers in *e rae* dances. Sometimes individuals travelling through the forest meet a *savei* whom they mistake for a fellow villager and are only aware that it is a spirit when that fellow villager tells them later that they were elsewhere at the time. *Buata* are grotesque giant spirits who inhabit a particular tree or have a hole at the base of a tree or rock. *Visu* fly through the air, their whole body lit up; however, they can be scared away by 'blowing a raspberry' with one's lips, sounding like a fart. *Kuara* is a *savei* spirit mounted on a bird and holding a spear.

Maututu stress the unpredictability and danger of encounters with all such spirits. When my village 'sister' Adi was processing sago in the swamplands, a black snake wrapped itself around her legs. She freed herself but her arms and legs became covered with black scales, and she fell sick 'close to death'. A black snake also appeared to the family when they occupied a block on the edge of the forest. Adi's husband found it wrapped around their radio one night and, having ushered his family outside, he killed it. However, a drop of its blood fell on his daughter and she fell sick and died in hospital the same day.

---

9   The galip nut season was seen as a time of increased sexual activity and elopements and was also a time when the spirit world intruded into village affairs.

10 The Maututu area is ringed by volcanoes, such as Pago to the west and Bamusi and Ulevun to the east, although only the extinct volcanic crater of Ivi is in the Bialla area. Volcanic fumes from these volcanoes drift into the Bialla area and can cause respiratory illness even today.

There are also spirits with whom people feel familiarity. *Taua* occupy sites in the forest considered sacred to a particular clan or lineage and may be identified as totems (*ruvu*) of the clan and/or lineage.[11] They may protect clan members but injure strangers. They are sometimes referred to as *la tahalo* (human) and may appear in human forms. A large snake, a *taua*, is said to occupy the bush near the Baikakea stream, a 'human', villagers say. On death, a person's spirit joins the *taua* of their clan at the sacred site, and when a child is sick a grandparent may journey to the site and place there a gold-lip shell or a spear in request for the child's recovery. After an hour or so, the valuable is recovered and taken home, its task effected. Maututu thus acknowledge spirits, whether they take natural or supernatural forms, as human in their relationships with people. They demonstrate 'capacities for conscious intentionality and agency' (Viveiros de Castro, 2012, p. 99). 'Wild' agents have the potential to engage in relations with those who occupy the 'home' space.

The juxtaposition of wild and home is also found in Maututu personality distinctions. Maututu, like the Bileki, categorise their fellows in terms of two broad personality types (Valentine, 1963, p. 29): men and women of anger/talk/movement/hyper-sexual activity (*tao la tulugala*); and men and women of shame/silence/sitting in secret (*tao la pou makovula*). Valentine (1963, p. 457) summarises the first type as individuals who, among other characteristics, are active, aggressive, explosive and impulsive, with shifting consciousness and oriented outward, while the 'home' type are passive, subdued, inhibited and oriented inward. Anger and explosive behaviour is of the wild; at the other extreme—of the hamlet—is shame and passivity. The times of *la gata*, according to Maututu storytellers, were dominated by people of anger and violence who had little respect (*tilogo*) or compassion (*gilogo*). Such men would chew ginger in the garden without drinking water and their 'livers' would become hot and their tempers brittle.[12] An angry man (*la tahalo la igototolola*) might spear his wife, brother, father or clan mate.

Maututu storytellers explore these personality types through humorous tales of rivalry between 'Orphan Dog' and 'Big Man Wallaby' (Guinness, 1973). The Maututu term for orphan is *latula gola* (child of *gola*, a chew of food or betel nut transferred to someone incapable of chewing, such as infants or toothless old men and women). The orphan, thus, is seen as handicapped

---

11 This term became used to refer to the Christian God.
12 Ginger is a key ingredient in both sorcery and healing spells. It may also stimulate a person to fits of anger.

by the absence of parents and close kin. On the other hand, the *tahalo auru* (big man) is known for his network of kin and affiliates who cooperate with him in organising large feasts (*la mage*). The genre of stories featuring Orphan Dog and Big Man Wallaby exaggerate the distinction between a figure of shame and a bombastic leader. Village dogs spend much of the day lying in the dirt and ashes around a house, active only when they fight over scraps of food randomly thrown their way or over a bitch in heat. Humans pay them no attention apart from kicking them out of the way or throwing stones in their direction to break up the squealing fights. But they are essential to the hunter in sniffing out and chasing wild pigs and wallabies. While a pig is usually cornered by a pack of dogs and can then be speared, wallabies can outwit dogs by jumping over logs and creeks or suddenly turning to leap back over the pursuing dogs. Hunters recount with humour encounters in the forest between their dogs and wallabies, which are not prized game like wild pigs.

In this genre, Orphan Dog is derided by Wallaby as lazy and good for nothing or *vauta* (deaf, foolish, forgetful, mad).[13] He is the epitome of the *tao la pou makovula*. At the other extreme, Wallaby is portrayed, sarcastically, as a 'big man' (*tahalo auru*). Wallaby is unpredictable, a figure of impetuosity, anger and aggression. In the best-known story of this genre, the two figures constantly deceive each other. Wallaby tricks Orphan Dog into eating an unfamiliar wild 'fruit'—in reality, Wallaby's faecal droppings. He also tricks Orphan Dog into burning his paws/palms on the hot coals on which Wallaby is roasting wild breadfruit seeds. In response, Orphan Dog tricks Wallaby into biting off his penis or poking his arms into a giant reef clam that amputates them (Guinness, 1973). Wallaby is referred to as a 'big man', but his behaviour destroys any respect he has in his community. He is not capable of sex nor of effectively building a house in the village and is eventually either killed or driven into the wild. He is despotic and violent rather than generous and caring of kin and wives, and his wife seeks other sexual partners, further inciting Wallaby's tyrannical outbursts. Orphan Dog, on the other hand, grows into a respected and sexually attractive young man because of his sensitivity to hamlet kin and ancestral spirits.

---

13   Sometimes the expatriate *kiap* or plantation manager was referred to as *latula gola*, reflective of Maututu judgements of the white *masta*, who sat around all day rather than going to the gardens or doing other manual work, and who was seemingly without social connections.

Big man Wallaby held a feast to initiate his two sons by crowning their heads with a feathered headdress. His nephew Orphan, exhausted from working alone in the gardens, lay ignored in the ashes of his fire. Wallaby derided him, suggesting that his two sons in their finery would inspire Orphan's wives to desert him. Orphan responded by setting up his bird nets high in the mangrove trees and netting many kinds of bird. As he did so the crumbs from the yam he was eating fell to the ground and were noticed by his spirit grandparent.[14] The spirit called him down and when Orphan hesitated through fear of being eaten the spirit grandparent asked rather to share his yam. He told Orphan to roast the birds he had eaten, feathers and all, and share them with his family, and then return next day with a fibre string.

The next day Orphan again netted birds in the same spot and tied them alive with the string, which he handed to his grandparent. The spirit advised Orphan to take no part in Wallaby's feast preparations. This only increased Wallaby's jibes. Orphan confided to his wives that he was staying with his forest grandparent and that on the day of the dance festival they should go out on the forest path to await his arrival. At the festival as Wallaby's two sons were paraded there was a huge disturbance as Orphan made his appearance, carried by wild spirits who danced and hooted while trees fell around them, his head crowned with live birds. No-one could see the spirits but Wallaby's betel nut palms collapsed to their song. The wives of Wallaby and those of his two sons ran to Orphan. Orphan instructed them to place gifts of taro and pig on the forest track for the spirits to take away, and he and the women departed to his grandparent's hamlet. When Wallaby and his sons tried to prevent them from leaving, Orphan speared the big man in his armpits and his tail such that he whimpered to his sons for help. Orphan and the women did not return.

In village life, the individual who does not cultivate relations with others is perceived as dangerous. They are seen to spend much time out of the hamlet, *ogala* (in the wild), cultivating harmful attributes, such as sorcery that they acquire from *la moimosi* (strangers). Maututu attribute sorcery to those who are socially distant, such as an unmarried man or one who suffers disabilities that make it difficult for him to take part in social life. The sorcerer (usually male) is marked by his restlessness (*tulugala*) and solitariness. Maututu perceive such persons as socially irresponsible. The sorcerer belongs to the wild, loitering in the forest beyond the village to waylay hapless villagers. There he renders them unconscious, before extracting their liver (the 'core of life'), sewing them up and restoring them to consciousness. However, on return to the village, they fade away within a few days and die. Thus, when

---

14 The term for grandparent, *tubu*, is not gender specific.

a hamlet resident unexpectedly falls sick or weak he/she is assumed to have had an encounter with a sorcerer or harmful spirit. An 'angry' resident might even pay a sorcerer to kill an enemy. Some Maututu in the 1960s and 1970s denied that sorcery was still practised. But, in 1968, a sorcery package of hair and dirt was found in the church. People claimed it was left there by someone supplicating the Christian God to kill their victim. One woman, Ita, told me of the day she lost her daughter. She and her daughter were in the garden when she saw two men from 'across the mountains' standing nearby. She and her daughter hurried home but by the time they arrived her eight-year-old daughter's eye was swollen right out of its socket; she died later that same day.

Marilyn Strathern (1980) records a similar juxtaposition of wild and home among the Hageners, people from the Mount Hagen area in the Western Highlands Province of PNG. In her account, wild and domestic differ in terms of essence or character, and spirits may be recognised as 'wild' or 'good'. Hageners associate the domestic with confinement, the mundane and the dull, and the wild with the exotic and the foreign. According to her: 'Wild is best thought of as a category of power located outside the bounds of those relationships that rest on nurture' (Strathern, 1980, p. 199). While Hagen males have more ready access to the spirit world and to exotic powers, Strathern warns against assuming that Hageners make any categorical association of males with the wild and females with the domestic. Similarly, the Maututu distinction of wild and home constitutes a perspectival framework in which multiple realities can be conceived, whether of human and animal, of human and spirit, of personality types or of moral behaviour, or, indeed, of gendered relations.

Wild and domestic in gender relations

Some of the stories narrated above indicate the centrality to Maututu of gender relations, particularly those of sexual relations and marriage. Orphan Dog, for example, triumphs as the husband of multiple wives, and it is clear that these women make a decision to join him. While the stories link women with *o-luma* (home) and men with the wild outside, Orphan Dog departs with his wives for the 'wild' abode of his spirit grandparent. Other myths narrate how woman taught man to have sex with her, how she discovered the coconut or fruit tree, and how she established relations with the spirit world. But in these myths, as in their daily lives, women preserved the domestic settlement and, together with men, worked the village gardens on the margin of the forest. Men penetrated the deeper forest, encountering wild game and wild spirits. Women only ventured there to harvest the wild almond trees or to get to another settlement—and not without the risk of harm by spirits or strangers.

However, any association of female gender with the domestic and male with the wild is confounded by the pattern of women marrying into the hamlet of their husband and, in so doing, initiating a new matrilineage in the hamlet. In such exogamous marriages, her children acknowledged their matrilineage-mates, particularly their mother's brother, living in another hamlet, and it was expected that adolescents would live for some time with their mother's brother in his hamlet. The matrilineage (*maratatila*: from *mara* 'side', *tatila* 'mothers') of a 'big man' and his brothers might comprise the core of a hamlet; yet, invariably, their close kin lived outside in the origin hamlet of their mother. Thus, the women at 'home' never lost their association with their outside origin place and kin.

It is difficult to determine the nature of gender relations in the pre-colonial and early colonial years, before mission teaching imposed a range of new gender norms. Gender relations may have been more fraught. An elder told me in 1972 that in the past there was intense scrutiny of contact between a man and a woman outside marriage. If a man returned to his house and found another man who was not a close family member or friend sitting there, he would spear him immediately. If a man encountered a married woman on the track, he would step aside with his back to the track until she passed and would break off a branch of a tree at that spot. On returning home, the woman would report the meeting to her husband who would check whether there was evidence of a broken branch at the spot. If not, he would immediately spear the man. It was more usual for men in pre-contact times and into the 1960s to socialise and sleep in the men's house. They might go 'home' (*goluma*) to their wife to eat, but the women also brought cooked food to the men's house where it would be shared. An adolescent boy would leave his mother's 'home' and join the men's house, and even as a younger child would spend time there. Women at times were seen as dangerous to men, including their husbands. A man avoided sexual relations with his wife before hunting or fishing for fear that contact with her would spoil his hunt; a menstruating woman warned her husband to avoid her and took rigid precautions not to touch his food. When a woman became pregnant her husband would have no further sexual relations with her until the child was weaned at about three years old. Most feared in the spirit world was the *kalulu* (ghost) of women, Pigobara, who had died in childbirth. Pigobara chased men and attempted to stuff the umbilical cord down their throats or strangle them with it.

In certain ceremonies women became the 'wild' ones. At the feast to mark a girl's first menstruation, unmarried women chased the men, cutting them with stones, razors or sticks, burning them with firebrands or setting their clothes alight. Men told these stories and revealed such wounds as items of pride, but the wounds could be serious, leaving permanent scars on the man's body. Such personal attacks could also climax in sexual relations between the two. When *e rae* is performed by men, women are not mere spectators. While the men are absent on the village outskirts dressing themselves in the paraphernalia of the wild, the more 'extrovert' women of the host hamlet become the centre of attention. One or two women known for their greater assertiveness and mobility (*tao la tulugala*) become clowns, dressing like men and caricaturing male behaviours to the hilarity of the large crowd of attendees. As the male dancers emerge, women may dance alongside their favourite man, perhaps their son, husband or desired lover. They may snatch the long stalks of the pitpit grass (distinctively a female plant in the myths) and whip a male dancer whom they desire. A woman's violent attentions to the dancer may culminate in her chasing him into the forest, where sex may take place. This is called *vakakuala* (to make cry out; *kaku* is the cry a woman utters, often in pain, or the howl of the village dog). Chowning (1989, p. 86) considered that the *vakakuala* effectively contradicts the statement that men always take the initiative in sexual matters, concluding, rather, that it signifies a balance in the relative strengths of the two genders. She reported on the Bileki in the 1950s (p. 19):

> Prior to marriage a girl could travel to other villages, participate in many ceremonies and dances, and enjoy sexual affairs so long as she did not become pregnant or get a reputation for promiscuity. All this freedom ended with marriage; fidelity was enjoined on her and enforced by the close supervision of her mother-in-law, while her husband was expected to continue to enjoy himself until he became a grandfather.

Some contemporary Maututu women suggested to me that gender relations in these ancestral times were far more balanced than the present day. Lydia Gah, who was among the first Maututu women to complete high school in the 1970s and then a university degree, married a non-Maututu and worked for much of her life in other areas of PNG and Australia (Gah 2020). In her autobiography, she detailed the domestic violence she suffered from her first (non-Maututu) husband. In a moving poem she identifies such violence with a monster, not unlike some of the wild ogres of Maututu myths:

> Shrouded behind the mysticism of Melanesian culture,
> Lies an untouchable monster,
> Wracking the lives of blossoming roses,
> Once the pride of families, clans and tribes
> Yet, towering menacingly high above dark clouds
> The monster looks on with an intent to wreck one more life
> …
> The evil monster exists and perpetuates its destruction,
> Against women and innocent children in Melanesian societies.
>
> (Gah, 2020, pp. viii–ix)

White people (*wokakea*) as wild intruders

European settlers established coconut plantations in the Blanche Bay area of the Gazelle Peninsular in East New Britain from the 1870s. To protect German trading interests, the German Government annexed Kaiser Wilhelmsland (north-eastern New Guinea) and the Bismarck Archipelago (New Britain and New Ireland) in 1884. From 1885 to 1899, German New Guinea was a protectorate ruled by the Neu Guinea Compagnie, a plantation and trading company. It was replaced from 1900 to 1914 by the German colonial administration. Maututu first became aware of these 'outsiders' through trading contacts they had with the Tolai of East New Britain and the Duke of York Islands, who came to the Maututu coast in search of *la tubeli* (*tambu*/nassarius shell). In 1896–97, a German expedition investigating a smallpox epidemic visited the Nakanai north coast under Dr Habl, accompanied by a Catholic missionary, Father Rascher (van Rijswijck, 1966, pp. 5–6). In 1901, the Catholic Missionaries of the Sacred Heart built a sawmill to the north of Maututu territory to supply timber for their buildings on the Gazelle, and, in 1928, they established the Ulamona Mission there to provide services to the Meramera people (McKillop & Pearson, 1997). Possibly the first direct contact of Maututu with such strangers was in 1912 when the Neu Guinea Compagnie acquired under 'freehold title' 800 hectares at Bialla in the centre of the Maututu domain, probably by the payment of valued goods, such as steel axes, bush knives, tobacco and cloth, to the resident hamlet populations.[15] The company signalled its appropriation of the area by nailing a tin plate inscribed with its name to a tree by the seaside. However, it did not develop the site and no German manager settled in the area. Elders in the 1960s suggested to me that their ancestors continued to hunt in the forest and the streams in the 'freehold' area, unaware that their territory had been acquired by strangers.

There was a complete disregard among expatriates for how the 'natives' perceived their world and such 'outside' intruders. Expatriates brought a very different perspective to bear on their life in the administered territory. Albert Hahl, appointed imperial judge to the Gazelle in 1896, later governor of German Neu Guinea, recorded his earliest impressions of the few expatriates then living on the Gazelle as traders, planters and missionaries:

> The unanimous conclusion [of the expatriates] was that any economic progress depended on inducing the natives to work for the Europeans and on increasing the demand for trade goods, that is increasing the purchasing power of the natives. However one section of those Europeans with local experience ruled out all possibility of any influence over the natives. They maintained that the contrast between our way of life and their stone-age culture was so extreme that the weaker party must inevitably go under. In this the New Guinea natives would only be following in the footsteps of the Australian Aborigines and other extinct races. Others on the other hand maintained that it was in fact possible to exert an influence but that this must be left entirely to the missions. Any attempt by the Government to influence them by training them in habits of peace, obedience and external order must fail.
>
> (Hahl, 1980, pp. 9–10)

Clear in this assessment is that the native way of life was viewed as not only culturally distinct, but also inferior and largely irrelevant to European progress in the colony. It was up to the Europeans to 'develop' the land and generate profit from cash crops and other trade. Any humanitarian concern for the natives should be left to the missionaries who, of course, had their own ontological priorities. The outbreak of the First World War in 1914 brought a halt to German and Neu Guinea Compagnie ambitions but opened the way for other 'strangers' under an Australian administration.

---

15 The Neu Guinea Compagnie had extensive plantings in the Gazelle.

In 1914, Australian troops asserted military rule over German Neu Guinea. Seven years later, the Australian Government took over. As Filer and Lowe (2011, p. 156) note:

> When the Australian Government took formal control of the area in 1921 it promptly embarked on a programme of expropriating German land assets and selling them to new [European] owners in order to secure war reparations. This process was completed by 1927.

Valentine (1963) reviewed in detail the society of New Britain in the early years of the twentieth century, characterising it as a caste society, established first under German and then Australian colonial administrations, in which Europeans assumed their own superiority in respect of material welfare, social status and ideological convictions over the lower 'castes' of Asian and native peoples. To the expatriate planters, the native population was 'stone-age', lacking any appreciation for German habits of 'peace, obedience and external order'. However, Valentine (1963, pp. 378–79) notes that the native groups were open to change:

> The general posture of the native population in the contact period was one of acceptance of innovation … the generally peaceful nature of the process, and the continuous voluntary manifestation of native interest in alien ways shows that the native societies were basically open to change.

Because the Australian Government provided limited finance to the colony, most of the energies of the early administration were directed towards the expansion of European commercial activity, meaning that 'little time or effort was spent on the promotion of indigenous agricultural development' (Kean, 2000, p. 160). According to Kean (2000, p. 160), European settlers were opposed to any improvement in 'the socio-economic position of the indigenous peoples' and condemned any colonial officers who encouraged copra production among the villagers. Patrol officers (*kiap*) were commissioned to conduct census counts of the villagers, maintain order and collect a 'head' tax, which in turn was intended to force local populations to seek cash through wage labour or cash crops (Department of External Territories, 1968). In response, Maututu strove to keep the peace with the *kiap* and some took up work as 'work boy' on plantations on the Gazelle.

While the Missionaries of the Sacred Heart were building their base at Kokopo, an Australian man, George Brown, his wife and followers, pioneered the Methodist Overseas Mission on the Duke of York Islands off the coast of the Gazelle Peninsular from 1875, extending their reach to the Tolai village of Kabakada on Gazelle in the 1880s. Initially, Maututu heard of these Methodist mission activities from Tolai visitors to their settlements in search of *tambu* shell (Mumu, 2019). Mumu reported that, in 1903, two pastors, one of whom was Fijian, travelled down the Maututu coast to purchase land at three Maututu hamlets, Bubuu, Apupulu and Uase, for church building; however, no further action was taken there by the Methodist pastors for the next 15 years. According to Maututu accounts, two men from Apupulu, Ulalu and Malai of the Uge clan, went to Rabaul with one of these Tolai traders, and were presented with a leg of pork at a feast there. They asked to exchange this for a picture of Jesus and/or a 'Holy Book' (a Bible or hymn book) and returned with this book to Apupulu, bringing pastors with them.[16] When fellow villagers threatened to kill these outsiders, Ulalu and Malai protected them, enabling the first church to be established. Another local account suggests that Malai went to Rabaul for Bible training and to ask missionaries to come to the Maututu. Malai returned from this trip with 'a large book written by Jesus himself' that he had exchanged for a leg of pork. On his return, he wrapped the Bible and left it on the shelf. When ships arrived offshore to recruit labour for the plantations and missions further east, the Bible was placed at the hamlet entrance to save residents from such recruitment.[17]

These Maututu accounts emphasised the wildness of the outsiders their ancestors encountered from the distant Gazelle. Maututu hamlets were raided for labour and they in turn sought to defend their hamlets by the spear and by acquiring strong spiritual powers from the missionaries. Their attainment of these outside powers was due to the agency of exceptional local men, who continue to be lauded by Maututu churches. According to mission accounts, in 1918, the missionary John Cox, who was one of the original expatriate founders of the Methodist Mission at Kabakada, visited Uase and Bubuu hamlets with his colleagues Osea and Margetts on reconnaissance. They were met by warriors flourishing spears on the beach;

---

16 In his research, Roy Mumu, a Bileki man from Galilo village dates this visit of Malai and Ulalu to 1899. Their request was accompanied with the gift of a live pig to Reverend William Chambers, the chairman stationed at the Methodist Church at Kabakada. According to Roy Mumu, it was not until 1917 that the synod assigned a Samoan pastor to Bubuu village, although the pastor appears to have been stationed instead at Galilo in Hoskins.

17 It is unknown whether this reference is to blackbirding, which from the 1860s recruited tens of thousands of Pacific Islanders, including from the islands of PNG, to work on Queensland plantations. This practice was outlawed in 1901 when the Immigration Restriction Act was passed. This story may refer to ships from the plantations in Rabaul that recruited labour all along the coast.

however, the singing of hymns by Cox's party won the villagers over. They left pastors at the two villages, Kepas To Kapes at Uase and Sakius To Mala at Bubuu (Threlfold, 1975). More Methodist pastors, recruited from Samoa and Fiji, arrived in other Maututu villages in the mid-1920s, supervised by Australian clergy stationed in Rabaul and Hoskins.

Chowning (1969, p. 31) suggests that these Polynesian and Fijian missionaries were the proponents of various changes among the Lakalai, introducing outrigger canoes, plaited mats and metal graters for scraping out coconut flesh to produce coconut cream for cooking. Indeed, all these as well as hymn books and Bible translations in the Tolai language Kuanua of the Duke of York Islands are still in use today. Maututu also attribute a number of changes to the influence of the missions: the introduction of *la malo* (laplap cloths) worn by men and women; the fashion of cutting their hair short and combing it into curls instead of leaving it in greased bundles down their backs; washing three times a day; building Tolai-style homes of thatch raised on posts, instead of houses on the ground walled with bark; the decline of warfare between hamlets; and a reduction in intra-clan marriage and polygamy in line with church teachings about incest. By 1927, schools had been set up by these Methodist pastors in key Maututu hamlets. Uase village, where a pastor was resident from 1918, was reported by the district officer in 1925 as a 'model village' with its improved housing, church and mission school.

Maututu thus responded enthusiastically to the strange manners of these outsiders, their spirits and their books and rituals, and in dialogue with the pastors fashioned their own interpretations of Christian rituals and teachings based on their local ontology. I return in the next chapter to consider the dynamics of this alliance between Maututu and outsiders. However, in conversations I had in 1969 a key memory of the early years of the church was the anxiety that drove early attendance: hamlet residents believed that if they did not continue to attend church and believe (*tautauoilo*, store inside) then they would return to the days of fighting, sickness and death, and face an everlasting punishment of fire. Methodist teachings had seemingly expanded Maututu sensibilities towards the unpredictable 'outside' while at the same time offering them means to accost those wild forces.

One significant intervention demanded by the government *kiap* and the missionary pastors was the amalgamation of the scattered Maututu hamlets into larger villages that could more readily be incorporated into outside administrative practices. Increasingly in the 1930s the colonial authorities expected village units to contribute labour to government-ordained tasks. Maututu oral historians mentioned to me that the *polisboi* (native police) used to beat both men and women to keep them at work.[18] This coercive approach appears to have stopped after the administration appointed *luluai* (village headman) and *tultul* (village secretary) to organise the administration tasks in native settlements.[19] These village leaders tended to be selected by the *kiap* rather than by the people, which led to some strange appointments. In Mataruru, for example, a Papuan was selected as *tultul* because his Tok Pisin was fluent, although he spoke no local language and was marginal in the village. Lare of Uase claimed he was pressured by the *kiap* to become *luluai*. The *luluai* and *tultul* collected the annual tax of either 10 shillings, a spear or a gold-lip shell, and summoned villagers to meet when the *kiap* came to administer regulations. They were responsible for ensuring coconuts were planted in the hamlets and for the maintenance of the local access track. The *luluai* administered judgements in the case of local crimes such as adultery, usually exacting fines, and could assign *big het* (big head, arrogant people, troublemakers) who challenged his authority to jail in Talasea. Such banishment to remote, wild zones raised considerable alarm for Maututu, forcing their submission to the directions of government through *luluai* and *kiap*.

During the 1930s, the Australian colonial administration continued to build its own legibility along the New Britain coast, but this was thrown into a state of chaos with the violence of the Pacific War. In February 1942, Japanese forces captured Rabaul as their base for the Pacific War, from there pushing along the New Britain coast towards the mainland and Port Moresby. In West New Britain, many Maututu fled inland to escape Japanese coastal patrols, living in caves or the sites of former hamlets in the deep forest, afraid to light fires for fear of detection by the belligerent outsiders. There were an estimated 5,000 Japanese troops based in Hoskins in 1942. Japanese patrols through the Maututu area ransacked gardens and cut down coconut palms to access the nuts. The few Maututu who remained in coastal hamlets were killed by bombs or by Japanese raiding parties or recruited as porters for the Japanese.

---

18 The Tolai in eastern New Britain organised a mass strike in 1929 to protest their low wages and status, and through the 1930s there were increasing cases of attacks on Europeans. In 1940, the Tolai on the Duke of York Islands voiced their discontent through the Dog Movement, which was in response to the alienation of their land and inadequate schooling for their children (Kean, 2000; Valentine, 1958).
19 These local administrative positions were created under the German administration and retained by the Australian administration.

Villagers reported being confused as to how to respond to the war. Allied force coastwatchers holed up in isolated watch points in the Nakanai Mountains, including the Uasilau area south of the Maututu, sought the cooperation of local populations to bring them details of Japanese troop movements. However, there was considerable suspicion on all sides, with Nakanai both aiding and opposing Japanese forces, and being punished by both sides for disloyalty. Allied forces fought back against the Japanese forces, first along the Kokoda Trail on the mainland and then, from 1943 to 1945, towards Rabaul along the coast of New Britain. In October 1944, the Australian 36th Infantry Battalion landed at Hoskins to take over from American forces and, in December, moved up the coast by barge to Bialla Plantation, where two companies established a forward base from where they began patrolling east (Long, 1963).

This was a time of extreme chaos, according to Maututu recollections, when wild forces dominated daily life. The war years are remembered as 'dark' years (*la masori*) when most Maututu lost their hamlets and gardens and were forced to live in the forest. Many locals died of tuberculosis during the war, and the infection's persistence after the war demoralised communities even when they returned to former hamlet sites. In 1949, the death rate from tuberculosis was so grave that villagers again fled to their mountain hamlets in an attempt to escape it.

Several men told me of working for the Allies in the later stages of the war, as carriers and as fighters, even though they regarded the Australian forces as ungrateful outsiders. For example, Tagorobo told me he was paid £54 for his war services by the Australians. He added:

> The Australians only delivered beatings, jail and hard work. After the war the War Damages Commission took count of animals, houses, trees and other possessions lost in the war, but no compensation was ever forthcoming. We fought for them, but they did not pay us well. They were scared of the Japanese, and it was we and the Americans who fought up the front. Today it is the *kiap* who push us around, but they are 'small men' [in contrast to Maututu 'big men'].

Tagorobo contrasted the 'white men' (*wokakea*) Australians to the 'Black Americans' (*wokurukuru*) who related quite differently to villagers. The Americans, he remembered, would chat with them and give them food and equipment and talk about their 'home' in Africa. As they had accepted the Fijian pastors before the war, the Maututu welcomed these 'Black' Americans into their 'home', whereas *wokakeu*, like the government *kiap*, remained as strangers and interlopers to Maututu. In contrast to the disdain shown by the *wokakea*, *wokurukuru* earned Maututu respect through relating to them in a different manner and through the redistribution of exchange goods.

This half century of expatriate administration and enterprise in the Bialla area alerted Maututu to the strangeness and wildness of *wokakea/masta* behaviours and assumptions. The Australian administration's appointment of village headmen with the powers to tax and exact punishment, their views of land as a marketable commodity, their insistence on larger village settlements that ignored patterns of shifting agriculture linked to hamlets, their incapacity to engage in mutual exchange and respect, and the mutual suspicion between parties that arose during the war all clashed with Maututu values. There would have been those who interpreted the random killings and the outbreaks of tuberculosis as further evidence that these wild agents would continue to threaten Maututu lives at 'home'.

The ethnographer as outsider

> Like the environment that the Kubo had always experienced,
> they [expatriate outsiders] were potentially beneficent but always
> unpredictable.
>
> (Minnegal & Dwyer, 2017, p. 236)

I must have been viewed in this way when I first entered the hamlet of Baikakea in 1968. I spoke neither the Maututu language nor Tok Pisin. I was an unknown quantity and therefore unpredictable, without kin ties or exchange relations within the community. Two relationships may have eased my entry, ameliorating my 'wildness'. The first of these was the invitation I had received from a US ex-serviceman, Fred Hargesheimer, to join the Airmen's Memorial School (AMS) in Ewasse, West New Britain. According to Hargesheimer's (2005) account of the school's establishment, it 'fell from the sky'. Hargesheimer was a US pilot whose plane was shot down over New Britain in June 1943. He barely survived in the forest before being found a month later by Meramera villagers of Ea Ea/Nantambu who hid him from the Japanese occupation forces. After five months he was rescued by submarine. Almost two decades later he raised funds for the Airmen's Memorial Foundation and negotiated with the colonial administration and the Methodist Church to build a school to serve the Meramera and Maututu populations.

Figure 1.5: Baikakea village, 1969
Source: Author.

After the school opened in 1965, the parents impressed on Hargesheimer that they were concerned that their children, who spent so much time at school and walking to school (often an hour), had no chance to grow up as 'Maututu'. Under the Australian administration, the school curriculum was taught in English and its frame of reference reflected Anglo-Australian ontological perspectives. Subsequently, the AMS Board, consisting of Maututu representatives, asked that Maututu language and culture be introduced into the school curriculum. I was invited as a volunteer to expedite such a program. The Parents' Association suggested that I should live in Baikakea, where villagers still lived in 'traditional' ways (Figure 1.5). I suspect they thought I would absorb something of what it meant to be 'Maututu' while living there, and so it was with some pride that Baikakea entertained the notion of welcoming an outsider into their community. When I arrived in October 1968, I was guided into Baikakea by a local school boy, Saole, whose English was fluent enough to smooth my introduction to hamlet life and who remained a friend until his death in 2017. This was the second relationship that eased my entry to Maututu life.

A male outsider visiting a Maututu settlement in those days would normally go directly to the men's house, where they would be offered food and a place to sleep. But they might also be offered a place with the *baramana* (young men), which is where I first settled.[20] I vividly remember waking one night to surreal wailings coming from the adjacent hamlet. I was alone and the hamlet around me was deathly quiet. I ventured to the adjacent hamlet to find it alive with villagers. The most prestigious man in the village had just died and everyone had gathered at the men's house to mourn his passing. Looking back on this moment, it was a clear demonstration of the community voicing their oneness in the face of spiritual uncertainty. The 'wild' was dramatically present that night, in the death itself and in their piercing wailing.

After several weeks I was invited to join the household of Tauvere and Koma and their three young children, Makoa, Kautu and Siamate. Tauvere became my 'father', and Koma my 'mother', and I was recognised as a member of Koma's clan, Kabuliala. Because Tauvere's first wife had died, I also recognised his daughter by that marriage, Adi, as my sister, and her clan, Ugeuge, also became my adopted clan as I was a similar age to her. I remained in their home for the following 10 months and during a later visit of two months in 1972. Tauvere was regarded as senior man of the village and had a long association with the Department of Agriculture, Stock and Fisheries (DASF), first as a trainee and then as a village cocoa development worker travelling throughout West New Britain. He became my primary mentor. While I always remained an outsider, Maututu had thus extended to me a relationship built on exchange—of food, material items, stories, cooperation and, ultimately, they hoped, a better school experience for their children.

I spent the initial months learning Maututu language as I accompanied villagers wherever their daily activities took them. We cleared the forest and worked the gardens, hunted 'up' into the mountains, fished out on the reefs, gathered shell in the sea grass, and participated in festivals and inter-village congregations. I resisted using either English or Tok Pisin in the village in order that my Maututu language fluency improve. As it improved, I was able to hold more in-depth interviews and search out the senior men and women who were to guide me in preparing school materials. These were not only living in Baikakea but throughout the Maututu area, so I walked around the villages, often staying for several nights with village hosts. Situated close to Bialla Plantation, where a trade store was located, were the Maututu villages of Uase (Ewasse) in the south and Gomu in the north. Further

---

20 *Baramana* is a Kuanua term, introduced to Maututu by the early Tolai missionaries. The Maututu *baramana* typically did not cook at their house but were fed by their female kin elsewhere in the hamlet.

south of Uase were Matililiu and Mataruru, and to the north of Gomu the villages of Apupulu, Baikakea and Bubuu. Inland of Gomu was the hamlet of Urumaili, that was later recognised as a separate village. The inland (*oilo*) people of Mataruru, Urumaili and Baikakea were generally recognised as having more familiarity with Maututu 'traditions' and the forest domain, while the coastal people of Matalilu, Uase, Gomu, Apupulu and Bubuu were thought to depend more on the marine environment.

My own ontological training began with the narration of myths that different village elders insisted I record for later use in the school. Many men and women entertained me with stories, but I particularly relied on senior men and women for their versions of Maututu myths. There was something in the language, dramatic turn of phrase and song lines that instilled authority to their telling of the myths, and Maututu recognised these senior narrators as producing the most authoritative versions. They directed me to particular elders: Ipa in Baikakea; Migu and, later, his son Kau in Gomu/Urumaili; Boea and Kiapa in Mataruru (Figures 1.6 and 1.7).

Figure 1.6: Migu, storyteller and hunter, 1969
Source: Author.

Figure 1.7: Kau, son of Migu, at forest hunting lodge, 1974
Source: Author.

I recorded the narratives on audio tape and would play the recordings to enthusiastic audiences in whichever village I was spending the night. This would encourage others to share stories with me, including older women. These stories would vary immensely in length and depth of imagery. While men and women enjoyed narrating stories and everyday events, all recognised the wisdom and depth of the narration by these few elders. Others might tell the same myths, but their versions lacked the intensity of detail and imagery that the experts provided. When these experts narrated myths, adults and children sat entranced by the vitality of the story, however familiar it may have been to them. Strengthened and sacralised through the words and songs of the myth-tellers, these narratives had agency, working to shape the world of their audience.[21] I matched these stories by observing and discussing everyday happenings with everyone in the villages. The relationships I gained from visiting all the villages allowed me to finally introduce lesson materials in the school, including written materials in Maututu language and craft and skill classes taught by senior men and women.[22]

---

21 Myths about a particular 'hero' generally included his identifying song.

22 Those initial 12 months living in Baikakea and working throughout the Maututu villages also enabled me to complete a master's degree in anthropology at the University of Sydney. My thesis, submitted in 1973, focused on Maututu mythology (Guinness, 1973).

I returned in 1973 for another 18 months in Baikakea during which time I was employed by the DASF as a field officer to strengthen cocoa production, pig breeding and marine fishing across Maututu and Meramera villages and to prepare Maututu villagers for the pending influx of oil palm settlers. I was employed on local wages and encouraged by DASF to work from my village base, with the provision of a motor bike to move around the area. Though an outsider, and with employment associated with an outside body, I felt accepted within the Maututu communities because of my kin relationships and my school contributions. The DASF financed the construction of a small house for me in Baikakea; when I left, that house became the home of my 'brother' Dome. In my DASF capacity, I held numerous village meetings, worked closely with the secretary and directors of the Maututu Cooperative Society and sought to bring local priorities to the attention of the few *masta* (white people) who lived in the area—the school principal, the *kiap*, the manager of Bialla Plantation and his wife, an Australian timber operator and family living near Bubuu, and the business development field officer who visited regularly from Hoskins.

I left PNG in 1975 as the nation achieved its independence, not to return for over 30 years.[23] In 2009, Lydia Gah, who had married an Australian and settled in Queensland, surprised me with a phone call and encouraged me to return, as my 'mother' Koma was gravely sick, and my 'family' wanted me 'home'. I was unable to get back before her death but arrived later to renew contacts with friends and family. Over the years since then I have visited Bialla six times, each time for about a month when I could find time away from university teaching. The changes I encountered were dramatic, as I recount in this book, but the village relationships I had experienced four decades before remained intact. I am forever grateful to my Maututu friends and family that I have been able to share deeply in their lives as I have tried to understand how they view the many radical changes they have experienced from colonialism to industrialisation.

My own ontological position needs scrutiny. It could be seen as presumptuous for an outsider to attempt to delineate Maututu ontological perspectives. As Robbins (2008) remarked, any interpretation can only be grasped as one of many possible accounts, and so I make no claim to

---

23   I did field work in Indonesia and Malaysia and taught in Indonesian and Australian universities. This fieldwork included studies of resettlement schemes (Transmigrasi in Indonesia, FELDA in Malaysia) where oil palm, among other crops, was being developed. I spent time with settlers and with administrators and company managers, understanding the very different expectations, experiences and aspirations they were investing in the development (Guinness, 1982; Suratman & Guinness, 1977).

have mastered Maututu ontological perspectives. I merely suggest an interpretation that reflects my lived experience and training in their villages. In the tasks I performed for the AMS and DASF, I was constantly wrestling with ontological differences in interpreting the development mindset of the colonial and 'self-government' administrations, and, later, the industrial capitalism of Japanese and Belgian oil palm companies. I was constantly aware of the distinct, and diverse, aspirations and values of Maututu villagers. The expectation of government—my employer—was that the blueprint of the PNG administration's development program needed translation, not interpretation, let alone consultation and debate. Olivier de Sardan (2005, pp. 168–69) commented that development agents play a role 'as mediators between types of knowledge … between technical-scientific and popular knowledge'. However, he added that the development agent:

> is not trained to mediate between different types of knowledge; instead, it is expected that he will assume various pedagogical roles, in order to cast light on those who are still in the dark … [he] is the person responsible for 'grafting' the technical message (originating in a cosmopolitan, scientific terminology) onto a system of significations that is peculiar to the rural population in question.
>
> (Olivier de Sardan, 2005, pp. 168–69)

As both a development agent and an anthropologist with a strong desire to accurately record Maututu views and aspirations, I was constantly entangled in the disjunction of multiple ontologies (Roberts, 2013). I saw my task as not only interpreting government directions for villagers, but also understanding and communicating to *wokakea* the distinctive village perspectives. This was by no means straightforward, as outsiders were not always interested in hearing what villagers thought, and my own capacity to communicate Maututu viewpoints needed time to 'mature'.

Olivier de Sardan (2005, p. 199) writes that:

> the social scientist who sets himself the task of elucidating peasant logics or of opposing them to development logics is not a mere spectator: he himself is involved in logics that influence his scientific practice (logics of professional recognition, or power, of credit 'capturing', etc) … According to Bachelard's famous expression, which is still valid today, 'scientific knowledge in particular is constructed through a continuous, unrelenting fight against error, by means of meticulous criticism, intellectual polemic, theoretical and methodological vigilance and of constant examination of acquired knowledge. Action on the other hand comprises arbitration, ambiguities, compromise, wagers, will and emergencies'.

There is always the challenge for the ethnographer, as articulated by Marilyn Strathern (1987, p. 257), of 'how to create an awareness of different social worlds when all at one's disposal is terms which belong to one's own' (cited in Viveiros de Castro, 2015). Viveiros de Castro (2015, p. 14) concludes about the ethnographic exercise:

> It means to be able to speak well to the people you study [and] … to speak about them to them in ways they do not find offensive or ridiculous. They do not need to agree with you completely—they will never do so anyway.

Paige West (2016, p. 112), who has been both an academic and activist in PNG, suggests that her role is 'to understand the worlds that people are living, in the terms that they are living them'. I follow her advice in using stories told by villagers 'to represent philosophical propositions or narratives of philosophy'—the study of the nature of reality or existence. She augments these with her own 'ethnographic vignettes that illustrate philosophical principles', and her aim is to allow 'indigenous philosophical theory to have the same explanatory power as other forms of theoretical abstraction' (West, 2016, p. 136).

Many people shared their experiences and perspectives with me; however, this book is my story about their lives, written in a style of narrative that is distinctively of my academic training rather than strategically theirs. Maututu constitute some of the critical audiences who will, I hope, engage with what I write here. While I attempt to see things 'through their eyes', I ultimately present only versions of what they see and have reported to me. Therefore, a key contribution an ethnographer can make is to remain aware and interested in the variable ways in which diverse peoples and societies interact with global changes and to point out the value of such adaptations. I try to provide as much ethnographic material as possible to allow readers to see through my depiction and come to their own understandings.

Conclusion

In this opening chapter I have demonstrated an ontological framework built on the tension between the wild and unpredictable outside and the home sustained through exchange relationships centred on *la hulumu*. Home in some contexts is epitomised in the single *mautu* 'hamlet', and at other times extended to neighbouring hamlets (*maututu*) *oale, omuli, orae* and *olau*. Central to the Maututu ontology is the relationship of 'home' to the vastness of the 'wild'. The unpredictability of the wild was experienced in the storms and volcanic eruptions and, on a daily basis, the actions of strangers, sorcerers and spirits. It was also recognised in the encounters with colonial regimes, and Japanese and Allied military forces.

The ontological framing through this juxtaposition of the two domains is identified in this chapter with an indigenous consideration of a range of important issues, such as relations with the spirit world, the forging of the ideal personality, the nurturing of community relations, partnerships between men and women, and dealing with unpredictable outsiders. In all such issues, Maututu recognise the tension between wild and home counterparts and attempt engagement. Strangers are brought into the men's house, spirits and sorcerers are confronted, outside women are incorporated into the home of their husband, and 'wild' personalities are tempered by community action. Maututu ontological engagement with such issues recognises the potential inspiration and enrichment that may come from such wild counterparts, just as they depend on harnessing the richness of the forest for their gardens. I return to this engagement in the next chapter.

I have contrasted the Maututu perspective with that of the colonial regimes intent on the commercial development of the land and the subjugation of 'stone-age' peoples. The 'natives' were of little value to expatriates unless they could be employed in colonial undertakings. Control rather than exchange dominated this perspective.

However, Maututu recognised in some encounters with expatriate outsiders the potential for exchange relationships and a tempering of the wild for the enrichment of home. They welcomed mission pastors, forged friendships with Black American soldiers and cooperated in establishing the AMS. As an outsider, I was a beneficiary of their intent to engage positively with outsiders.

In the chapters that follow I examine whether Maututu ontological preference for creative engagement with the wild explains something of how Maututu have responded to the immense changes they have experienced since the beginning of the twentieth century. I present this history as struggles across multiple ontological worlds as Maututu 'pursue their own priorities and understandings in tandem with their engagement with outsiders' (Escobar, 2016, p. 20).

2

Partners

In the previous chapter I introduced the distinction Maututu make between the domestic world and the outside forest, and the importance they attach to the wild domain and its elements as both a locus of danger and unpredictability and source of inspiration and energy. It is clear from Maututu stories that they see themselves as always entangled with 'wild' elements beyond their hamlet and home and recognise the benefits that can emerge from engaging with these outside forces. These outside agents are wild in the sense of being outside village control, unsupervised, unpredictable, chaotic and encountered in a zone of extreme danger. The myths explore engagement and entanglement with these agents. Men penetrate deep into the forest or beyond the coastal reefs, where they encounter such dangers. Women, more commonly associated with 'home', also engage with wild forces, but these are generally closer to home in the gardens or at the bounds of the village space. The home realm is always under threat from the wild and, if not defended, will revert back to wild, just like abandoned gardens and hamlet sites. On the other hand, the wild offers benefits to the village, as in the fertility that the forest brings to the soil. Gardens cannot be worked to advantage for more than three years, after which the exhausted soil is allowed to revert to forest, often interspersed with some cultivated plants such as coconut and betel nut palms planted in the old garden. The wild is thus a source of both richness and destructive forces, and that provides the dynamic of Maututu life. As I will explore in myths and Maututu response to outside 'development' programs, villagers focus on establishing a balance or partnership with the wild, not by destroying it (which they admit is inconceivable) but entangling with it, absorbing its energies and ideas to enrich village life. Figuratively, the garden is the site where the entanglement of domestic and wild is most keenly negotiated.

Never in their stories nor in their historical recollections did Maututu entertain the idea of isolating themselves from the wild. The outside was a constant presence even at 'home'. Trading exchanges with outsiders had existed for generations. For example, obsidian had spread along the coast through exchange from its source in the Talasea Peninsular, and was exchanged by the Maututu and Meramera to the mountain Maenge, together with stone tools (Lattas, 2011). In exchange Maututu acquired bark cloth and woven baskets from the Maenge/Mengen. From at least the late nineteenth century when more seaworthy vessels were built, Tolai from the Gazelle area visited the Bialla area to trade gold-lip shells from the Duke of York Islands for nassa shells (*tambu, la tubeli*) collected by Maututu from the seagrasses offshore from their hamlets (Simet, 1991). Chowning (1978) dates such Tolai sea journeys to the Nakanai area with the introduction to the Gazelle of plank boats in about 1899. The *tambu* that Tolai acquired from the Maututu became a prestige good and currency for the Tolai, while the gold-lip shells became the key prestige good for Maututu. They decorated these shells with bead-like nuts and woven fibres, named individual shell valuables and traced their passage through subsequent exchanges. The richness of the outside was also recognised in the words of their sacred songs and their dances, which were said to derive from the language of the bush Mengen (Maenge). This long historical engagement with outside peoples presented to Maututu the opportunity to compare their own lifeways and perspectives with outsiders, and to adopt materials and ideas from beyond 'home'.

Partners in myth

I begin the exploration of this ontological frame of 'partnership' by considering the most important/sacred myth told to me. Unlike many of the narratives, this one, whether narrated by Migu or Boea or Kiapa, had no accompanying song.

Origin myth of Kalakala and Koi

In the long-ago, an old woman Bulaso was sweeping the hamlet of rubbish. She was the only inhabitant left in this hamlet because a giant *buata* (wild spirit being) called Vulutaola who lived in a large tree just outside the hamlet had snatched up and devoured all its other residents. She swept to the edge of the settlement two betel nuts, one a domestic betel nut (*kalakala*) and the other a wild betel nut (*koi*), but both rolled back to her feet. She swept them away but when they again returned she picked them up and put them in an empty half coconut shell in her cooking house. On resuming her sweeping she was shocked to hear voices from inside the house. Rushing in she found two young men, Kalakala and Koi, sitting on the bench where she had left the coconut shell. 'Quiet', she whispered, 'Vulutaola will hear you and devour us all'. The young men quickly gained an account of how the *buata* had terrorised the hamlet, and they vowed to take revenge. They found a mosquito in the stream nearby in the forest and sent it up into the *koimo* (*Octomeles sumatrana*) tree where Vulutaola was settling in for the night. The mosquito buzzed in his ear but he brushed it away. Twice more the mosquito buzzed in his ear, until finally there was no response. Vulutaola was fast asleep. Informed by the mosquito that the *buata* was asleep, the young men stuck spears in the ground, point up, at the base of the tree and climbed into the tree. They attacked Vulutaola with their many spears and then tipped him onto the spears below where he hung dead.

They returned with triumphant shouts to the hamlet but Bulaso warned them: 'Don't get too excited, another *buata* called Kitumagola lives just beyond the hamlet boundary in a fenced enclosure. Her facial hair is straggly and her tusk teeth curl upwards over her cheek. She is very dangerous'. The young men hurried off to find a mouse to help them. The mouse dug under the fence of the *buata*'s enclosure and emerged in the kitchen where Kitumagola was sitting. 'Grandmother', the mouse said to the *buata*, 'let me give you a shave'.[1] As the mouse began the shave it said: 'Grandmother, your tusk teeth are in the way. Loosen your teeth so I do not cut myself'. Kitumagola loosened her teeth and put them on the ground, and mouse furtively swept them into the tunnel it had dug on entry, and scurried away to Kalakala and Koi to inform them it had disarmed Kitumagola. They rushed into the compound and speared the *buata* to death. Finally they could celebrate the freedom of the hamlet and Bulaso joined them this time, even claiming that she had killed the *buata*. Koi, who came from the wild betel nut, was angry with Bulaso for claiming all the credit and impetuously killed her.

---

1   *Pupu* (grandmother) may designate a specific kin relationship but is a term also used to address any elder or being of respect.

Kalakala and Koi had a sister who married into a hamlet high in the caldera of the volcano Mount Ivi. But she was mistreated by her husband who fed her rotten sago grubs. Kalakala and Koi heard about this and asked advice of their grandparent the frog at the forest stream.[2] 'Grandparent', they said, 'what shall we do?' 'Take two large wild taro leaves and use them to catch the spray when I jump into the stream'. They wrapped up the spray in the leaves and hurried up to the mountain hamlet. Koi could scarcely contain his curiosity and let some of the spray escape where it cascaded down the slopes as new streams. The brothers called their sister out of the hamlet and placed her in a tall banana palm with their dogs. Then they released the spray onto the hamlet, and it swelled and swelled, flooding the hamlet and drowning its residents. When the waters threatened the sister's position in the banana clump, the dogs lapped it down again. The waters rushed out of the huge lake created in the crater of Mount Ivi, and cascaded down the mountain, a river now called Lovo 'flying' river. The brothers ran each side of it, trying to contain it, but it rushed on. Where Koi on the north bank outran Kalakala, the river turned southward, and was finally slowed in the Obu lagoon on the coast before entering the sea. Thus Kalakala and Koi were responsible for many of the physical features of the landscape and for bringing peace to the people.

The myth juxtaposes the two realms of wild forest and hamlet home. 'At home' is a solitary old woman in a small hamlet that she preserves by sweeping forest refuse to the domestic boundary. She lives in terror of the overshadowing forest and its *buata* Vulutaola, who had eaten all the other residents. The wild is swallowing the hamlet. She is unable to engage with the forest. It is a dramatic portrayal of a past when the ancestors carved tiny settlements in the vast jungle. The old woman Bulaso has no freedom and lives in constant terror. She cannot access her gardens nor does she enjoy the company of kin and neighbours. There is no partnership possible between the wild and home.

However, the potential of partnership emerges from the rubbish Bulaso desperately sweeps away. The partnership of the two brothers, Kalakala, emerging from a domestic betel nut, and Koi, from a wild betel nut, is captured by the old woman as she places them together in the coconut shell. For Maututu, the betel nut is a prime agent of sociality, harvested from multiple palms scattered throughout the hamlet and gardens. It is distributed in bunches to guests, particularly at feast exchanges, and is carried constantly in men's and women's baskets to be shared with whomever they fall into

---

2   Maututu language does not nominate gender in the grandparent and grandchild generations.

conversation. The wild betel nut, however, is treated more cautiously for its violent 'kick'. It can induce anger and unpredictable behaviour. It is the partnership of Kalakala and Koi that frees the old woman and reconstitutes the hamlet. To slay the two *buata*, the brothers build partnerships with forest agents, the mosquito, the mouse and the 'grandparent' frog. These partnerships are constituted as kin relationships, between humans and non-humans. Maututu clans and lineages recognise particular species of plant, fish and animal as clan/lineage totems and therefore kin, and certain locations in the wild are sacred clan sites because of their association with such ancestral kin. Such partnerships of human and non-human actors are central to many ontologies. 'Animism is an ontology which postulates the social character of relations between human and non humans' (Viveiros de Castro, 2012, p. 86). Referencing Ingold (1994), Viveiros de Castro (2012, p. 88) argues that animism is 'founded on the immediate interagentive engagement between humans and animals'. Of another Papua New Guinea (PNG) people, the Biangai (upper Bulolo, Morobe), Halvacsz (2020, p. 50) notes that 'worlds are layered with human and non-human agencies … that are related to one another through kinship'.

Figure 2.1: Lamo Auru lake, 1974
Source: Author.

The wild *buata*, on the other hand, can never be recruited into such a partnership because their wildness cannot be appeased, so they must be opposed. Some wild agents, like the sorcerers threatening Maututu lives, can never be trusted to form a partnership. But the partnership of the brothers allows the hamlet to engage with the outside world, eventuating in the magnificent lake of Lamo Auru (Lake Hargy) and the mighty river Lovo on which a hydro-electricity station now stands. The partnership of home and wild creates a revivifying force that rescues Bulaso and, later, the brothers' sister (Figure 2.1).

The following story further attests to the dangers of encountering spirits of the wild but shows how an openness to partnership brings rewards.

> Sailogo was hunting when his dogs barked at an object on the ground, mistaking it for a pig. They bit it and shook it. It was a coconut but Sailogo had never seen one before. He thought it might be food, so he climbed the palm above to pick one, open it up and eat the flesh. At that moment Laveutu, the *taua* spirit that owned the palm emerged, sending the cockatoos screeching away. He accosted Sailogo: 'Who do you think you are? Is this your palm? What is your clan?' 'I am a Mapa man', said Sailogo. 'That is alright then, climb down over me.' Sailogo did not want to descend, as the spirit's skin was very cold and he thought he would die. 'Are you afraid of me? Are you really a Mapa man?' Sailogo braced his ankles with a vine ready to descend. 'You don't need that, just hold onto me.' Sailogo climbed onto his folded arms, then down onto his thighs. Laveutu was standing on his tail wound around the palm. Sailogo reached the ground and moved slowly away. 'Where are you?' said Laveutu but Sailogo had fled. The next day another man, Silegalua, went hunting and his dogs barked at the coconut. He climbed the palm only to be surprised by Laveutu. 'What clan are you?' 'I am a Kabulu man', Silegalua answered. Laveutu swallowed him. After that Laveutu moved away, his head like a human head resting at the source of the Aliai stream, and his body like that of an eel with his tail reaching the shore. Sailogo took the coconuts and planted them at home, and today they still stand, much higher than the coconuts we got from the Tolai in Rabaul. This is the origin of the mountain coconut.

Another story tells of fire and ginger-based medication as gifts from the spirits of the sky, once again negotiated by an older woman abandoned with her grandchild at 'home'. The stories embolden villagers to remain open to outside surprises. Maututu would have sympathy for the views of the Kubo people in the inner lowlands of PNG, as:

> Kubo attend closely to the subtleties of what the environment is doing … there is always the possibility that the environment, or unseen forces that lurk within it, may withhold what is desired.
>
> (Minnegal & Dwyer, 2017, pp. 233–34)

For the Maututu, however, the outside environment can also be a source of great value.

The balanced personality of prominent dividuals

Valentine (1963, p. 448), in his analysis of personality types among the Bileki Nakanai, described:

> leading personalities who may combine, for example, a tendency to angry responses, verbal expressiveness, physical mobility and uninhibited sexuality with care in observing customary proprieties, a high degree of concentrated attention and achievement in certain traditional skills.

Such leaders had a balance of the personality characteristics of 'men of anger' and 'men of shame'.

In the 1960s, Maututu told me that they saw their ancestors as *vogari te la igogolu* (hardworkers) who would, therefore, spear a lazy man. The most prominent men might be known as *la tahalo la vuluti* (men of wealth), *la vuluti* referring foremost to the holding of exchange items, such as gold-lip shell and pigs, and possession of powerful armbands. Very few leading residents had worn the *suara*[3] wristband that signified they were respected over a wide area, not just for their supernatural knowledge but also for their ability to accumulate and distribute wealth and to bring peace between hamlets. I was told of two such *suara*, Soa Ubia, who lived in the Central Nakanai/Loso/Ouka village of Uasilau, and Boas Kule, who lived in the Bileki village of Galilo on the Hoskins Peninsular, both outside the Maututu homeland, but recognised by Maututu for their outstanding character.

---

3   All village men and women wore wristbands as ceremonial regalia. Certain men wore particular wristbands, such as the *suara*, as the repositories of spirit power that bolstered the authority of the wearer.

I was told of only one *suara* among the Maututu, Dome, who had fled from Kapore in Hoskins when Pago erupted and gained the respect of all Maututu until his death in 1942. Dome was marked initially as an assertive and unpredictable 'man of anger' who would readily spear a man who annoyed him, but he became a more balanced personality, culminating in his acquisition of the *suara* wristband whose resident spirit (*savei*) became his partner.[4] The value of the wristband was reflected in the 10 *tuali* (gold-lip shells) with which he acquired it from its previous owner in Hoskins. He then established himself as a pre-eminent 'big man', respected across many hamlets. If he approached a couple to arrange the marriage of their daughter they could not refuse, but he would guarantee all the necessary marriage payments. When he held a feast, he himself would contribute up to 20 pigs and all in the village would work in his gardens and be fed by him at the end of each day of work, the feast enrichening their whole community. Dome's transformation to a wise and productive leader was thus portrayed in these accounts as built on a partnership with the spirit of the wristband, community cooperation and his generosity in exchange relations. He also won respect by moderating the 'wild' elements of his personality—his anger and impetuosity—and by developing wisdom (*la mari*), compassion (*la gilogo*) and respect (*la tilogo*) that attracted partnership with others. The wild in his persona was not extinguished but balanced by other 'home' attributes cultivated through relationships. Yet he remained dangerous, even to his closest associates. If someone trod in the *buai* (betel juice) he had spat on the ground they would fall sick, even die, unless he healed them with the ginger he always carried with him. If someone took a betel nut from his basket, that person would die. In the men's house, no-one would walk behind him or make a noise. A snake, another 'wild' companion, slept in the doorway of his men's house, and anyone except his wife who stepped over it would die. When he visited another's house, they would present him with a *tuali* to ensure the *savei* of the *suara* did not become angry and *bili* (overwhelm, kill) them. In the event of such a 'wild' occurrence, wealth items were presented to the *suara* who then revived his host. Dome died in 1942 of pneumonia before he could introduce another to the wristband *savei*, and so it was regarded as too dangerous for anyone else to wear and was buried with him.

---

4   The significance of this close partnership between human and spirit will be explored later.

The *suara* were exceptional among big men for their relationship with spirit agents that gave them powers. There were other men who were not *suara* but performed healing services in their own and other hamlets. Healers in the 1960s were in high demand and were said to complement the modern medicine that the colonial administrators were introducing. Their 'patients' would bring the healer a ginger root grown in their house garden, which the healer placed under his pillow when he slept. The ginger was of the wild—hot, angry—though grown in the gardens. As he slept, the healer's *kalulu* (spirit) journeyed to distant abodes of the spirits where he identified and countered the spiritual source of the patient's distress. On waking he sent the ginger root back to the owner with instructions to chew and spit the ginger over the affected part of the body. Such healers were familiar with the 'wild' outside and able to challenge the spirits they encountered there. The healer in sleep would *lovo* (fly) to the hideout of the *buata* spirit who held the *halulu* (shadow) of the sick person. These *buata* inhabited specific sites, such as Olea near Gomu or Eriga near Baikakea. The healer would cut his way with a knife through the forest as he flew, and villagers, on observing the cut fronds of coconut falling to the ground, would say 'there goes Siloe' or 'there goes Galewa', the healers. Knife in hand, they would fight the *buata* and win back the *halulu* by cutting the skin of the *buata*. Siloe was also said to travel in his sleep to his son who was at school in Lae and to deliver to him portions of pork and taro from the *mage* feast, some clean clothing or money. He would even recruit a *savei* bush spirit to impersonate him in the village while he travelled elsewhere. Villagers, in answer to my queries, suggested he could even carry me to Australia if I had forgotten anything, and return with me the next morning.

Most healers had a personality tending more to the *tao la pou makovula* (introvert, man of shame) and took a low profile in village politics, but their alter-image portrayed them contesting wild spirits and traversing the outside in order to restore social relations in the village. Many were respected myth-tellers and renowned hunters who roamed the forest alone in search of game. Although generally not the patrons of large feasts or known for their assertive social presence, they nonetheless embodied a balance of both assertive and reclusive personality traits that was highly respected.

Home community and its partners

The Maututu big man (*tahalo auru*), by the force of his personality and strength of his exchange relationships, drew kin and exchange partners to share a men's house (*la hulumu*) and hamlet (*mautu*). In the early years of the Australian administration, such hamlets were scattered through the forested coastline and slopes of Mount Ivi. The survey of the Bialla Plantation area by Barry (1933) gives a good indication of the early dispersal of the population in hamlets.[5] In 1933, the hamlet populations were listed as Kapei, 98; Papaha, 25; Uawa, 60; Kaiamamo, 57; Wilelo, 79; Suvia, 17; Loimo, 34; Baikakea, 30; Morosiros, 21; Malamake, 49; and Maga, 33. These figures indicate that the scattered hamlets ranged from about 5 to 20 households.

Karakara refers to the group of people who settle together in the hamlet, who converse together.[6] *Vai-karakara* means 'speaking together', the prefix *vai* referring to the act of making or causing mutuality. The *karakara* was centred on the lineage of the big man and his siblings and at least one other lineage linked by affinal ties, such as that of the big man's wife. The big man could have more than one wife, adding considerably to the size of the *karakara*. The *karakara* might also be augmented by single men or couples attracted by the energy and charisma of the big man. Goodenough referred to the *karakara* of the Bileki Nakanai as 'nodal kindred', a grouping that included a core sibling set, or a pairing of sibling sets, sons and wards of these founders, clan mates and phratry mates, who were tied together by kin ties to each other. Goodenough (1962, p. 9) called it 'the most important single unit of cooperative action in Lakalai'.[7] Maututu elders named for me the paired lineages associated with each former hamlet site: Tobaobao was home to Vorega and Kabulu Vauvahu lineages; Tobiso was home to Vorega and Giloiloli lineages; Baikakea Kabili was home to Biso and Uge lineages; and Kahe, where the village of Baikakea is now situated, was home to three lineages—Kabulu, Uge and Biso. Hamlet membership was and is significant in the way Maututu form partnerships.

---

5   The survey listed the hectares occupied by each hamlet, ranging from 9 to 556 hectares, presumably noting the garden areas, but the largest figures are hard to explain for such small populations.

6   One villager translated this word as 'mob' and referenced the Australian use of that word.

7   Among the neighbouring Maenge (Mengen), the *galiau* is comparable to such a nodal kindred, an instrument of cooperative action, preparing festivals or cultivating ceremonial gardens, whose core is made of a local descent matrilineal group but included in-marrying males and females and descendants in the patriline of core members, who 'usually live adjacent to one another in the same hamlet' (Panoff, 1976, p. 186).

The men's house (*hulumu*) was central to hamlet activities when I first lived there in 1968–75. In clearing the soil, the *karakara* men would work together, felling and burning the dense foliage, led by their 'big man' (Figures 2.2 and 2.3). Their wives or, in the case of single men, their sisters or mothers would then join in the clearing and burning of the cut vegetation, the weeding and the planting. Each couple would be assigned a section of the cleared soil, demarcated with felled timber laid along the plot boundary. That couple would enjoy exclusive access to the produce of that section. Frequently, a large garden clearing would be pioneered by a 'big man' when he planned to hold a *mage* feast to commemorate an important lineage event, such as the rituals of a firstborn, or the commemoration of the death of a lineage elder. In these cases, the taro and sweet potato from the various contiguous gardens were harvested at the same time by a large group of village women and men, not just the couple who had tended the gardens, in preparation for the feast at which prominent outsiders were presented with baskets of food—fish, pork, betel nut, etc. Such events carried the name of the 'big man' and his *karakara* who sponsored them. Notwithstanding these ceremonial demands, other produce on each couple's garden, such as bananas, cassava, beans, chillies, tomatoes, eggplant and pumpkin, could be used for the individual household's personal consumption, and they could plant coconut and betel palms to which they had exclusive access.

Figure 2.2: Children play in a half-completed canoe while their parents burn off newly cleared gardens, 1969
Source: Author.

Figure 2.3: Father caring for infant during garden work, 1969
Source: Author.

The *karakara* was also identified with the big man's *galamo* (slit-gong) that was stored in the men's house. On ceremonial occasions, the hamlet group of men and women sang around that slit-gong and danced before it. The hamlet, at larger *mage* ceremonies, was represented by these same dancers or singers gathered at the slit-gong. The host of the *mage* invited other big men and their *karakara* to attend and to perform their dances, though the performers risked being flayed with rattan by the women of the host hamlet. The host distributed pigs, other foodstuffs and betel nut to the invited *karakara*, while not hesitating to criticise the quality of their performance at the slit-gong. Their standing as 'outsiders' was thus reiterated. Interchange between *karakara* was frequently very competitive, drawing attention not just to the talents of its men and women but to the strengths of their ancestors. This centrality of the hamlet and *karakara* in Maututu affairs continued despite the Australian administration's 1930s amalgamation of hamlets into villages (Figures 2.4 and 2.5).

Figure 2.4: Dismantling of food display and its distribution at a *mage* feast, 1969

Source: Author.

Figure 2.5: Dismantling the stands of food baskets at a *mage* feast, 1974

Source: Author.

In 1972, Mapulo Gaa, a big man of Gomu, challenged the young men of his hamlet who were spending their money on alcohol and lazing about to support him in holding a *mage* for his first child's initiation. He explained to me that preparing for the *mage* festival—organising its food distributions and dance performances—would test their resolve and their strength. 'The ways of the ancestors are difficult (*vogari*)', he said. 'To hold a *mage* allows key events of recent times to be commemorated, but more importantly galvanises the community to renew their pride and re-engage with other *karakara*.' His challenge was most immediately directed at those of his *karakara*, and, indirectly, at the youth of other *karakara*. He announced that at the feast he would present a large portion of food to particular 'big men' from outside *karakara*, and such gifts would impose on them the obligation to hold an exchange feast at a later time. When Mapulo, several days before the *mage*, brought out the slit-gong, announcing nights of singing and dancing, he made a presentation of baskets of young taro to a renowned hunter, Liulai from Baikakea, to hunt for pigs. Toruga, big man of the Baikakea Kabulu clan and clansman of Liulai, was annoyed that Liulai chose to hunt for Mapulo rather than work on his local *karakara* garden, and angrily cursed Liulai, who subsequently failed to spear any pigs. Liulai reported what had happened to Mapulo, who then made a formal challenge to Toruga by presenting him with baskets of young taro. Toruga and his *karakara* were thus put under obligation to return the feast in due time.

Mapulo Gaa identified with the hamlet of Urumaili higher up the slopes from other Gomu hamlets. Urumaili had been decimated by sorcery and feuding in the past. His challenge to the young men led to an incident later that year when they dissociated themselves from the slit-gong of the coastal hamlet (*la galamo olau*) to renew their identity with their origin *karakara*. They brought out their 'inland slit-gong' (*la galamo orai*) with the claim that they sang real Maututu songs (known as *la suluko*), not the songs of the Uasilau-Silanga Uasi/Pelevavu people, known as *la masegi*, that were being sung by the coastal group. This challenge, fuelled by alcohol, led to fighting between the two groups of youths, during which the slit-gong of the coastal hamlet was destroyed. The village leader (*kansil*) ordered the two groups to sing off to the remaining slit-gong until morning. The inland group invoked the spirits of their ancestors to join them to boost the strength of their singing and they outlasted their rivals. Their performance at the slit-gong led to the reinvigoration of their inland *karakara* and their return to that site.

Among the Maututu, the *karakara* has continued to be important in village affairs, even acquiring new functions. For example, in 2018, the church leadership in Baikakea instituted a novel way to raise funds for church buildings and pastor support, identifying 10 former male leaders and listing their descendants as 10 groups responsible for raising funds. This was an innovation of the *karakara* system, as these groups referred not to lineages but to those kin who would have supported that particular leader and who were mostly resident in a specific hamlet.

Matrilineages as linking home and outside

Strathern (1988) argued that personhood in PNG societies is embodied in the relationships that exist through acts of exchange. As distinct from 'modern' perspectives that stress the 'individual', she proffered the term 'dividual' to indicate the personhood in PNG that is tied to social relationships. Paige West (2021, p. 114), in her work in the Eastern Highlands of PNG, reflected similarly that 'the body is composed of relations'. Relationships are vital to Maututu, consolidating *karakara* cooperation and support for the 'big man'. The core of that solidarity rests on lineage membership and on marriage exchanges between lineages. 'Dividuals' are known as 'father of …' or 'mother of …' rather than by their personal name, or are referred to by their relationship with the speaker, such as *tailagu* (my cross-cousin), *isagu* (my aunt), *pupu* (my grandparent), etc. Each relationship is constituted through continuous food exchanges or cooperation in gardening and other activities. Rather than use personal names, Maututu refer to each other as *taogu* (my namesake), *tabu* (my in-law), *tabaragu* (my brother) and *kadere* (my friend, Tok Pisin), terms that stress the nature of their relationship.

Maututu trace their spiritual and social identity through their mother and, through their mother, claim membership in her matrilineage. Through her and her siblings, particularly her brothers, children become acquainted with lineage ancestors; sacred locations (*olu*), such as a reef, mountain or stream; and natural species, such as wallabies, cassowaries or turtles, that they recognise as ancestral *ruvu* (totems) and of especial value to their lineage and clan mates. They may not consume their *ruvu* because these share a matrilineal bond and may, in some contexts, be regarded as ancestors of the lineage. Lineages acknowledge a sacred association with their *olu*, a feature on the landscape such as a mountain or a waterway from where ancestors are thought to have originated or where they now gather. For example, Kabulu

Buleha lineage recognises a cassowary that lives on the reef off Bialla where it walks on the sea floor and also wanders up into the mountains that source the Tiauru River.[8] Members of other Kabulu lineages recognise the same *ruvu*, but may trace their origin to different sites scattered over Nakanai territory from Hoskins to Lolobau. Members of the extended *maratatila* (clan) recognise each other as kin because they share these common *ruvu* and *olu*.[9] They may also recognise other *maratatila* who acknowledge the same *ruvu* or sacred site *olu* as being closely related to them, though not of the same *maratatila*. The *maratatila* may also include a number of people adopted into the group.[10] For example, when a child's mother dies in childbirth or during the child's infancy, the child is brought up by another woman and may be adopted into that woman's *maratatila*—but not always, as those adults most concerned for the child will make a decision about the lineage of the child, which is partly dependent on how conscious the child has become of their birth mother's group.

Maututu are definite about the *maratatila* identity of each other—that is, one belongs to only one *maratatila*. It is within the localised lineages, rather than the more extensive clans, that genealogical ties are likely to be rehearsed. For example, the Kabuliala clan at Gomu has three lineages: Kabuliala Laulalu, whose ancestor came from Urumaili and who claim affiliation with soil in Urumaili; Kabuliala Kairokaroka, whose ancestors and soil are in Gomu; and Kabuliala Latoto, whose soil and specific *olu* are at Lolobau Island among the Meramera people. They all have common clan membership with Kabuliala people in Baikakea village, who nevertheless constitute another lineage. The Kabulu clan in Baikakea listed nine lineages—Buleha, Vavaa, Maugegete, Bolu, Sarukuruku, Guvilogo, Matamuli, Matalogo and Bamusi—and each of these had specific origins, taboos and totems as well as sharing in a common totemic affiliation with the turtle, cassowary, hornbill and white cockatoo. Two of these Kabulu lineages were specifically listed by my informants as *kaluvuti* (finished, died out). In Mataruru, Kabulu and Kabulu-mosi clans were said to have been one clan in the past. They divided when fighting broke out between clan members and they became

---

8   Kabulu is the wider clan; Kabulu Buleha the lineage.

9   *Mara-tatlla* is derived from *tatila* (mothers) and *mara* (meaning 'bunch' in some compounds).

10   My sense of the Maututu term *maratatila* (clan, lineage) is that, in the past, and to a lesser extent today, it primarily designates a link between the living and dead, defined partly by totemic associations—that is, the living and dead of a *maratatila* share respect for particular totemic animals, fish, plants or sites. Second, one's *maratatila* determines how one engages with others—members of one's *maratatila* are related to as siblings, mothers, mother's brothers, etc, while non-members may be defined by in-law designations indicating various avoidance relations, or as one's father's kin.

mosi (strangers) to the other. But they continued to share the *olu* (sacred sites) of Buleha and Paialo and the *ruvu* of the cassowary, white cockatoo and hornbill.

In this way, Nakanai all along the coast from Hoskins to Barema recognise common clan membership and can extend those memberships to neighbouring Meramera people and even Tolai people—that is, those neighbouring groups who share the matrilineal principle. In more recent times, when persons from further afield have married into Maututu families, lineage membership has been expanded to recognise them on the basis of shared totemic species or even a historic association. In these ways, lineage and clan identity is affirmed and strengthened through spiritual associations as much as through blood ties, providing ways in which lineages can be rejuvenated through incorporating others into exchange relations. Thus, kinship through lineage is constantly reconstructed in context yet remains the core of identity. Lineages link those at 'home' with outsiders, not only in other hamlets but also ancestral spirits, totemic species and sacred sites in the forest who together constitute the unity and cooperation vital in everyday and ritual occasions. More dramatically, the *maratatila* can recognise 'blood ties' with potentially a wide range of strangers *moimosi*.

Although the Maututu *maratatila* is founded on the birth ties between a mother and her children, the group is constantly finding expression through the sharing of food and hospitality, and through adoption and support. This becomes clear in bridewealth considerations. Bridewealth is collected by the father(s) and mother(s) and mother's brother and lineage of the prospective husband to present to the kin and lineage of the prospective wife, but Maututu see it not as marking exclusive lineage membership but as recognising the groups who have cared (*gogo*) for the prospective husband or wife. Those of the same lineage name who have not rendered care may not be recognised as kin in the activation of such exchanges. For example, in 1968, Adi, an Uge lineage woman from Baikakea, married a Kabulu lineage man from Apupulu village, and his Apupulu kin made a bridewealth payment to Adi's father and her mother's lineage. Adi's mother had died soon after childbirth and Adi, as an infant, was cared for by women of the Giloilouli lineage, who also were recognised in distribution of the bridewealth. Later, an Uge clan brother returned from Rabaul and demanded seven tins of *tubeli* shell from Apupulu as his share of bridewealth. Apupulu kin were indignant because they had already paid a large bridewealth, but Adi's father was also indignant because this kinsman had never looked after his lineage sister, though he shared her parents' house when they 'adopted' him.

When Adi and her husband later moved to live in Bubuu with Kabulu lineage kin, Apupulu kin demanded the bridewealth be returned to them by the Kabulu lineage in Bubuu. The Apupulu kin declared that the couple had deserted the husband's lineage in Apupulu, including the husband's younger brother, and their plantings of cocoa and coconuts in that settlement, but, most importantly, that their children would no longer grow up in Apupulu to contribute to the strength of their father's hamlet.

Almost inevitably, because hamlet populations are small, marriages bring together a man and a woman of different hamlets, the partnerships with outsiders forming the 'dividual' husband and wife. If the couple are in a sexual relationship prior to marriage, their kin see this relationship with an outsider as highly dangerous. However, once an exchange of valuables and food is arranged to seal the marriage, the outsider becomes 'at home'. The bride moves to the hamlet of her husband, and the lineages of husband and wife become closely aligned in the many exchanges throughout the life of the couple. Parents aim to celebrate a number of occasions in the life of their child, especially in the life of the first child (*posolagu*), and each occasion constitutes another moment to make presentations between the lineages and kin of the mother and father. The mother's brother is expected to pass onto his sisters' children his knowledge and some of his property, such as betel nut palms, slit-gongs, canoes, spears and the like, and they may spend some years in their adolescence living with him. In former days, but to a less extent today, the mother's brothers or mother's mother's brothers were responsible for the ear-piercing, nose-piercing and hair decoration ceremonies that marked a child's growing up. A man therefore has to balance his relationship with his own children and his sister's children in another hamlet, and he shares knowledge and valuables with them all. This link between lineages is, in principle, consolidated through later generation marriages. In the case of divorce, young children normally stay with the father in his hamlet, and if he has other wives are cared for by them. The bridewealth is not returned because the marriage has resulted in children for the man and his hamlet. On the other hand, if a childless woman refuses to stay with her husband her kin return the bridewealth.[11]

---

11 Some suggested that, in the past, her brothers might kill her for burdening them with the return of the valuables.

Such flexible mechanisms of constituting kin through social action were put under pressure by the intrusions of the colonial administration, church missions and even ethnographers who had the effect of rigidifying kinship membership. The Australian administration sought to define clans and lineages by formally listing their membership, just as they sought to formally define clan territories, in a dogmatic, exclusive and permanent way that did not correspond with the more fluid indigenous notions of recognising others through kinship. It led, as we shall see later, to more recent attempts by outside bodies to rectify local indigenous 'error' in determining clan membership, another example of ontological friction. Martin (2006, p. 30), in his study of the matrilineal Tolai society of East New Britain, suggests that names of matrilineal descent groups (*vunatarai*) should not be interpreted as designating a delimited social group, as they can refer to a range of different levels of descent group identity, from moiety to lineage sections. He indicates that outside pressures such as government policies or mining royalty negotiations can create these social identities in new and exclusive forms, but that these emerging social groups must be seen as contextual. Bolyanatz (2000, p. 16), ethnographer of the matrilineal Sursurunga of New Ireland, referred to 'activated matriliny, or conspicuous social relations', thus rejecting the rigidity of clan and lineage formulations that assign membership according to strict principles of descent. Maututu constantly identify *maratatila* as meaningful groups in social action, but these clans and lineages are constantly being reconstituted as people contribute to, or withdraw from, activities of the group, and outsiders are incorporated into *maratatila* as adopted members. In that sense, what is evident from practice and context is far more important than the ideology of genealogical rights through birth.

Gender balance

The relationship between men and women, as husband and wife, brother and sister, or as garden partners, suggests that 'dividuals' mature through the forging of relations perceived in terms of wild–home partnerships. In myths, women are more typically of the 'home', their husbands of the 'wild'. A woman marrying into a hamlet is of the 'outside' and her children are encouraged to keep associating with their mother's brother 'outside'. The lineage, in its membership, links dividuals of two or more hamlets, and these links are constantly invigorated through the exchange of valuables and food, particularly at *mage* feasts.

Women's agency in contributing to hamlet vitality is celebrated in many of the myths. They negotiate with spirits, summon sexual partners, and abandon tyrannical husbands. One myth, that of Gavemo, ends with the phrase 'That day was the women's day'. This story uses the familiar mythemes of the arrogant big man Wallaby and his sister's son Orphan.

The men in Wallaby's *karakara* went hunting pigs in preparation for a big feast; Orphan was expected to marry Wallaby's daughter but he did not join the hunt. Instead Orphan was tasked with carrying the game back to the wife of Wallaby and her daughter who roasted the pork for the feast. One day as he carried the pigs into the hamlet Orphan caught sight of the sexual organs of Wallaby's wife and innocently asked her about them, because he had no knowledge of how sexual relations were conducted. Wallaby's wife explained sex to Orphan. This happened repeatedly over several days and Wallaby, suspicious of how long Orphan was taking to deliver the pigs, tailed him home and from his hiding spot heard their conversation. Wallaby exploded in anger, shaming Orphan.

Next day the shamed Gavemo dressed in his finery, climbed on the roof ridge of the house, and set fire to the house, singing his name as he burnt to death. But a spit of his fat lodged in a banana bunch growing nearby and Wallaby's wife noticed it and stored the bunch in the house rafters. In the subsequent days Gavemo came back to life in that banana bunch and was discovered there by the two women. Wallaby's wife and daughter then secretly redirected their feast preparations, no longer to Gavemo's funeral but to a celebration of his rebirth. It became a feast for Gavemo, and Wallaby was ignored. Gavemo was brought out by the two women, and he and the two women distributed the food. That day became the women's day.

In this myth, it is the strength of the mother–daughter relationship (and through them the matrilineage) that nurtures Gavemo to manhood. He is not of their lineage but his role as future procreator of their lineage is instilled in him by his future mother-in-law as vital to the wellbeing of the community. Orphan transforms from a maligned loner to a mature man ready for marriage.

The following story of Samsam captures the initiative of women in marital relationships.

> A young 'strong-eyed' woman had rejected all men's advances until a young
> man from up in the mountains decided to woo her. He threw two charmed
> coconut leaf midribs provided by his grandparent from the crown of a tree near
> his compound directly into her house far away near the coast. She was curious
> as to who would approach her in this way and her thoughts became restless.
> Finally, Samsam appeared, singing his song searching for his charmed midribs,
> going from house to house to enquire after them. When he reached her house,
> she enticed him in and, blocking the door, had sex with him. The villagers
> objected to her relationship with this mountain 'wild' man, but she insisted on
> her choice and returned with Samsam to the village of his grandparent.

Samsam is the 'wild', spirit-aided hunter from the mountain region, but
his sights and spears are set on his future wife at 'home'. She is not only
the pioneer of this new affinal relationship with the outsider but also is the
origin of her lineage in his remote community.

In another myth, young women actually venture into the wild to collect
galip almond nuts (*la uele*).

> It was the season of galip harvest when two young women went far into
> the forest in search of the nuts. They came to a tree where Litu was shaking the
> nuts to the ground. The women collected the nuts. They viewed his legbands
> and armbands lying at the base of the tree and desired him, and when he
> descended they invited him to have sex with them. They then carried the nuts
> home. The girls were smitten in their love for Litu. They refused their father's
> best food and had no interest in the young men he called each night as their
> suitors to sing to the slit-gong. Their thoughts were only for Litu. So their
> father sent kingfisher to scour the mountain slopes for the remote village of
> the man who was distracting the girls. When kingfisher came to Litu's hamlet,
> he recognised the subject of the women's infatuation and invited Litu to sing to
> the slit-gong in the women's village. Litu protested that he had no kin to join
> him, as he and his mother lived alone. However, kingfisher insisted he accept
> the invitation. After kingfisher departed, Litu spat ginger towards the wild
> betel palm and men, women and children dropped from its branches. As his
> new-found *karakara* journeyed to the coast in their finery, a great wind tore
> down trees along their path. As he entered the village, the two young women
> husked the galip nuts they had collected from him and fed him. When big
> man Wallaby challenged his right to marry the women, Litu speared him in the
> buttocks and departed with the young women.

Like Samsam, Litu is associated with the wild. He lives in the mountains and has spirit partners and powerful ginger magic. The girls as active agents respond to this wildness. The forging of productive and intimate relations between the wild man and the village girls exemplifies the richness Maututu envisage in partnerships between the domestic world and what the wider environment outside has to offer them. It is a relationship in which both parties have agency and respect.

Negotiating partnerships with outsiders

There is, thus, in the Maututu ontological frame, a focus on a partnership of home with the wild, whether humans with spirits, female with male, or home kin with those in outside hamlets. Villagers saw the forest world outside their hamlet as suffused in unbounded richness and spiritual energy that could be dangerous but could also be harnessed to benefit the dividual and the community. This was an ontological perspective that was vastly different to that of the colonial outsiders who were disposed to suppress the Maututu 'home' by imposing the 'wild' on them. I focus on two innovations by outsiders to 'develop' native society, through local government and local schooling, to illustrate how Maututu negotiated these innovations.

Local government

In the prewar years, Australian patrol officers (*kiap*) periodically visited Maututu from their headquarters in Hoskins. They appointed local leaders (*luluai, tultul*) to administer regulations and collect taxes, but this did not result in the 'free, close and permanent' association that the Australian administration envisaged (Mortimer, 1979, p. 184). Further administration reforms led to the establishment of local government councils. These were established throughout PNG after the passage of the Village Councils Ordinance in 1950 as a means of cultivating a closer association of expatriate *kiap* with 'natives'. The Tolai of the Gazelle Peninsular led the way by rapidly establishing five councils in the 1950s (Salisbury, 1970), but it was not until 1967 that the Nakanai Council was set up, bringing together under one local government body the Meramera people north of Maututu, the Maututu people at Bialla and the Central Nakanai around the resettlement sites of Uasilau-Silanga. Maututu were daunted by the prospect of cooperating with the larger Uasilau-Silanga population from the interior of the island, but they were encouraged when the new patrol post was established at Ewasse (beside Uase village) and an expatriate *kiap* appointed to live there and to advise the council. The challenge for the Maututu, as for their council neighbours, was to build respect and cooperation beyond their own linguistic and political communities.

The first elected president (Figure 2.6) of the council was the former *luluai* of Gomu/Apupulu and chairman of the Maututu Cooperative Society, Mapulo Gaa. Born about 1930, he had only received a year or so of primary education. Through his earlier time as *luluai*, Gaa had won the respect of *kiap*, *didiman* (agricultural field officers) and the Bialla Plantation manager, and his leadership led to the council receiving early strong support from these expatriates. A *kiap*'s patrol report at the time opined that he was the 'only influential leader among the Maututu' (Department of External Territories, 1968). Gaa suggested to me that, at the time, he was the only one who could 'follow white man's thinking quickly enough' and that others could not express themselves in front of the *masta kiap*. He was thus able to cultivate partnerships with both expatriates and the mountain communities, bridging the ontological divides. The council's population was about 6,300 at the time (*Post Courier*, 1970), of whom about a thousand were Maututu (see Table A.1).

Figure 2.6: Mapulo Gaa, 1969
Source: Author.

The council comprised 18 councillors (*kansil*, replacing the *luluai*), each with oversight over two or three villages. They had the task of articulating the demands of the administration with their own community priorities. Councils were intended to take responsibility for the maintenance of law and order and 'good government' and to facilitate the provision of public services out of local peoples' resources (AL Epstein, 1969, pp. 264–65). Council meetings were run according to a set agenda presided over by the *kiap* but chaired by the president, with a regular finance report. In each village, the *kansil* member was assisted by a *komiti* (committee man), who organised collective labour, called meetings and liaised with government. The *komiti* collected the head tax of K10 for men and K5 for women, which they sent to the executive officer of the council. From the head tax fund, the council financed building improvements, such as community halls built by residents in each village, a water tank in Gomu and a health clinic in Gigipuna. Each *kansil* member received an honorarium of K20 for attendance at council meetings, but otherwise *kansil* and *komiti* were unpaid.

Expatriate expectations were in tension with native viewpoints. For example, in 1970, the Nakanai Council, under pressure from the *kiap*, passed a pig law, requiring owners to fence village pigs on the edge of the village in order to improve family health. However, this ignored Maututu preference that pigs forage for food around the houses and kitchens, cleaning up waste, and that they sleep underneath the house where owners could watch over them. The *kiap* patrol report following the application of the council ruling observed 'the devastating effect on traditional village life' of this rule, as owners preferred to sell their pigs rather than fence them and be forced to feed them' (Department of External Territories, 1968). The decline in pig numbers threatened local capacity to hold customary rituals and ceremonies, and the council at a subsequent meeting rescinded the law.

While the administration sought to create a stable leadership with whom they could negotiate, Maututu preferred the position of *kansil* to be rotated among prominent dividuals. In Baikakea, Tauvere, highly respected in Baikakea and Bubuu because of his leadership in cocoa planting, was elected the first *kansil* representing the two Maututu villages and the Mengen village of Gigipuna. In subsequent years, he was replaced by Kasivalo from Bubuu, then Vaisisi from Baikakea and then Lapou from Bubuu, reflecting local preference to alternate the role between these two villages. Similarly, the *kansil* position for Ewasse, Matililiu and Mataruru, and that for Gomu (including Urumaili) and Apupulu, was rotated among the constituent villages. These *kansil* were expected by villagers to have the personalities of 'true big men'—men of compassion and balanced temperaments, who earned respect not through their abrasive behaviour but through careful consideration of local concerns. The *komiti*, on the other hand, although nominated by villagers were seen as enacting the demands of the *kiap*, and were often characterised as aggressive, impetuous and with angry temperaments (*la tahalo la igototolola*). They were expected to intervene in village disputes but it was more often the *kansil* who reconciled the disputants. The *komiti* ensured that the villagers fulfilled the orders of the *kiap*. On 'government day' (each Monday), the *komiti* would assign someone to draw water for the school, or collect and sew roof thatch for the Cocoa Society fermentery, or collect *tubeli* shell to pay their tax, or to maintain roads. A few would be sent to council 'headquarters' at Ewasse to cut grass or perform other tasks there. It was common in village meetings for *komiti* to call out 'laggards' who were not contributing enough labour to the various activities, and senior men would criticise young men for not turning up to clean the council headquarters.

Engagement with these outside forces was, wherever possible, on Maututu terms. The authority of *kansil* and *komiti*, formally with the backing of council and *kiap*, was largely based on their acceptance within the community. When, at rare times, the *komiti* appealed to the *kiap*—usually when instructions from the *kiap* were being ignored by the community—fellow villagers would become indignant with him. The *kiap*'s authority, stemming from the colonial administration, had little traction in the village, and was only tolerated by villagers in those spheres managed by expatriates, such as around the council headquarters, school and Bialla Plantation. In village affairs, the *kansil* and *komiti* were expected to keep the *kiap* at a distance rather than draw him and police into community matters. Their leadership was built on consultation in the community.

A frequent accusation aired at the village meetings before the *komiti* was adultery. The council formally designated a fine of A$1,000 for adultery and when such a matter was sent to the *kiap* he would impose the full fine, in a literal reading of the council's intent. Villagers, on the other hand, saw the nominated amount simply as reflecting expatriate priorities. In 1969, the *kansil* in Baikakea-Bubuu presided over a case of a villager who had sexual relations with a married woman. After witnesses were called and the man admitted the liaison, the *kansil* threatened a fine of A$100 but finally determined a fine of A$10. He added that if the woman had been unmarried no wrong would have been done, thus ignoring formal church teaching about sexual relations before marriage. This same *kansil* also heard the case of a married man who had propositioned a single woman and sought to work love magic on her. She complained to her male kin of this behaviour and the married man was fined A$2.

Villagers did not hesitate to resist council demands when these were seen as undermining community. For example, the opening of the council headquarters in April 1969 required the levelling and clearing of an airstrip at Ewasse for the arrival of dignitaries. Maututu were conscripted over several weeks to get this work done, supervised by the *kiap*. At one point, a worker let out a yell of exhaustion as he struck his spade into the ground, something villagers regularly did as they worked their own gardens, but the *kiap* interpreted this as insolence and, with clenched fists, advanced on the man. The villager grabbed the *kiap*'s wrists to prevent him striking out and in the ensuing scuffle the *kiap* fell into the ditch. At this point, the *kiap* told the village *komiti* to summon a policeman, which he did, and in the following days 13 of the workers were tried for insubordination before a court run by the *kiap* at Hoskins patrol post. Found guilty, they were sentenced to jail in Hoskins for periods varying from two to five months. In later discussions villagers strongly condemned the *komiti* who had done the *kiap*'s bidding to fetch the police. In retelling the incident, these villagers judged the *kiap* as not worthy of their respect, and, decades later, were still telling the story with great pride. The Ewasse *kiap* himself misinterpreted what had occurred when he remarked later to me 'these villagers do not realise that it is for the good of their own Council that they are doing this work'.

Though they struggled to engage this *kiap* in partnership, they were enthusiastic in using the council through the *kansil* and *komiti* to bring in changes in 'home' arrangements that reflected community concerns. For example, the 'government day' instituted by council led to the adoption of other days of the week for 'home' concerns. Tuesday was youth (*baramana*) day, reserved for the youth group to work on their cocoa blocks or other activities; Wednesday was set aside for working at the church or in the pastor's garden; Thursday was for the Women's Fellowship; and Friday was for work on family cocoa blocks. Villagers sought to adopt new 'modern' patterns when these articulated with their 'home' priorities.

Local schooling

These accommodations of 'home' with outsider demands were also evident in Maututu willingness to engage with schooling developments. Up to 1964, all local schooling was conducted by Methodist pastors in individual villages. Pastors who had little or no teacher training generally taught to Grades 2–3, focusing on literacy. The one or two children who went further in education had to board at schools in Hoskins and Rabaul. When plans for the Airmen's Memorial School (AMS) were announced in 1963, Maututu villagers eagerly supported the scheme as it offered full primary schooling without the necessity of leaving home. A Parents and Citizens Association (P&C) was formed to support the school, and in the next few years village carpenters helped to build permanent material classrooms and teachers' houses. The Nakanai Council also took a keen interest in the school. Mapulo Gaa, as council president, persuaded the Airmen's Memorial Foundation (AMF) to purchase a block of land in the planned resettlement scheme and to plant it with coconuts as a way of supporting the school financially. In his thinking, if funding ceased from the AMF, the school would have this reserve source of funds.[12]

The AMS opened in 1964 with an Australian headmaster, four native teachers, four classrooms and around 100 children, mostly from the nearby pastor schools of Matililiu and Uase, enrolled in Grades 1–4.[13] In 1966, children from the northern Maututu villages joined the school in large numbers after the pastor school at Apupulu was closed. By 1968, Preparatory and Grades 5 and 6 classes had been added, so that local children could complete their primary schooling in the Bialla area while living at home (Table A.2). In 1969, it was still rare for children to go beyond primary school, and many did not complete Grade 6. At the time, I counted only 13 Maututu youth across all villages who had attended one or more years at high school in Rabaul.[14] However, by 1972, a third of the Grade 6 graduates from AMS continued to high school, opening opportunities to gain employment as teachers and medical workers or as 'missionaries' (church pastors and lay preachers).[15]

The school thus bridged expatriate and local aspirations, with parents keen to adopt outside ways if they could be brought into line with local priorities. One concern of the P&C in those early years was that the school

---

12 A few years later, this block was planted in oil palm managed by Hargy Oil Palm in the interests of the school.

13 In the first intake in 1964, the average age of those admitted to Preparatory was 6 years old, Standard 1 was 8.5 years, Standard 2 was 11.5 years, and Standard 3 was 14 years, thus indicating the serious lack of consistent schooling in the pastor schools up to that time.

14 Girls were just as likely as boys to attend school at AMS, although, in the 1960s, it was still unusual for girls to leave the area for secondary school.

15 Moramora Technical College, Vunerima Technological College, Vunapope High School, Teacher Training College and Salelubu Agricultural College.

was exclusively focusing on education in the expatriate language (English) and culture (educational syllabus) and marginalising local *kastom* (culture). Children were penalised for speaking in local language in the classroom and playground. The parents pointed out that their children were often absent from home from dawn to dusk due to the distance they had to walk and could not therefore be grounded in local cultural priorities. The AMF agreed to employ an ethnographer who would study local language and *kastom* and introduce these into the school program. This led to my recruitment to introduce local cultural practices to the classroom by using village elders as instructors, and to initiate a literacy program in the Maututu language for school children. Parents repeatedly expressed to me their concern that abandoning local ways would not only disorientate the children from local ontological perspectives but also undermine Maututu political and cultural identity as the area began to open up.[16] There was a sense even in these early years that the AMS was a Maututu school and needed to be closely watched to ensure that local interests were served. At one P&C meeting, this included berating the expatriate headmaster for being absent from the school in class time.

Conclusion

This chapter has explored the Maututu understanding of the partnership between home and the wild outside. Not only are dividuals formed through relationships, as has been demonstrated elsewhere in PNG, but also, importantly, through partnerships with the wild: indeed, this is how the most creative relationships are formed. The analysis has shown that relations between humans and spirits, villagers and forest species, women and men, *karakara* and outside lineages, and docile and explosive personality traits all illustrate this principle of articulating home and wild elements.

This set the pattern for Maututu responses to colonial and church developments. While the colonial administration sought to impose radical change on hamlet communities, in line with expatriate ontological perspectives, local residents sought to ameliorate these demands by moulding them to local interests. Appointed leaders largely supported community

16 The colonial objection to indigenous language and culture was overturned after independence. In 2014, village schools under village teachers taught reading and writing up to Grade 2 in the local language before students went onto the government primary school in Grade 3, where English became the language of instruction.

rather than *kiap* concerns, the local school promoted 'home' concerns, hamlets retained their prominence despite village amalgamation, and the weekly allocation of tasks balanced *gavman* (government) duties with community priorities. In welcoming the 'modern' changes that outsiders brought, local communities prided themselves on material transformations of their 'home' settlement—for example, the health posts and water tanks, the 'modern' church buildings (corrugated iron, cement floor and fibro sheeting) in Matililiu and Gomu, and the school and council headquarters near Uase. These symbols of outside 'development' became the focus of 'home' identity. The following chapters will explore this process more specifically in agricultural developments that brought into stark contrast the tension arising between outside and local ontologies.

3

Foreign crops and home initiatives

When German planters acquired 2,000 hectares of land at Bialla in 1912, none of the hamlet residents who received their gifts as payment would have been aware that this extensive area, so casually acquired by the visiting seamen, had been delineated by boundaries on colonial maps. Maututu villagers would not have understood the concept of 'purchase of freehold title'. As we shall see below, Maututu perceptions of 'soil' contrasted with the European notion of 'freehold title' over land. Was there any notification at the time that hamlet populations residing in the Bialla area would be required to vacate the delineated land or that valuable wild forest was destined to be felled for a coconut plantation? For Maututu, exchange was a valuable complement to local production, but it never included landed resources such as trees or the land itself. Rather than representing a 'sale' of land, the exchange of goods probably signified to Maututu that the German visitors acknowledged Maututu affiliation with the area.

In 1933, the Australian administration conducted a survey of the Bialla Plantation area through Mr Barry of the Native Affairs Department. Barry concluded that the Neu Guinea Compagnie had 'illegally' acquired much of the Bialla Plantation in 1912, as it was not 'waste and ownerless' land. The survey documented 15 Maututu hamlets occupying 1,679 hectares within the area acquired by the company—that is, 84 per cent of the total area—and Barry (1933) concluded that the residents should be compensated for these lands.[1] In the legal settlement, Barry determined that 800 hectares

---

1   Gomu residents in 1969 suggested that the Bialla land adjacent to their village 'belonged' to two clans, Kabuliala on the seaward half and Kabulu on the inland half.

of coastal land acquired but not planted by the Neu Guinea Compagnie be returned to the Maututu, to be replaced by another 800 hectares further inland of Bialla to reinstate the Bialla freehold title to 2,000 hectares. The ruling thus recognised Maututu sovereignty over soil from Gomu to Bubuu to the north of Bialla that was originally included in the Neu Guinea Compagnie land. The administration paid Maututu a price per hectare for the replacement area, and, in doing so, perhaps for the first time, alerted Maututu to this strange colonial custom of measuring and valuing soil as a material commodity that could be traded. In indigenous terms, the cash paid was more likely to have been seen as an exchange for the use of the soil. Fifty years later, Maututu from Urumaili, Gomu and Uase asserted their right to reclaim these soils on the basis that their ancestors could not have understood the colonial concept of 'purchase'.

The newly acquired 800 hectares were identified by Barry as 'wasted' area that the plantation could 'improve' through agricultural development. But Maututu would have seen such 'wasted' areas in a quite different way. For them, secondary and primary forest represented future sites of gardens and settlement. They recognised that soils could only be used for three or so years before their fertility was exhausted and they were returned to the wild for regeneration. Home production needed to build on wild fertility. The abundance of former hamlet and garden sites throughout the forest, even on the acquired block, was testimony to this pattern of regeneration.

In 1969, I was told by Council Chairman Mapulo:

> in our grandparents' time the law was not strong in reference to land ownership, and it was only when the government sat down with us to delineate land rights that people themselves marked their land. Before that it was simply a matter of saying that such and such a lineage was the original clearer of a site.

Mapulo had recently returned from an official tour, undertaken by Papua New Guinea (PNG) council presidents, to Australia that included a meeting with the 'Demarcation Committee' in Canberra. On his return, he reported to a village meeting that councils in Australia controlled land and could commandeer it if owners did not pay their taxes. When questioned, Mapulo offered his view that the colonial administration had bought land in West New Britain to protect it from Chinese traders and *masta* (white Australians), who would otherwise *gris* (bribe) clan leaders to steal their soil. The term he used for the government acquisition was *lotorobo* (protect by purchase), seemingly acknowledging a continued association of Maututu with such soils.

Victoria Stead (2013, p. 26), an observer of change on the Oro coast of mainland PNG, explains that 'ontologically distinct ways of being in the world are entangled with one another and the ambivalences of this multiplicity engender the possibility of creativity as well as of insecurity'. In her analysis, 'modern and customary forms of social relations can exist coterminously' (Stead, 2013, p. 19). Stead prefers the term entanglement for such analyses, where local forms are not absorbed into a new hybrid modernity but rather local and global configurations jostle for meaning in their entanglement. There is an 'articulation' between customary and modern ways of being and seeing, they overlap and generate friction as people negotiate the way forward. The 1968–69 discussions with me of 'land' demarcation and purchase indicated that local ontological perceptions of *la magasa* (soil) differed from, yet existed alongside, the colonial administration's formulation of 'land' as an alienable property.

In his studies of PNG societies, Rumsey (2006) differentiates three models for thinking about articulations between indigenous and expatriate viewpoints. As an exemplar of the first of these, he cites Sahlins's model of 'develop-man' that envisages people 'devising on their own heritage, acting according to their own categories, logics, understandings'. In this model, Sahlins (1992) proposed a radical disjunction between tradition and modernity. He described Pacific peoples as yearning to retain *kastom* (traditional culture) even as they grappled with the pressures and aspirations of development and modernity. For his second model, Rumsey cites Robbins who proposed that, in certain circumstances, people 'take on an entirely new culture on its own terms', such as through the Christian charismatic movement. The third model is exemplified by what Clifford (2001) calls 'processing the new through dynamic traditional structures'. In this model, indigenous peoples 'reconfigure themselves, drawing selectively on remembered past[s]' in affirming their autonomy to both insiders and outsiders. Rumsey (2006, p. 61) refers to this process as 'contingent juxtaposition, the bringing together of previously isolated entities or categories in a way that reveals something theretofore concealed or latent in each'.

In this chapter I examine this juxtaposition of diverse ontological understandings of soil and 'agricultural development', and how Maututu attempted to articulate their home ontological framework with outsiders' demands.

On home soil (*la magasa*)

Maututu use the term *la magasa* when talking of land areas significant to them. I shall use the term 'soil' rather than 'land' to distinguish their ontological understanding from that reflected in the administration's registration of 'land' as a bounded and transactable asset. For a variety of reasons, such as seeking fertile garden sites or escaping friction within *karakara* and lineage groups, individual households within Maututu hamlets regularly dispersed and cleared new gardens. This 'soil' then became permanently associated with the pioneers and their grouping of *karakara* and *maratatila*. The original clearer was said to have *vaipalahia la magasa* (revealed/brought into existence the soil from the past) and his *karakara egite tomi tahaloa vamuli* (kin all affiliated with it after that).[2] Individual men, on their hunting trips through the forest, would discover fruit trees, wild betel nut or sago palms and mark those as affiliated with them, but such claims did not extend to the soil on which the tree stood unless they also cleared that soil for gardens. Once the soil was abandoned to forest regrowth, another dividual could clear it, but only with the approval of the lineage who had pioneer association with it. Thus, throughout the forest, *la magasa* marked an affiliation between *karakara* or lineage and that site. In addition, while lineages recognised exclusive association with sacred *ruvu* sites (*la olu*), those sites did not constitute claims to the wider areas around them. *La magasa* and *la olu* were identified by the site centre, not its boundaries. In 1968–69, the extent of village, hamlet or lineage territory was not demarcated. Farmers marked the boundaries of their individual garden plots, but, beyond those, the only boundary was one imagined by the colonial administration.

In the days before extensive commercialisation of agriculture in the area, lineages and *karakara* rarely objected to individuals clearing primary or secondary forest. Utilisation of that soil was temporary and served to reflect or create strong links among kin and neighbours. Indeed, lineages might allow others to farm the soil because the 'name' of the pioneer lineage would be enhanced by the later lineage's activity, while the soil always remained affiliated with the pioneering lineage. Tauvere commented to me in 1969:

---

2   *Vai-palahia* has the sense of bringing into existence or into the present. *Palaha* refers to the past, always associated with ancestors, so there is a sense here also of bringing the ancestors into the affairs of the present through the clearing of land that they inhabited in the past. *Tahalo* refers to 'man', so *tahaloa* is an action that links a human with the soil.

> In the past we planted our coconuts, betel nuts, pepper vines, breadfruit and galip trees wherever we liked, on the soil of any lineage, and these plantings could be passed onto our children, sister's children or other kin. In the same way we planted our gardens on any soil, and when they became overgrown and reforested anyone could open them up again.

Maututu ontological understandings of soil were far removed from colonial aspirations for the development of PNG land. In 1958, Minister for Territories Paul Hasluck stated:

> Government's land policy is to respect native ownership of land and to ensure that enough land is reserved to native inhabitants to meet their present and prospective needs. Land can only be acquired from native owners … if [they] are willing to sell.
>
> (National Archives of Australia [NAA], 1947–63)

A letter dated 24 August 1961 from Administrator Cleland to Department Secretary Lambert in Canberra noted that:

> suitable land is bought provided a) owners are unanimously willing to sell, b) land is surplus to their present requirements and those of foreseeable future, c) it is generally suited to agricultural/ pastoral use.
>
> (NAA, 1947–63)

Hasluck noted in 1962 that the major problem for government in the coming years would be finding land for native settlers who had no land of their own. In October 1962, the departmental record added: 'The Minister believes that sooner or later consideration will have to be given to some degree of coercion or compulsion in obtaining native owned land to satisfy demand [by land-poor indigenes]' (NAA, 1947–63). An Australian External Affairs special issue on land tenure in PNG (Sack, 1971) noted that the European concept of alienability of land was foreign to traditional systems of land tenure, but that this was rarely acknowledged. The author noted that:

1. natives still believe their land is not really alienated
2. that to be paid for the land acknowledged the person's rights to the land
3. natives do not seem to be sure whether a 'big man' was entitled to dispose of land.

Victoria Stead, citing Filer (2014), suggested that a PNG national ideology of land ownership arose during this time, stimulated by both colonial and post-colonial land policies:

> The national ideology of landownership declares all indigenous citizens to be customary landowners, it denies the possibility of waste or vacant land, it identifies clans as the foundational social unit of the nation, and it establishes rent or resource compensation (paid to 'customary landowners' whose land or natural resources are subject to commercial exploitation) as a principal mode of income and the predominant means of accessing 'development'.
>
> (Stead, 2017b, p. 358)

Significant here is the ideology's assumption that the clan is both the foundational social unit and landholding unit, and that arrangements can therefore be made to purchase surplus land from clans for the purposes of national economic growth. Stead concluded:

> The introduction of practices of land formalisation brings into being a whole new system and structure of knowing and governing land. Abstracted from the intimate and particular relations of belonging—defined through new practices of boundary making—land is stripped of its own agentive capacity and potential, and customary communities' autonomy over their own land similarly diminishes.
>
> (Stead, 2017b, p. 374)

Soil for the Maututu was not a commodity to be bought and sold. Rather, as Stead remarks, land/soil has 'agentive capacity'—it carries and expresses the affiliations that generations of Maututu have with it; they have *tahaloa* (personed) it. For generations, Maututu had built relations with the soil and its wild residents, and had welcomed outsiders to settle with their *karakara* and use their soil. As Curry and Koczberski (2009, p. 99) note:

> the social relationships from which land rights are derived and accorded their moral legitimacy are not pre-given, nor unchanging; rather they must be constructed and carefully maintained and from their presence, resources rights flow.

Maututu neighbours from a wide kin base frequently cooperated to clear gardens, there being no sense of lineage exclusivity when it came to cultivation of the soil; rather, soil worked to create kinship links. For example, in the 1970s in Baikakea, an elder in the Kabulu clan gave permission for his wife's brother (who had no children) from the Uge clan to plant coconuts on soil associated with Kabulu ancestors, and these palms were later inherited by his Uge sister's children. At both stages, when the Uge man first planted and then when the palms were inherited, the Kabulu lineage members were consulted and the soil remained affiliated with their lineage, although utilised by Uge members. The coconuts did not determine ownership of the soil, but the use of the soil reinforced the close links between Kabulu and Uge lineages. Vegter (2005, pp. 553–54) explains that common property regimes in PNG mean that:

> property is not necessarily defined as the right of persons over things, but as obligations owed between persons with respect to things … Such ownership provides an incentive structure that enhances coordination, cooperation and investment among resource-using groups.

Alex Golub (2007, p. 41) adds: 'land tenure in Papua New Guinea is characterized less by routine implementation of an established order and more by a generative ambiguity'. Such flexibility was at odds with a colonial administration anxious to demarcate 'land' and list its clan 'owners'. In administrative and business discourses, natives were increasingly defined in terms of the 'land' they purportedly owned and the administrative villages in which they resettled. But ideas of 'landholding' and 'village' reflected a very different ontology espoused by global investors and colonial governments, at odds with how Maututu affiliated with sites and accessed soil for gardening and gathering. There was, and remains, a strong distinction between the 'land' envisaged by expatriates, government and developers, and the soil (*la magasa*) that Maututu cultivate, and between the 'village' defined by its administrative boundaries, and the specific sites, such as *la olu* (sacred location, mountain) or *la mautu* (hamlet), that Maututu share with the spirits of ancestral kinsfolk. For the Maututu, such sites are integral to their sense of wellbeing and identity; however, for successive administrations intent on 'opening up the land', people can be resettled in new sites and their identity defined in terms of formalised village and clan. It is the tension between such different ontologies of being that most threatened Maututu engagement with outside forces of modernity.

This ontological friction in regard to soil/land was not easily resolved. In August 1960, Native Lands Commissioner Read, in determining clan ownership of the land in the Nakanai area, assigned much of the land to pairs of clans (External Territories, 1968, p. 57). But while hamlet leaders may have indicated to the commissioner that particular lineages were linked in a particular hamlet, there was no formal pairing of clans across Maututu society, unlike in neighbouring Silanga.[3] What Maututu did recognise was

---

3   In the population of Silanga, where Nakanai and non-Nakanai were jointly resettled, van Rijswijck (1966, p. 7) reports that 'the traditional kinship system is based on the principle of dual organization. Every individual belongs to one of two main exogamous clans whose membership is determined matrilineally.' She adds that on Chowning's authority this is different to the coastal Nakanai (van Rijswijck 1966) The Tolai term *vunatarai* refers not just to 'clans/lineages' but to two moieties into which all lineages are located (Martin, 2006, p. 30).

the grouping of lineage members organised by each 'big man' and focused on his *karakara* and *hulumu* and the *mage* that he sponsored. Under the Land Titles Commission Act passed in 1962, Land Demarcation Committees were set up in each area, including a representative from each village,[4] with the aim of making 'land' available for 'development'. The committees worked on the colonial assumption that land could be divided into clan domains that were owned according to Western notions of property. In addition, the committees focused only on current settlements and demarcated more remote areas as 'empty'. The colonial administration insisted at the time that these vast swathes of jungle inland from the Maututu villages were extra to 'native' needs and should be purchased for economic expansion, despite the history of Maututu ancestors occupying those sites.

Home plantings and foreign plantations

A Maututu myth recounts the arrival of coconuts in the area as the outcome of a violent struggle at sea between the 'home' hero and a monster fish.

Ture, his brother-in-law and other youth canoed to the island to shoot birds. Late in the afternoon only Ture had not returned to the canoes, so the men paddled home. Ture finally reached the beach but there was no canoe for him. He constructed a raft and paddled out with all the pigeons he had shot. It was slow and exhausting by raft. Suddenly a large fish broke the surface beside him and threatened to capsize the raft. Ture threw the pigeons, one by one, to the fish until there was none left. The fish consumed the logs of the raft one by one until only one log remained, as Ture sang his mournful song. Ture cut off his own leg and threw it to the fish, then the other leg, then other parts of his body, and still the fish menaced him. Finally only Ture's head remained, floating on the ocean. Ture's sister, informed by her husband, waited anxiously on the beach. Her brother's head floated to her on the tide, and she buried it carefully inside her house. Days later the head sprouted and over time bore coconut fruit. She fed the fruit to her child who was crying from hunger and the child grew fat. Some time later another sister noticed how chubby the child had become and asked for the coconut. Now the coconut has been planted throughout the villages.

---

4   Among Maututu these were the recognised big men of each village (Mataimi, Valu, Peni, Mapulo Gaa, Ubi and Kiapa).

The dead Ture, at risk of becoming a wild spirit, is incorporated back 'home' as a coconut by his sister, his lineage partner, another example of the riches that emerge in the myths from such encounters of home and wild. Several other myths narrated the discovery of wild coconuts and their subsequent cultivation at home.

Coconuts were also introduced into New Britain by the colonial outsiders. The Gazelle Peninsular was the centre for expatriate coconut plantations from the 1880s. In the early 1900s, Maututu coconut growers may have sold their coconuts to the German plantations or Chinese traders opening up on the Gazelle, and, once Bialla Plantation began production, they were able to sell their coconuts and copra there.[5] In time, both the administration, intent on collecting cash taxes, and the plantation managers, interested in expanding the copra exports, encouraged Maututu to plant coconut palms more extensively. The villagers did this—not in the ordered line of palms typical of expatriate plantations, but in clusters near their hamlets, allowing men and women to pick coconuts daily for household consumption.

Prior to Barry's 1933 survey of Bialla, the *Rabaul Times*, on 21 October 1927, announced the sale of approximately 2,000 hectares in Bialla, described as 'expropriated property that had not been surveyed nor entered in the "ground book", but when entered it was expected the title would be freehold'. This implies that little work had been done by the Neu Guinea Compagnie to transform the Bialla area into a plantation and that the area had been ignored by the Australian postwar administration until 1927. Four people tendered to purchase the property, three of whom were returned Australian soldiers. An Australian-born, German-ancestry settler Frederick Werner tendered by far the highest bid at £800, which was accepted and the sale completed in February 1928, with a loan recorded of £130 from the shipping and plantation company Burns Philp (BP).[6] Werner, born at Newelton (or Nevilton?) in Queensland in 1902, had arrived with his parents in New Guinea in 1903 at a time when Governor Hahl was recruiting specifically German farmers from Queensland to open plantations in German New Guinea (Filer & Lowe, 2011). Werner's tender application listed his residence as Baining on the Gazelle Peninsular; however, it noted that he had also resided at Talasea and Rabaul, both centres of early century German plantations. It is not clear that Werner took up residence at Bialla

---

5   Bolyanatz (2000) indicates that people on New Ireland, adjacent to Rabaul, from the 1920s sold copra for cash to Chinese traders but that the price they received for their wet or dry coconut from the traders discouraged their effort.

6   In 1927, the land of Bialla was valued at 5 shillings a hectare, valuing the Bialla plantation at £500.

immediately, but records indicate that in 1931 BP controlled Bialla's agricultural production as mortgager. All produce had to be delivered to BP and all labour engaged through BP. All transport of goods and persons was also done through BP. Such contractual commerce was far distant from hamlet patterns of growing coconuts cooperatively for food.

By 1937, Werner had fully paid off his debt to BP and had the property ownership conveyed to him. Perhaps its success to that point was due more to BP's oversight than Werner's management, for soon afterwards Werner sought another mortgager. A Plantation Inspection Report in March 1948 indicated that a Japanese plantation owner, Nagahama, had acquired a controlling interest in Bialla, appointing a fellow Japanese called Mori to run the plantation. However, at the beginning of the Pacific War, both Bialla and Nagahama's other plantation property were seized by the controller of enemy property.[7] The controller's subsequent report indicated that, of the 5,000 acres (2,024 hectares) in Bialla, only a fifth of the area, or 1,012 acres, was under coconuts, with an annual prewar production of 175 tons. The report mentioned that another area of Bialla, cleared around 1937, was choked with vines and apparently not yet planted.

Bialla Plantation, and its occupant Werner, must have been viewed by Maututu as unpredictably 'wild'. JK McCarthy, assistant district officer at Talasea, reported that the prewar Bialla Plantation had been badly managed and was suffering from 'gross negligence': buildings were 'decayed' and Frederik Werner operated without any vehicles and with only a small dinghy.[8] According to McCarthy, Werner 'led a life of dissipation and was frequently intoxicated' and the condition of Bialla did not improve under the Japanese manager, Mori. Maututu memories of 'Masta Fred' recorded that one of his sisters had married a Japanese man, possibly Mori, and that they would hike inland to the Lamo Auru Lake on Sundays for recreation. Werner would get so drunk on these trips that he had to be carried home, presumably by his plantation labourers. There was even a story told by a later manager that, on one occasion, Masta Fred had allowed himself to be beaten up for his 'past sins' (perhaps his drunken orgies?). Werner apparently remained a German patriot, the Australian administration describing him as a Nazi supporter. He had a German passport, had applied for membership of the Nazi Party and spoke positively of the mistreatment of Jews and Poles by

---

7   The controller noted that Nagahama held a mortgage over Bialla, but the colonial government could find no record of the value of that mortgage, estimating it to be substantial, between £4,700 and £8,000.

8   McCarthy, postwar, became district administrator in Madang (HN Nelson, 2000).

the Nazis, as reported by the Commonwealth Investigation Board (NAA, 1946–48). As a result, he was forced to leave New Guinea in August 1940 to enter internment at Tatura, Victoria, Australia, for six and half years. Bialla Plantation was abandoned for the rest of the war.

In 1947, following his release from internment, Werner applied to return to Bialla to resume ownership of the plantation. Despite objections from the Department of External Affairs that he had been a Nazi sympathiser, the Commonwealth Investigative Unit reported in September 1948 that he had been living quietly in Sydney for the previous 18 months and raised no objection to his return (NAA, 1946–48). The Bialla Plantation suffered little damage during the war, despite its occupation by both Japanese and Allied forces (Figure 3.1). The 1948 Plantation Inspection Report noted that its rehabilitation would require 80 labourers. The report also noted that the 'rich deep basaltic chocolate loam' of Bialla would make it ideal for cocoa. Indeed, William Mossman, inspector of agriculture since 1931, had submitted his own tender application to the custodian of enemy property in July 1947 to lease Bialla for the cultivation of cocoa. Werner's application was preferred and he arrived in September 1948 to resume his occupancy of Bialla. In the early 1950s, Werner began to plant cocoa by logging uncleared areas.

Figure 3.1: Bialla Plantation, 1969
Source: Author.

Werner and his managers exemplified a plantation economy established on what to the Maututu were strange practices. Native labour was employed on minimal wages and conditions to cultivate the crop and were accommodated in male barracks within the plantation. The plantation owner had total authority over his labour force, including the ability to use harsh penalties and firearms if the labour force rebelled. According to Maututu villagers, the initial labour force consisted mainly of Bileki Nakanai from Hoskins, recruited on 18-month contracts for £1 10s a month, with a severance pay of £25. Later, the workforce was recruited from the Simbu people of the Eastern Highlands.[9] Labourers started work at 6 am and spent the day cutting grass and extracting the white flesh from coconuts. Local Maututu despised working for the plantation, calling it 'work fit only for Simbu'.[10] These highland labourers were not welcome in Maututu villages, wary as Maututu were of potential sorcery, the rape of women and other violence.

Maututu remained wary of the plantation despite increased interaction between them and subsequent plantation managers. Local villagers performed short-term work on the plantation, when the meagre pay was attractively complemented with handouts of rice and tobacco. One or two took on specified longer-term roles at Bialla. Joseph was the cook at the Bialla manager's house for 14 years from 1954. He also scaled rations and was allowed to use the manager's shotgun and motorboat. With Joseph's help, the manager, through the plantation store, sold basic goods to plantation labourers and to villagers, stocking machetes, axes and tobacco, as well as foods such as rice, sugar and tinned meats and even shotguns and cartridges for hunting. However, in general, Werner and his managers did not encourage close relations with the villagers. They could be abusive to Maututu shoppers in the plantation store and were seen as stingy in the low prices they paid for Maututu produce. The manager I observed in 1968–69 treated Maututu with disdain, accusing them of laziness, poor care of their coconuts and cocoa, and promiscuity. In time, the plantation store became the supplier of cartons of beer to Maututu. The village men who shared these cartons of beer invariably became intoxicated, leading to raucous and sometimes violent behaviour at home in the hamlets, further antagonising 'home' residents against the plantation. The Bialla Plantation, through its outside labour force and its sale of alcohol through the store, thus posed serious threats to Maututu 'home' populations.

---

9   Silanga was a major initiative of the Catholic Mission to bring inland peoples (Ouka-Loso Nakanai, Sa Mamusi and Uase) closer to the coast and introduce them to cash cropping. In 1954, the 'lessee' of Bialla plantation agreed to buy 10 bags of sweet potatoes a week from settlers at Silanga in order to feed the labour force and to pick up those bags with its 'crashboat' at Lasibu on the coast (van Rijswijck, 1966).

10   Throughout the Gazelle plantation, managers generally found local natives reluctant to enter their labour force if these locals had access to their own gardens.

Village cocoa

Cocoa was introduced on the Gazelle Peninsular in 1949 through the establishment by the Australian administration of an agricultural extension station at Keravat and extension facilities at Taliligap and the Tolai Cocoa Project (Kean, 2000). From there, in the 1950s, cocoa spread throughout PNG. By 1962, Werner was reported to have planted 368 hectares of the 2,000 hectare Bialla estate with 30,000 cocoa trees interspersed with coconut palms as shade trees.

Maututu engaged with this new crop as positively as they had earlier planted coconut palms.[11] But there was an important difference. Coconuts were desired as domestic food. The coconut flesh could be processed by the household to add to their meals of taro, sweet potato, cassava and other vegetables. However, cocoa had no domestic use and, unlike coconut, never featured in the mythology. The only Maututu use for cocoa was as a cash crop, sold initially as wet beans and later processed as dried beans.

The adoption of cocoa demonstrated Maututu willingness to work together with outside agents to achieve something of value for the home society. Department of Agriculture field officers (*didiman*) were based in Salelubu, a half-day's journey away in the Nakanai Mountains, where their primary focus was on the Uasilau-Silanga resettlement scheme where cocoa was being promoted. In 1954–55, several Maututu were sent by the *didiman* to Taliligap agricultural college in Rabaul to undertake training in cocoa production. One of these, Tauvere, journeyed from Baikakea to Salelubu in perhaps 1955 to ask agricultural officers for assistance in bringing cocoa to the Maututu villagers.[12] At that time, Bialla Plantation was trialling cocoa and the first village cocoa had been planted between Apupulu and Gomu

---

11 While the administration encouraged villagers to grow coconuts, they discouraged indigenous processing of copra, preferring that they sold the nuts to the expatriate plantations. Jack McCarthy was removed from his position as assistant district officer in Kavieng in 1932 after he antagonised expatriate plantation owners by encouraging the people to process their own copra in hot air driers (HN Nelson, 2000).

12 In 1953, the Bialla plantation supplied 8,000 coconut seedlings to the Central Nakanai resettlement site of Silanga in exchange for labour from Central Nakanai to work at Bialla. In 1959, government established large cocoa plantings in the resettlement of mountain peoples at Uasilau and Silanga in the Central Nakanai mountains, although individuals had brought cocoa seeds there from as early as 1953 (van Rijswijck, 1966, p. 13). The agricultural station of Salelubu was established there to guide cocoa developments, including agricultural projects among Maututu. Maututu also attended Salelubu in the 1960s for up to 12 months to receive training in cocoa development. The development of cocoa in Maututu villages appears then to have been driven and managed largely as a village initiative.

by Tolai visitors. The expatriate *didiman* insisted that the Tolai plantings be rooted out because the blocks had not been properly marked out. He then encouraged the agricultural trainees to begin village plantings. From 1956 the trainees, including Tauvere, marked out and planted the first block near the coastal village of Apupulu. The main reason Tauvere gave me for selecting Apupulu for the community block was its proximity to coastal vessels that moored off the beach at Apupulu. He and other leaders had confidence that they could build cooperation across hamlets, lineages and villages to ensure the success of the new crop. Villagers from all four northern villages, Bubuu, Baikakea, Apupulu and Gomu, took part in the first block and referred to the cocoa as the *kampani* (company, communal plot). Unlike household food gardens, coconut or betel nut palms, cocoa was seen as an inter-village cooperative farming venture.

However, this 'native' *kampani* model did not convince either *didiman* or *kiap*, both of whom predicted that disputes would arise due to multiple clans and villages sharing the one plantation of cocoa. They demanded that the *kampani* 'land' be formalised under the ownership of clan and village. The expatriate assumption was that cocoa cultivation locked land away from other uses, and that unless ownership of the land was formalised and plantings restricted to those owners, serious conflicts would arise. While the administration officers focused on ownership of land and village exclusivity as essential to the future of the cash crop, the Maututu regarded cooperative labour among lineages as determining who should benefit from the crop. Land boundaries were irrelevant to their agricultural concerns. The friction between outside and home views led to an impasse; in the end, outside villagers abandoned the Apupulu block.

Tauvere marked out another *kampani* block in Baikakea, exclusively for Baikakea residents. *Kampani* became inclusive of all those who invested energy in the new crop. There appears to have been no sense that a particular lineage had exclusive claim to the cocoa planted there. Although this second plot appears to have accommodated the *didiman*'s insistence on village proprietorship, the block's cocoa was still a group concern, with trustees appointed in the village to use the cash from cocoa sales for community concerns. This pattern was followed elsewhere. In Uase, a *kampani* block of cocoa was jointly planted by *baramana* (youth) from Uase and Matililiu, although it was increasingly worked only by the Uase youth. These *kampani* blocks were planted to financially support village groups, such as the church, the women's group or the youth group, and it was these groups who planted and harvested the cocoa. A decade later, in 1968, when

I lived there, *kampani* continued to cultivate cocoa blocks in Baikakea and Apupulu, and the respective trustees used the two accrued funds to help needy families with cash expenses, such as school fees and clothing, or to hold *kapti* to further build the account.[13] The *kampani* processed the wet beans through a fermenting and drying process in the village but depended on the Bialla Plantation to alert them to the arrival of coastal shipping for transport of the beans to Rabaul. Banking was done through the plantation store, with the Rabaul merchants crediting the *kampani* account on delivery. Trustees then withdrew the funds at the store. Few villagers had bank accounts at the time and *kampani* participants were not always confident of the trustees' skills in managing the account. Some of their distrust was fuelled by allegations made publicly by the expatriate store manager that the trustees were misappropriating the funds.[14]

Eventually, with the success of the *kampani* blocks, cocoa plantings were expanded through household plots. Maututu began to plant cocoa on their abandoned garden sites. Many planted cocoa interspersed with their coconut and betel nut palms, and regarded all such cash crops grown on soil the family had cleared as the property of the household who planted them. The soil, on the other hand, continued to be identified with the hamlet group and with lineage ancestors who had pioneered farming in that space. Indeed, in those years, the Maututu agricultural trainees encouraged villagers to plant cocoa wherever it was convenient with no thought of which lineage was associated with the soil. Some of the plantings of cocoa were even made in neighbouring villages, where lineage links could be claimed. Apupulu and Bubuu residents, for example, planted blocks in Baikakea, closer to the fermentary and drier that began to operate there. However, this did not raise concerns among Baikakea residents about loss of their 'land', as feared by administration officers, because all soil was seen as borrowed for the period of planting, rather than alienated.[15] The expansion of cocoa blocks was a source of pride for the whole village and village leaders determined that every Friday villagers would labour collectively on group cocoa blocks, such as those of the youth group (*baramana*) or the women's association or the church.

---

13 *Kapti*, a Tok Pisin term, refers to a publicised event in the village where a group raised money by selling cooked food and beverages, sometimes including alcohol.

14 As a *didiman* myself, in 1973–75 I took over as the business development officer to train villagers in managing bank accounts.

15 Van Rijswijck (1966) refers to a similar view in Silanga where Wulai, the Nakanai head of clan and *luluai*, invited other villages to occupy his clan land but refused to sell the land to them. Instead *luluai* from these mountain villages gave him traditional valuables and Wulai retained his status as 'father' of the resettlement scheme.

In 1968–69, Maututu pointed out to me that the Bileki of the Hoskins Peninsular had reacted very differently to cocoa development. The Kivung millenarian movement among the Bileki rejected cash cropping, preferring to look to spirit agents to bring them prosperity; they had also rejected the establishment of a local council (Jebens, 2004, 2010). On his return from Australia in 1969, Nakanai Council President Mapulo Gaa passed through Hoskins and confronted the leader of the Kivung movement. He said to him:

> I witnessed in Sydney how the white men make trade goods in factories. It is wrong to suggest that they stole these goods from the ancestors. That is why we Maututu are embracing the local government council rather than the Kivung movement.

The Maututu claimed to have never engaged in millenarian practices that rejected cash crops.[16] On the contrary, Maututu cocoa trainees took cocoa to the Mengen village of Gigipuna, where the Kivung movement was strong. Two Gigipuna men, Wawage and his brother, refused to join the movement and instead approached Tauvere to introduce cocoa to the village. They proceeded to demonstrate to Gigipuna neighbours that they could earn cash through cocoa and through the holding of *kapti* (food fairs). In this way they persuaded others to plant cocoa. Gigipuna became a major producer of cocoa, at first on the *kampani* basis, aided by Maututu trainees. This then spread to household plots, as had happened among Maututu, with the Gigipuna growers incorporated into the Maututu Cooperative Society (see below). In the first years of harvesting, Gigipuna men, women and children carried the wet cocoa beans on their backs (women) and shoulders (men) 20 kilometres to Baikakea, where they sold them at the fermentary. Maututu, for their part, welcomed this partnership with the 'wild' mountain people.

As cocoa planting expanded on former food gardens around the settlement, new food gardens had to be located further away from the hamlet, requiring more work for those carrying the heavy tubers home. Over time, Maututu became more concerned with planting cocoa where their clan and lineage had claims to soil, indicating their awareness of tensions arising from the growing shortage of accessible soil. Among the Tolai on the Gazelle Peninsular, where cocoa was first planted, management of the crop increasingly demanded exclusivist claims to land and revenue, both by

---

16 Jebens (2004) quotes one Bileki big man as suggesting the Kivung movement did exist at Bialla, perhaps referring to practices at Gigipuna.

individual farmers and by individual lineages (Martin, 2006). Some Maututu began to plant specifically on soils formally affiliated with their father or with their mother's brother, and planned blocks for both their children and sister's children on soil affiliated with their lineage.[17] For example, Rausi, who had no children of his own, planted his cocoa on Kabulu soil because his father was Kabulu, even though he and his mother were of the Biso clan (Figure 3.2). As he put it, the Kabulu lineage had *vaipalahia* (brought him into existence) and, in recognition of that fact, he planned to pass on those trees on Kabulu soil to Kabulu men whom he addressed as 'sons', 'because the semen of my older brother impregnated their Kabulu mothers'. One block of his cocoa, however, was planted on Biso soil to be passed on to his sister's son. Another senior man informed me that his cocoa would be inherited by his son, but not by his daughter, because her husband had 'exchanged valuables' for her. If his son did not survive him, the trees would go to his sister's daughter's children and to his daughter's daughter.

Figure 3.2: Rausi and 'grandson' Taba in front of Rausi's kitchen and elevated sleep house; Taba was the *posolagu* of a Kabulu man, 1969
Source: Author.

---

17 I am suggesting here that 'clan land' demarcated by the administration ignored the important village distinction between lineage proprietors of the soil and the wider clan who recognised common affiliation with *ruvu* species and sites.

There was thus a variety of ways in which Maututu reconciled rights to soil with kinship. As Curry and Koczberski (2009, p. 101) observed, in reference to Nakanai, the social relationships on which the moral legitimacy of access to soil/land are accorded 'are not pre-given, nor unchanging: rather, they must be constructed and carefully maintained and from their presence, resource rights flow'.[18] In 2013, for example, I recorded those who had planted cocoa or coconuts on a large strip of soil stretching from Baikakea village inland—soil that was identified at that time with the Biso lineage. The Biso lineage had been more prominent in the 1960s when a group of three Biso brothers were leading men in the community, among them *Kansil* Vaisisi who had two wives of different lineages. Of 22 persons who had perennial crops on the land in 2013, only four were from the Biso lineage that 'owned' the soil. Of the remainder, eight were the children of Biso fathers, seven were sponsored by Biso as friends or adopted family, two had claims through their mother's fathers and one only seemed to have a claim because he had randomly planted the land with coconuts when it was not tightly monitored. Thus, while it was clear that people were justifying their claims in terms of the pioneer *maratatila* of the soil, their claims were varied and by no means limited to membership of a strictly defined genealogical lineage or clan. The soil was recognised by all as being affiliated to the Biso lineage, clearly distinguished from soil affiliated to other lineages, the result of the historical opening of the soil by the three Biso brothers.

There were occasional disputes when the right to plant cocoa in a certain location was questioned. Koasiro, for example, abandoned one of his cocoa blocks in Bubuu because another lineage was protesting his occupation of the soil. But for the majority, even those who harvested their cocoa on soil not associated with their lineage, production of cocoa continued without dispute, and might only be challenged when they sought to replace ageing cocoa. That is, their rights to use the soil extended for the life of the crop they planted. This represented application to cocoa farming of the understanding of gardens as 'soil' for the temporary use of whomever puts in the energy to fell and clear the forest. Such use did not supplant the claim of the lineage group to have prior and deeper connection with the soil by virtue of what their ancestors had done.

---

18 Martin (2006) discusses the relation of the Tolai *vunatarai* (clans) to land in the Matupi area of Gazelle, indicating that this relationship changed as land pressures built up with cash cropping. There was a 'tendency to attempt to constitute the *vunatarai* as a local land-based descent group, as a discrete owner of land and to minimise claims made on the basis of reciprocal interdependence that threaten that identity' (Martin, 2006, p. 40). It would appear that such 'landholding' groups among the Maututu emerged only later in the oil palm era, as access to soil became competitive.

According to the East Nakanai Crop Census (16 villages) of 1969, the 7 Maututu villages had planted over 50,000 of the almost 70,000 cocoa trees (71 per cent) despite comprising less than 50 per cent of the population. In almost all villages in 1969, immature, non-fruit-bearing cocoa trees represented one-quarter or more of plantings, indicating the rapid expansion of the crop, fuelled by the access the crop gave villagers to the cash they required for school costs, government tax and the purchase of store commodities (see Table 3.1).

Table 3.1: Cash crop census 1969–70

Population 1973	Village	Cocoa 1969	Coconuts 1969	% mature cocoa	% mature coconut	Cocoa 1970	Coconut 1970
144	Apupulu	3,996	5,850	90	60	4,256	4,698
141	Baikakea	11,462	16,575	70	70	31,158	15,856
132	Bubuu	5,500	2,000	80	80	2,119	1,374
228	Uase	8,755	2,348	75	75	2,750	7,910
220	Gomu	7,832	3,000	50	90	9,178	5,692
186	Matililiu	6,754	6,820	75	60	5,272	5,246
52	Mataruru	6,500	4,000	70	75	5,600	1,182
1170	Total Maututu	50,799	40,593	–	–	60,333	41,958
73	Gigipuna	4,822	1,500	75	90	6,965	625
–	Baia	1,000	3,500		50	–	–
–	Baobao	1,500	2,643	50	70	–	–
–	Nantambu	1,500	1,000	60	75	–	–
–	Noau	–	1,500	–	50	–	–
–	Ubili	6,500	16,919	80	70	–	–
–	Potou	–	1,000	–	90	–	–
–	Piapia	500	650	90	80	–	–
–	Total	69,347	70,805	72.7	72.8	–	–

Note: Maututu villages in italics. The figures for 1970 are taken from patrol officers' reports, which, on their admission, required further checking. The 1973 population numbers are also from patrol reports but are much more likely to be accurate. The patrol reports noted a Maututu population of 1,071 in 1970, and a Meramera population (Baia, Nantambu, Noau, Ubili) of 1,092. The total Maututu crop figures are roughly consistent, indicating additional planting, particularly of cocoa in Baikakea, during 1969–70. Not too much more should be drawn from comparing these rough figures village by village over the two years, as trees may have been counted in one village one year and in its neighbour the next.

Source: Author's research.

Despite the enthusiasm for cocoa among Maututu, neither the administration nor the villagers promoted it as replacing food gardens. Rather, cocoa became the main source of disposable income, principally to buy commodities from the plantation store and, later, village stores. Packaged foods, cigarettes, clothes, lamps and torches, and beer were procured. On the week of 7 April 1969, for example, I calculated that the average sale of cocoa by 50 growers was A$2.90 per grower; on 28 April, the average for 50 growers was A$2.40; on 9 May, among 43 growers, the average was A$3.80.[19] This cash remained fluid, rather than banked. It seldom covered the purchase of larger items. Only the occasional villager owned a sewing machine, a guitar, a bicycle or a watch, as this would have required the banking of cocoa income over weeks and months. School fees, clothes, lamps and other household necessities were far more likely to exhaust such funds. Few Maututu children attended high school, which would have demanded some of this cash for fees, books or uniforms. Village organisations, such as the church, women's group or youth group took advantage of this influx of cash by holding *kapti* at which they sold cooked food and sometimes alcohol in order to raise funds for their activities. Cash was also used, like customary valuables, to request cooperation. For example, in November 1969, two Kabulu clan elders sent A$2 to Gomu village as a request to residents there to come to Baikakea to clear a large garden and plant it with taro for a feast. Thirty men and 30 women arrived the next day and, with Baikakea residents, planted the garden and were rewarded with a large meal at the end of the afternoon. For daily requirements, food gardens, rather than cocoa earnings, were essential to sustain each household.

Maututu Cooperative Society as an extension of 'home'

In the early years of the twentieth century, Maututu were scattered in small hamlets that, despite inter-hamlet marriages, remained suspicious of, even hostile to, each other. Maututu came to recognise their shared interests with the introduction from the outside of the Methodist Diocese, Airmen's Memorial School (AMS) and Nakanai Council. Through these, they extended notions

---

19   In the mid-1960s, villagers could sell *tambu* shell to Tolai for between 5s and £1 per small tin. Some Maututu employed hill people on their cocoa blocks for 5s a day. Decimal currency was introduced in PNG in February 1966 and replaced with PNG's own decimal currency of kina and toea in 1975. The Catholic sawmill in Ulamona in 1969 paid wages of A$17 a month for a new worker and A$30 a month for a carpenter.

of 'home' to include the wider Maututu community. The same was true of the initial plantings of cocoa on multi-hamlet *kampani* blocks. The Maututu Cooperative Society became remarkable in fostering cooperation beyond *kampani* blocks with all Maututu villages, and even with the Mengen mountain people of Gigipuna. Like the *kampani* blocks, it represented a new type of 'home' enterprise. Tauvere and other trainees had pioneered the planting of cocoa in all these villages, but they were wary of their growing dependence on the expatriate plantation manager to whom they sold the wet beans. They identified this outsider as hostile to local interests.

In 1956, Mapulo Gaa from Gomu-Urumaili, who would later become president of both the Nakanai Council and AMS Board, formed the Maututu Cooperative Society. He was then *luluai* in Gomu and recognised, even by adjacent villages, as a 'big man'. His reputation and the enthusiasm of trainees like Tauvere brought the proposal to fruition. Mapulo invited fellow villagers to canoe five days down the coast to Talasea to consult administration officers about setting up their own cooperative society.[20] The initial aim was to process coconuts into copra and market this directly to Rabaul with the help of coastal vessels. The *kiap* supported their venture, advising them to collect £5 from each farmer, many of whom had spare cash due to working in Rabaul on plantations and through selling *tambu* shell to Tolai. Mapulo invited all Maututu to join the proposed cooperative and over 100 joined in its first months in 1956. He asked each village to nominate one 'big man' as a director of the Maututu Cooperative Board, and it was on the basis of their participation that the society gained the backing of all Maututu.

These initial years of the Maututu Cooperative Society were, thus, a time of great enthusiasm because it symbolised their consolidation of 'home' in partnership with, but not dependent on, outside administration officers, and freed them from dependence on the more hostile plantation manager. Each settlement was keen to be seen as cultivating modern ways (*tavulovulo halaba*/fresh ways). The first copra drier for the Maututu Cooperative was built in Apupulu, followed by driers in Gomu and Uase. To reduce their reliance on the Bialla store, the society built its own trade store in Bubuu, where cargo vessels could moor in the deep water inside the coral reef to offload the goods the society ordered from Rabaul merchants. When the seas at Bubuu proved too rough to land the cargo, the society directors moved

---

20 In the 1960s, the Cooperatives Section was part of the Department of District Services and Native Affairs.

the trade store to Apupulu. The first delivery there of cargo in 1962 was so plentiful that some had to be stacked outside the store shed. An Apupulu youth with secondary education was appointed as manager of the store and as financial secretary for the society, responsible for all purchases of coconuts and copra from villagers.

Maututu were driven by priorities that differed from the administration's goals of developing business enterprise. Trade stores and copra and cocoa processing facilities were seen as prestige goods more than capital enterprises. Curry and Koczberski (2013) suggest that village trade stores (and other ventures such as cooperatives) in PNG should not be evaluated in terms of their profitability, but rather in terms of the enterprise's capacity to supply and distribute valuables. Curry (1999) observed that most trade stores in PNG drew on a wide network of kin to pool capital and labour, serving to promote that group's identity and status. 'Trade stores are vehicles for gift exchange' and become 'the physical representation of modernity in the heart of the village, thus reflecting the group's success in engaging in the modern world' (Curry, 1999, p. 295). These authors documented how business capital was often spent not in building up stock and profit but in distribution as gifts by the storekeeper. The Apupulu storekeeper allowed customers to have goods on credit that was never paid back. Although business development officers considered such loss of capital a failure, the group that sponsored the trade store saw redistribution as key to its success and were willing to raise new capital through *kapti* or sales of copra to restock the trade store when its goods were exhausted.

However, the extension of these 'home' enterprises to serve all Maututu was fraught. Those in other villages were disillusioned when the Apupul storekeeper favoured only his own kin and hamlet neighbours. The society directors did not have the accounting acumen to challenge his management and when the secretary indulged himself with new clothes or shared alcohol with friends, directors could not determine if he did this with his wages or with society funds. One of the two storekeepers from Apupulu allegedly embezzled A$1,200 of trade store funds in the mid-1960s, for which he was jailed by the colonial administration after they conducted an audit. On his release from jail, he was reinstated as secretary by the directors because there were no others in Apupulu with the necessary skills. Because the store was located in Apupulu it needed to be managed by someone from there. However, his handling of the store continued to rankle the wider Maututu community.

Meanwhile, administration officers were keen to develop the processing of cocoa under 'native' management. In 1963, according to Tauvere, the agricultural officer (*didiman*) based at Salelubu suggested a village fermentary and drier be constructed at Malasi near Kiava, half-way between Maututu territory and the Central Nakanai area of Silanga. But such a proposal, while no doubt more convenient for *didiman* supervision and seemingly meeting the needs of a much larger population of growers, did not appear to acknowledge that Malasi was in the Ata language territory, would have to be under Ata control and would only raise the profile of this group to the detriment of Maututu. After protest from Maututu, the *didiman* proposed that the fermentary and drier should be in Apupulu close to where the copra drier was operating and where the dry beans could be loaded onto visiting trading vessels. It is not clear whether any consultation with Maututu was undertaken in coming to this solution. Finally, Tauvere made the trip to Salelubu by canoe and foot to successfully convince the agricultural officers that Baikakea was a better location, as, by that time, Baikakea had by far the largest area of cocoa plantings.

As with the earlier consultations in establishing the Maututu Cooperative Society, Tauvere demonstrated the benefits of negotiating with expatriate officials to construct beneficial partnerships, despite their differing ontological priorities. The *didiman* in their decisions prioritised technical efficiency and market access. Apupulu was more accessible by boat for the loading of the dry beans, and at that time more men in Apupulu had gained secondary education and employment outside, making them more familiar with outsider demands. Baikakea, on the other hand, had always been more isolated inland, was seen as more 'traditional' and was also more distant from the anchorages at Apupulu or Bialla. However, for Baikakea growers, their proposal was based not just on the area of their cocoa plantings but also on their desire for a symbol of modernity in the village. Apupulu, Gomu and Uase had their copra driers, and Apupulu, and for a while Bubuu, their trade store, and Baikakea pushed for their own 'modern' enterprise. The *didiman* was swayed by Tauvere's dedication to cocoa planting, despite the decision attracting the derision of the Bialla Plantation manager, who declared that the native enterprise would never produce quality cocoa beans.

The Baikakea enterprise had many challenges. The poor condition of drier and storage shed meant that beans from the Maututu Cooperative Society were often of poorer quality, earning the growers lower prices. The first palm-thatched drier in Baikakea fell into disrepair in the late 1960s. The society was forced to seek assistance from the Bialla manager when cargo ships abandoned the Apupulu loading port and only stopped at Bialla wharf. Under administration pressure, he allowed them access to the wharf but did not allow society produce to be stored at the port nor did he alert them to the arrival of the coastal ships. More often a villager passing by the wharf would carry the news of a ship's arrival, at which point men and women on foot rushed the dry beans the 4 kilometres to the wharf, hoping the ship was still there for loading.

As these challenges escalated in 1968, expatriate officers from the Cooperatives Section conducted a financial review of the Maututu Cooperative Society (see Table A.3). This showed that the trade store in Apupulu had suffered large losses in 1966–68, as had their marketing of copra. However, after an initial loss from production in 1964–65, cocoa showed a profit up to 1966–67, when its contribution far exceeded that of copra and the trade store. The next year, cocoa processing operated at a loss, with the deterioration of the fermentary and drier in Baikakea, forcing members to sell their produce to Bialla Plantation.[21] In response to these ongoing challenges, the cooperatives officer persuaded the society directors to relocate the society trade store from Apupulu to Baikakea so that the chairman could directly monitor it. The Apupulu store manager/society secretary was replaced by a younger (high school–educated) man from Baikakea.[22] The cooperatives officer was focused on society finances, but the directors needed to satisfy the demands of multiple communities for a share of the 'modernity' that the cooperative represented. At one point, the chairman of the society, Toruga from Baikakea, offered loans of A$1,000 to assist any society member to start up trade stores, purchase pig wire, or erect permanent material houses or copra driers. This was his acknowledgement of the importance of distributing prestige to the wider Maututu population. Only when benefits were widely shared would the Maututu Cooperative Society be truly embraced as 'home'.

21　At the time of the 1968 audit, A$90 in cash for dry beans was owed to Gigipuna growers and there were outstanding debts at the trade store of A$180. See Table A.3.

22　The patrol reports of 1970 noted that the situation of the society store was made even more dire by the fact that the nearest cooperative department office was in Talasea 'eighty miles away'.

Engaging with outsiders — antagonism and partnership

During my stay in 1968–69, Baikakea began work on a new fermentary and drier using permanent materials, under direction from the expatriate *didiman*. In his visit in January 1969, the *didiman* challenged Maututu to produce 50 bags every two months to pay off society debts and thus open the way to purchasing a tractor to ease transportation to the wharf. Baikakea and Bubuu villagers responded in multiple ways to his challenge. In addition to raising money through harvesting their cash crops of cocoa and coconuts, the *baramana* group held a large *kapti*, at which they marketed local produce of *tubeli* shell, sago and *sisi* shellfish. Two bags of rice were purchased for the preparation of cooked dishes of coconut rice with garnish complemented by sweet tea.

This merely increased the hostility of the Bialla manager who had benefited from the purchase of Maututu cocoa at minimal prices when their drier collapsed. He closed the wharf at Bialla to all society shipments in February 1969 and later claimed to me that he had made a profit of A$2,000 for an outlay of A$1,500 on Maututu cocoa sold to him. He worked to foster distrust among Maututu visiting his store, alerting them to what he claimed was mishandling of the society enterprise. He continued to accuse Baikakea farmers of pigheadedness and stupidity for not selling all their cocoa crop to him. His reasoning was that individual farmers could make more money by selling to him. In stressing individual profit as the motivation for development he failed to understand the importance of the society as a statement of Maututu partnership with the outside, and their resistance to falling once again into submission to his often-unpredictable ways that undermined any relationship or partnership with villagers. The villagers responded to him, saying that it was their cocoa produce and their spending in his trade store that had clearly contributed to his success, including the investments he had made in extensions to his house. In their view, he was obliged to redistribute some of this bounty to villagers and to partner with them to further their development.

Despite the plantation manager's hostility, partnership with other outsiders proved beneficial. The cooperatives officer provided ongoing support and I helped to keep communication open with other expatriates.[23]

---

23   In 1970, the Cooperatives Section was absorbed into the Department of Trade and Industry with a brief to encourage all business development in villages.

Fred Hargesheimer, founder of the AMS at Ewasse, was teaching at the school that year and offered the society the use of the AMS tractor to transport bags of cocoa beans to the port (Figure 3.3). Society members contrasted his generosity with the 'greediness' of the Bialla manager. By 1973, when I returned to Bialla, the new fermentary and drier were in operation with a warehouse constructed of bush materials nearby. With the aid of the AMS tractor, produce was reaching the market promptly and society revenue was improving. The society was able, in 1973, to purchase the tractor from AMS and, in 1974, directors added a Toyota Land Cruiser bought from a Rabaul dealer. These two vehicles allowed them to rush their dry beans to port whenever a ship called in, as well as provide transport of wet beans from other villages to the fermentary, saving growers considerable time and energy. The vehicles were also used by the society 'firemen' to transport firewood and could be hired by members to carry timber or wild pigs. They were not only an economic asset but also a source of prestige, particularly for Baikakea and Bubuu villages where they were located. In 1976, the society acquired a blue Isuzu truck as the volume of cocoa beans continued to grow and, for a time, they even used Mapulo's fermentary in Gomu as additional facilities for processing product (Figures 3.4 and 3.5).

Figure 3.3: Fred Hargesheimer used his tractor to aid the Maututu Cooperative Society, 1973
Source: Author.

Figure 3.4: Saole, driver of the Maututu Cooperative Society utility, 1974
Source: Author.

Figure 3.5: Society workers rest beside the cocoa drier and fermenting boxes, 1974
Source: Author.

As another outsider, I worked for the Department of Agriculture, Stock and Fisheries to support Maututu enterprise over the years 1973–75 when I was resident in Baikakea. My major contribution was helping the secretary manage society accounts and ensuring that the dry beans were promptly delivered to the wharf. My presence in a supporting role for the society also built some confidence in its operation in neighbouring villages. For example, when I first arrived, the secretary had not revised the purchase price for wet beans for several years, even though the global price had improved considerably. I explained to him that he could monitor the global prices through the radio and the directors agreed to adjust the purchase price accordingly. The rise in price attracted more to harvest their crop and sell to the society, including many from more distant villages. In addition, the improved finances allowed the society to distribute dividends annually.

This account of cocoa development demonstrates the prime value of partnership between home communities and outsiders. Maututu were drawn to the cocoa enterprise in terms of its prestige of 'modernity'. Cash crop income enabled villagers to expand their consumption of trade store goods and to meet schooling and other immediate needs, but the key benefits lay in how cocoa enhanced the community. The *kampani* and the Maututu Cooperative Society represented their interest in strengthening the 'home' group. They did that by recognising the need for collaboration with outsiders but not to the point of subordinating their priorities to those of the expatriates. They became skilled at processing quality cocoa bean but the distribution of benefits among members remained more important than capital investment. Soil remained affiliated with lineages rather than delineated as household ownership. Directors sought to be big men in their exchange relations rather than 'big shots' like the plantation manager (Martin, 2006).

Transformations in gender relations brought by cash cropping

The Australian administration, in its dealings with villages through expatriate *kiap*, *didiman*, cooperatives and business development officers, tended to focus on local men and neglect engagement with local women. This ignored the formidable role women played in 'home' activities, such as food gardens, rearing of pigs and chickens, lineage affairs and education of children. The village planting of coconuts was closely associated with women's agency, as in the myth cited earlier, and was seen as independent of outside agency. Expatriate assumptions around growing cocoa promoted men as trainees and planters, as well as managers of the fermentary and drier. Despite that, women assumed an equal share in growing and harvesting both coconuts and cocoa. While the family's cocoa block was cleared, marked and planted by men, the ongoing work of pruning, maintenance and harvesting was done by husband and wife, with either of them delivering the wet beans to the fermentary and collecting the payment. If the woman delivered the wet beans, then she received the cash directly from the society secretary. An unmarried woman or wife could also plant her own plot of cocoa with the help of a kinsman when needed. Women regularly condemned their husbands for spending agricultural income on alcohol rather than the upkeep of the family, and, for that reason, many wives preferred to be there when the cocoa was scaled and payments made. Thus, cocoa production, like garden production, allowed many women to meet their own cash needs as well as the cash needs of the family. Koczberski (2007) suggests that men in PNG insist on control over cash income in order to meet ceremonial and customary needs and to maintain male prestige and power. This was less the case in the matrilineal society of Maututu because women had equivalent access to cocoa income and were not averse to using it for their ceremonial and customary purposes. Women saw cocoa as a solution to the cash burdens they tended to carry, such as paying school expenses, buying clothes and imported foods such as rice, sugar and tinned fish. Cash was also used to meet kin obligations, such as payments of bridewealth and contributions to Women's Club activities. While male access to cash could result in drunken 'wild' behaviour that disrupted family and community life, both men and women used cash to improve their home life. There was some heated exchange at a village meeting in Baikakea in 1969 when one woman accused the men of not helping with cocoa and copra production on the Women's Club block. The men present strongly rejected her accusation and she was forced to qualify her statement to 'some of our husbands do not help us'. The men particularly stressed how they had marked out and sometimes cleaned the Women's Club block. However, perhaps chastened, they promised to provide more help each Thursday, the Women's Club day. Several women commented to me: 'the men are full of talk'.

Land transactions under agricultural development

In her book *Land's End* about Lauje cocoa smallholders in Indonesia, Li (2016) comes to the conclusion that cocoa, as a perennial crop, transformed land into private property, inevitably leading to the accumulation of land by some and landlessness for others. Such was not the Maututu experience. The planting of cocoa did not result in soil becoming private landed property. Unlike the Lauje, the Maututu did not incur debt in obtaining seedlings from the administration because they quickly propagated their own seedlings. For Maututu, *la magasa* (the soil) on which the cocoa was grown remained subject to the oversight of hamlet and lineage groups, rather than the ownership right of children or sisters' children. Throughout all these years, food production remained central to the livelihood of all Maututu families, and there remained enough soil for them to retain both garden and cocoa production.

However, a process similar to that noted by Li occurred among the Tolai of East New Britain. Particularly on Matupit Island where land was in short supply, cocoa was planted so extensively that there was a shortage of garden areas and some people were no longer able to access land. And yet the Tolai concept of the soil as subject to communal claims resembled that among the Maututu. AL Epstein (1969, p. 110) wrote at the height of the cocoa boom in the 1960s:

> In the Tolai vernacular there is indeed no term which corresponds to or otherwise adequately translates our own concepts of property and ownership ... Thus whereas we speak of property in the abstract, to the Tolai property always appears as a concrete and particular relationship ... *kaugu pia go*, this is my land ... may refer to a range of different interests in the land, and how it should be interpreted may depend not only on the context but also the personal knowledge and the speaker and his circumstances.

A later observer of Tolai cash cropping, Keir Martin (2006, p. 64), asserted that the non-alienability of links to the 'land' is the key difference distinguishing Tolai customary land from Western land as property. Such non-alienability is not primarily about a block of real estate but about a site where people trace their origin and their identity and construct their social relations. However, Martin indicated that control of land became much tighter as cocoa expanded. Under these mounting population pressures, Matupit land began to be bought and sold. But even when a father purchased land that he could pass onto his children without fear of lineage counter claims, such land became 'customary' in the next generation in that this land, following the death of the children, would revert to their lineage—that is, it could not be inherited by the sons' own children (Martin, 2006). Martin (2007, p. 56) observed that 'custom is as much a position taken on the morality of certain transactions as it is an empirical description of a juridical process to be preserved or reformed', and that, 'as land holding units, clan identities have perhaps become more unitary and fixed over the years' (Martin 2006, pp. 96–97). As the perennial cocoa crop locked away the soil from cycles of garden and forest interchange, local values were transformed without being abandoned. Among Maututu this transformation under cocoa did not involve the trading of 'soil' as landed property.

In the same decade, the Australian administration was embarking on a very different program of alienating and commodifying land in preparation for the resettlement of land-poor households from throughout PNG. The process that had begun with the 1933 land survey and subsequent purchase of village soils for restoring the full extent of the Bialla Plantation became a much starker reality in the 1960s as the administration negotiated the acquisition of vast areas of West New Britain for agricultural development. The administration faced a huge challenge of landlessness in the PNG Highlands and the Gazelle Peninsular, partly caused by expatriate plantations there acquiring the best land for their cash crops of coffee and cocoa, respectively (Rowley, 1972). At the time, the government presumed they had several decades in which to establish their targets of economic development prior to PNG attaining independence. In 1962, the Australian administration began negotiation with the owner of Bialla Plantation, Werner, who, in 1963, agreed to sell 1,700 hectares (4,201 acres) of Bialla to the government, followed by a later sale of 250 hectares.[24] The Land (Tenure Conversion) Act of 1963 permitted the transfer of customary land to individual freehold title, particularly to stimulate coffee cultivation in the PNG Highlands and oil palm in West New Britain and Popondetta.[25] In the Silanga-Uasilau area, the administration acquired native land for indigenous cultivation of cocoa in 1964.[26]

---

24 These sales appear to have seen the exit of Werner from Bialla. By the late 1960s, Burns Philp had taken full ownership of the Bialla plantation, which was managed by resident manager Merv King until 1976, even though, in 1970, the plantation was sold to Alois Akun and Co., a company based, from at least 1950, in Rabaul and with another office in Hong Kong. The patrol reports of August 1970 indicate that the plantation of 1,350 acres was fully planted in coconuts and, within two years, would be fully planted in cocoa, mostly interplanted with the coconuts. The figure of 1,350 acres acknowledged the large area of the original Bialla Plantation already sold off to the administration for oil palm and town developments.

25 But, in the end, few of the Land Tenure Conversion blocks were converted to freehold title (Koczberski, Curry & Anjen, 2012, p. 185).

26 In 1964, Father Wagner from the Catholic Mission in Silanga recorded the official purchase of the Silanga resettlement land from the Central Nakanai villagers: 'Today a milestone in Silanga's history: £13,764 paid out for 6,882 acres of the Silanga section of the Central Nakanai Settlement Scheme', an average price of £2 per acre/£4.10 per hectare (van Rijswijck, 1966). The land was immediately divided into blocks of 15 acres that were leased at a nominal sum to those households already settled there. Five acres on each block were marked for cash crops (van Rijswijck 1966).

The administration's 1962 plan for the Bialla area was to create 900 six-hectare smallholder plots, totalling 5,400 hectares, suitable for oil palm, alongside a nuclear plantation under a corporate producer with provision for road access to all blocks. Inclusive of other services, the program was estimated to cost £43,000, but this cost appears to have been considerably exceeded in the years that followed. In 1964, the administration obtained the thumbprints of Maututu villagers on documents for access to their soil stretching between the Tiauru and Barema rivers—that is, the entire inland territory above Maututu villages as far as the edge of the volcanic crater of Ivi. The acquired land was divided into two mega-blocks either side of Bialla. The Wilelo block, stretching from Bialla to the Barema River, consisted of 30,272 acres (12,256 hectares) and the Tiauru block, stretching from Bialla south to the Tiauru River, consisted of 10,689 acres (4,327 hectares). At this early stage, the administration had already tripled its original target for land acquisition, with seeming disregard for any potential expansion of oil palm to village holdings.

Not only was the administration's 'purchase' of land alien to Maututu understandings of soil, but also the payment of funds to Maututu was made according to expatriate determinations of who 'owned' the land (see Table 3.2). The Wilelo block payment of A$73,000, for example, was divided equally among four villages, Bubuu, Baikakea, Apupulu and Gomu.[27] This was not in accord with Maututu understandings that the entire Wilelo territory was affiliated primarily with the hamlet groups (*karakara*) of just the two villages of Bubuu and Baikakea, and the *karakara* of Urumaili. Maututu would have expected that an exchange of valuables for access to soil would have been delivered to 'big men' of lineages in Bubuu, Baikakea and Urumaili, and that they would have shared that with kin and affiliates mainly in their own *karakara*, but including kin in the other two villages of Gomu and Apupulu. The colonial government instead assumed that villages—a colonial construction—had pre-eminent control of land, and left it to village *luluai* in all four villages to determine the distribution of monies to the customary owners.[28] The seeming acceptance of these 'wild' arrangements by Maututu

---

27 Several villagers in 2008 claimed that the total payment in 1966 was A$272,000. Ilisi, former LLG chairman, reported that A$82,000 was paid for timber on Tiauru and Wilelo. Jackson Taba, a Maututu lawyer, claimed that a payment was made in 1964 of A$68,000 for purchase of timber. Tomarum who was national land commissioner until 2004, claims that oil palm land was not purchased, but only timber rights.

28 For the Tiauru block, Matararu villagers reported receiving A$10,000 as *la mapa la magasa* (price of soil), receiving A$47 a person. Further up the coast beyond the Barema River, 40,000 acres of forested land on the designated Soe block were acquired by the Australian administration in 1967, with part of the A$160,000 cash paid to Bubuu villagers. However, this territory was also affiliated with the Meramera people and the Land Division records that the people of Nuau village received A$70,000 for the Soe block, with payments of A$4,200 to each resident. In the Meramera area, two further blocks were acquired through a payment of A$73,000 for the Madudua block, with payments of A$300 each individual and A$55,000 for the Ibana block with payments of A$2,240 each.

was reflected in December 1968 when Gomu, Bubuu, Apupulu and Baikakea villagers again put their marks on a document for the 'sale' of 14,000 acres of soil in Wilelo, a total distribution of A$40,000.[29] Similarly, the Tiauru soils, including their timber, were acquired (10,689 acres in 1964 and 5,848 acres in 1968) from the three villages of Uase, Matililiu and Mataruru.

Table 3.2: Purchase of land and timber by Australian administration

Year	Name	Purpose	Acres	Price (A$)	Owners
1962	Bialla Plantation	Town/industrial	3,500	–	Plantation
1964	Silanga	Cocoa	6,882	£13,674	Uasilau-Silanga
1964	Tiauru and Wilelo	Timber	–	$64,000 or $82,000	Maututu
1964	Wilelo	Timber/oil palm?	30,272	$73,000	Bubuu-Gomu
1964	Tiauru	Timber/oil palm?	10,689	($10,000)	(Mataruru), Matililiu, Uase
1966	Hargy	Timber	–	$272,000	Maututu
1967	Soe	Timber/oil palm?	–	$160,000	Bubuu
1967	Madudua	Timber/palm oil?	–	$73,000	Meramera
1967	Ibana	Timber/oil palm?	–	$55,000	Meramera
1968	Wilelo	Timber/oil palm?	14,000	$40,000	Bubuu-Gomu
1968	Tiauru	Timber/oil palm?	5,848	–	Mataruru-Uase
1968	Tiauru–Wilelo coast strip	Timber	–	($76,000)	Maututu

Note: Decimal currency was introduced in 1966. The 1964 Tiauru payment to Mataruru was for a portion only of the block, possibly about 4,150 acres, with other claimants from Matililiu and Uase, the total price being around A$26,000. Grieve (1986) reports that more than 42,000 hectares of land in West New Britain were alienated from native control by the administration for oil palm and timber development in Bialla and Hoskins/Kimba. The incomplete list above already details almost 30,000 hectares in the Bialla area.

Source: Author's research.

The administration interpreted these payments as the purchase of timber and/or land based on an ontological understanding of timber and land as material assets. Maututu, on the other hand, did not conceive of their soil as a material asset that could be put on the market and saw these payments as granting access to soils that remained permanently in the keeping of

---

29 At same time, a local man working as cook and storekeeper at the Bialla Plantation was earning A$40 a month and a driver there was earning A$12 a month.

past, present and future generations of Maututu. Soil represented a living environment in which humans negotiated with forest inhabitants and ancestral spirits to allow them to grow food and to hunt for game. This tension between these two ontological positions was not always obvious to the two parties, because they did not consult with each other as to what they each understood they were doing. The colonial administration often acted as though natives would readily accept the ways of 'development' and, in doing so, accept the 'primitiveness' of their own native understandings. Their assumptions of native ignorance were only confirmed when most villagers were unable to read the contracts presented to them and signed with a cross or thumbprint rather than a signature.

A patrol report dated November 1968 documents negotiations with Maututu villagers over the second Wilelo block of 14,000 acres.[30] The surveyor took four and a half days to discuss and survey the relevant block and remarked that the people were familiar with this work, having been involved in several land investigations before. He commented:

> When the 'Declaration of Custom' was being completed the writer noticed that several people were listed several times in different clans with the same or different names and approximately one dozen were listed in the one clan twice under different names. On investigating this matter it was discovered that each of these villagers had rights to the land in one clan only.
>
> (Department of External Territories, 1968, p. 46)

Apparently, the surveyor—the powerful outsider—objected to individuals being listed several times, as though they were cheating the administration or their fellow villagers. His expectation appears to have been that land was divided exclusively among clans and that only clan members could have a right to any financial rewards from parting with that land. I was resident in the village at the time and observed the negotiation. The expatriate *masta mak* (surveyor) was 'abrupt, impatient, lacking any understanding of native custom, scarcely smiling, and generally looking as though he wanted to get out as quickly as possible' (see author's field notes, 10 December 1968). He cursed anyone who claimed access to soil from two clans in the one

---

30 Matililiu villagers in 1969 reported to me they had received A$8,000 as *la mapa la magasa* (value of soil), a sum they divided to four clans, who distributed the cash more widely through other clans. Individuals received A$20–40 from this payment.

village, or the one clan in two villages, and there was no acknowledgement that one clan (or lineage) might have claims over more soil than another. I noted at the time:

> It is no wonder that bad race relations develop when whites let blacks know they have no time for them, that they suspect them of cheating and theft, and that they despise their culture.

> (Field notes, 10 December 1968)

Faced with this colonial arrogance, each villager then listed themself in only one clan. But their initial naming of people associated with each area of soil recognised many beyond the clan who had an interest in that soil, not only those whose lineage ancestors had initially opened the soil, but also their kin from other lineages who had shared gardens or otherwise had close links with the core line.

The administration's handling of these payments provides vivid evidence of the distinction between administration and Maututu ontological assumptions. In the administration's wisdom, the government representative in the village, the *luluai*, was in the best position to distribute the cash and would give equal amounts to everyone. The *luluai*, however, acted on indigenous assumptions and passed the cash onto lineage heads for them to distribute in whatever way they decided to a wider network of kin and affiliates. In Baikakea, for example, Ove, as senior of the Vorega lineage, distributed A$4,600 to 14 members of his own lineage (7 of whom lived in the far village of Mataruru), as well as 4 in his nuclear family, 7 of his wife's lineage, 3 kin of his lineage mates, 11 of the dominant Kabulu lineage in the hamlet, 4 of whom had fathered Vorega members, 4 leaders of other lineages, 4 outsiders to the village and 15 other village residents. The payments varied from A$10 to A$200, with Ove taking a large share of A$400 for himself. The redistribution from this one lineage 'head' thus included lineage and non-lineage in the village and members of the clan living outside the village. The range of this distribution demonstrates how Maututu at the time were more concerned with consolidating a wide network of kin than asserting the exclusivity of a particular lineage in its affiliation with soil. These payments may have been even more widely distributed. Malalia in Baikakea reported to me that he had received A$100 each from different lineage heads, demonstrating that the payment for soil or timber was not seen by Maututu as 'purchase' of property but more, like bridewealth, as an acknowledgement of the wide network of kin who had contributed to the lineage's affairs or who were strongly associated with the lineage.[31] In their distribution of *la mapa*, lineage heads recognised wide ties of affiliation with lineage and clan members and with fellow residents.[32]

This sudden injection of large amounts of cash in the space of only a few years from timber and land purchases led to Maututu purchasing items such as aluminium boats with outboard motors (A$1,000), radios (A$30–40), bicycles (A$30–40), watches (A$10–60), shotguns (A$40–50), cameras (A$60), tape recorders and guitars. Some surplus cash was put into bank accounts, but this was quickly spent on purchases of clothes and food. It was a blaze of 'individual' consumption. However, when I arrived in 1968, there was little to show for this vast injection of cash. The boat motors had fallen into disrepair and rusted, and the boats were useless without them. On the other hand, contributions to bridewealth increased from A$2–10 to A$300 and even higher. In 1967, for example, bridewealth payments as large as A$1,800 were exchanged, and in 1968 the standard bridewealth was A$600–900, denominated in cash rather than in valuables such as *tuali* shells, pigs or cloth. The extraordinary influx of cash had no doubt encouraged the individual consumption promoted by the administration; however, over the longer period, villagers promoted increased distribution through exchanges. This period of cash bonanza did not last, after which most could only access further cash through their cocoa harvests. Five years later, with ready cash dwindling, the Nakanai Council regretted the inflation in bridewealth payments and established a limit of A$100 for future bridewealth.

Maututu were later to recognise that they had little sense of what the administration was doing, because it cut across their ontological sense that soil was inalienable, instilled with the spirits of ancestral and wild spirits, and renewed through cycles of forest regrowth. Administration surveys drew lines on maps to mark village and clan ownerships, whereas my own investigations in 1969 revealed that people prioritised not boundaries but ancestral sites. They would identify a section of forest by the site of a past

---

31 Martin (2006, p. 118) refers to Tolai bridewealth in the past as part of a cycle of reciprocal gift exchange constituted through exchange marriage between lineage sections, contrasting it to the 'bride price' inflation among Tolai in recent years that reflects the greed of some parents who treat their daughters as a commodity in the market. A similar tendency has emerged among Maututu where the marriage is contracted with distant families outside of the regular exchanges, for example, with those from another language/culture group who may demand inflated cash sums to finalise the marriage.

32 *La mapa* referred to a sum of valuables as the payment or value of something. *La tahalo/tavile la mapa* referred to someone of great value, such as a wife who brought great value to her husband and his kin, or a big man who brought value to all his *karakara*.

hamlet, a fruit tree or coconut or betel palm, naming the ancestors who inhabited the site. They had no understanding of my questions about the boundaries of such sites.

Conclusion

The history of cocoa development in West New Britain reveals the friction between the worldviews of the expatriate exponents of economic growth and the Maututu growers. Cocoa for the colonial agricultural officers and for the Bialla Plantation manager was a means to build financial resources, both for the individual growers and for the national economy. Together with other agricultural exports from PNG, it was seen as a key measure of 'development' and a step towards eventual independence for PNG. The government focus on export income drove the expansion of cocoa plantings and the careful application of fermenting and drying procedures to ensure the high quality of beans. For the village growers, on the other hand, cocoa was not the primary source of livelihood, which continued to be the food gardens, their domestic pig herds and their harvest of forest and marine resources. Cocoa provided them with disposable income to cover periodic needs, such as school uniforms and fees, government taxes and the purchase of exchange goods for ceremonial occasions. Just as importantly, it represented the prized goal of 'modernity'.

The Maututu adoption of cocoa must, therefore, be seen in contrast to both Lauje and Tolai processes. Cocoa plantings did not consume all Maututu soil and the soil on which cocoa was planted was not reconstituted as individual property. There was no pauperisation driven by cocoa plantings or cycles of debt, but, instead, cocoa became another cash crop alongside copra and betel nut, allowing villagers to enjoy some cash revenue secondary to their main subsistence crops. Koczberski, Curry and Anjen (2012, p.184) observed in PNG that, despite the cultivation of long-term perennials such as cocoa, 'land continues to be fundamental for household food production, and for sustaining spiritual beliefs, social and ritual activities, individual and group social identities, and for underpinning social organization'—that is, it is rarely commodified, even where it has been 'purchased' under German or Australian administrations. In Maututu terms, it still remains 'soil'.

The Maututu Cooperative Society was an example of home engagement with the unpredictable outside world. Villagers negotiated with these outside agents to bring benefits to the community in ways that they saw as strengthening the 'home'. The outside remained a force to be reckoned with, not only in the antagonism of the plantation manager or the remoteness of administration officers, but also in the opportunities the new cash provided. In confronting these unpredictable forces, Maututu strove to engage in beneficial ways. Cocoa—a strange non-food—became domesticated as a crop that allowed them to identify with the 'modernity' offered by the outside world. Their responses indicated that they were not blindly adopting the ways of expatriate strangers but fashioning these new opportunities to their own priorities. Cocoa financed 'modern' symbols such as permanent material buildings and vehicles within the village and became a favoured way for Maututu to financially support the village institutions that represented modernity to them. The Women's Club, the Youth Club and the village church had cocoa blocks and residents designated days each week when they allocated their labour to extract from these the means to finance the club or church. Their adoption of cocoa became a means by which communities could raise their status and meet communal priorities.

Maututu aspirations at the time were to benefit cash-wise from their relationships with expatriates and, at the same time, to consolidate their cultural identities within hamlet, lineage and village, while continuing to live in symbiosis with the forest from which they sustained their lifeways. Maututu expressed their progress in contrast to their 'backward' neighbours, the Mengen and Ata, or their cargo cultist West Nakanai (Bileki) kin. In his discussion of West Nakanai cargo discourses in the 1990s, Jebens (2004, p. 131) pointed to the ambivalence with which the West Nakanai considered Europeans:

> With their goods and their Christianity, Europeans do possess what the Nakanai lack. At the same time, however, people willingly point out that Europeans in turn have no knowledge of shame or respect, of hospitality or generosity, that is, of the very values that are seen as particularly characteristic of Nakanai culture.

West Nakanai saw the outsider Europeans as situated in a very different ontological space, with no value set on relationship. They also saw the Tolai of the Gazelle as 'greedy and selfish, that is "just like Europeans"' (Jebens 2004, p. 131). The Maututu had similar views of the 'greedy' European and 'big shot' Tolai and, like the West Nakanai Kivung movement, rejected those values. Their adoption of cocoa as a cash crop did not set out to mimic the outsider's vision of unilinear development but to engage with cocoa in terms of 'home' values. The Maututu Cooperative Society pioneered a relationality that became extended to all Maututu, even to a Mengen village, despite such hamlets and villages being viewed with distrust as outsiders in other contexts. As Curry and Koczberski (2013, p. 346) remarked: 'cocoa fermentaries, like cash crops, lend themselves to communal production practices through sharing of the asset of the gifting of labor'. This was feasible because running costs for the fermentary were kept low by Baikakea locals carrying out what maintenance was required.

However, society members from other villages rarely contributed labour at the drier and fermentary, signalling future tension over the standing of the society. Tension between communities grew around the distribution of society benefits. While the society enhanced the home community of Baikakea, where the assets and leadership were located, other villages looked for similar benefits for their home community. The success of the society led to demands from partner villages for their own driers, fermentaries and vehicles. This had the potential to devastate the society, as had happened with the earlier trade store. In terms of the outside logics of capitalist development, as espoused by the administration, it may have made sense to further consolidate the society's operations before expanding their assets elsewhere; however, in indigenous terms, these demands were difficult to counter. Every village wanted to boost its own 'modernity'. Aware of the difficulties that had closed the trade store, the society chairman resisted investment in other villages fearing that not enough funds would remain for critical maintenance when the rusting pipes allowed smoke to affect bean quality, or when vehicles became unroadworthy. But this only raised suspicion that the society chairman was being greedy (like his expatriate advisors) and was unduly advantaging his lineage and hamlet. The partnership between home and outsiders thus required mutual respect displayed through redistribution. The most enduring 'modern' enterprises were those that allowed exchange relations to flourish. Like a 'big man' planning an important *mage* feast, the success of the enterprise lay not in the stock of wealth he had laid aside but in the network of exchange partners willing to back the enterprise and, as a consequence, benefit from distribution.

Cocoa allowed dividual persons and lineages to contribute to such partnerships, but leaders of the Maututu Cooperative Society, for their part, needed to acknowledge partnership with outside groups by redistributing benefits to them. In *Sustainable Communities, Sustainable Development,* James et al. (2012, p. 23) call for 'a lived reconciliation—with all the continuing discomfort and tension that such a process entails—between ontologically different ways of doing things: tribal, traditional and modern'. Robbins (2010, p. 639) cites Badiou (2003), who argues that:

> Events that challenge societal norms need to recruit subjects who will be faithful to them, who will work to realize their consequences by radically transforming the state that preexists them.

Robbins (2010, p. 639) goes on to argue that such post-evental persons are 'divided' subjects—that is, they need to 'work constantly to overcome the particular life they have led in light of the newfound fidelity to the event and its universal implications'. This was the case for the society directors who sought to satisfy the market demands of cocoa production while remaining faithful to local exchange relations. Gewertz and Errington (2016, p. 376), writing of the Suabi of the PNG Sepik, refer to 'ontological bricolage' as an expression of 'shifting, situational, melded, often self-conscious, and sometimes critically appraised ways of being and acting in the world' as people 'slide in and out of multiple frames of reference'. Minnegal and Dwyer (2017, p. 8) write of the Kubo in PNG: 'They sought ways to draw the outside world into their own and, thereby, to gain access to and control over what they perceived as its future possibilities.' That was the dilemma that society leaders faced as they expanded the cooperative, building their relations with outsider communities through distribution while enhancing the modernity of the home. For the chairman, distribution was largely through the purchase of wet beans and the annual dividend to members, while, for other communities, distribution of 'modernity' was sought through investment in their own 'modern' structures.

By the end of the decade, the Maututu Cooperative Society had collapsed because these partnerships could not be sustained. In 1978, Apisai, after eight years as the society secretary/bookkeeper in Baikakea, was sent to Rabaul for accountancy training, encouraged by the independent PNG government's push to build local skills. This provided the opportunity for Gomu-Apupulu members of the society to demand that leadership pass to them. The positions of secretary/bookkeeper and chairman were assumed by Gomu-Apupulu men. The new secretary/bookkeeper was actually the former secretary at Apupulu who had been jailed for embezzlement. The new chairman was, at the same time, establishing his own fermentary and drier in Gomu, where another fermentary owned by the prominent leader Mapulo Gaa was already operating. The Toyota Land Cruiser and Isuzu were relocated to Gomu, away from the Baikakea fermentary. These arrangements undermined the Baikakea operations, as transport of both wet beans to the fermentary and dry beans to the port was disrupted. Growers in Gomu began to prefer fermentaries in their own village. The Land Cruiser began to be used to deliver wet beans to private fermentaries, further undermining the Baikakea operations. Eventually, society funds were squandered to the point that the Baikakea fermentary could not be maintained. Without a healthy bank balance, it was not long before the tractor and Land Cruiser were also inoperable, left to rust in the village.

The demise of the society reflected the challenges the directors had always had in satisfying the demands of multiple hamlets, and in office holders balancing their obligations to kin and neighbours with the market requirements of cocoa production. But, more significantly, it occurred in a period of violent challenge to Maututu framing of their world. The emerging industrialisation of West New Britain through logging and oil palm posed a critical challenge to the survival of relational ways of knowing the world and partnering with the wild outside.

4

The violence of logging and oil palm

Done right, palm oil should generate wealth and employment for local communities. Done wrong, oil palm estates can lead to land alienation, loss of livelihoods, social conflicts, exploitative labor relations and degraded ecosystems.

(Colchester et al., 2006, p. 11)

Industrialisation came to West New Britain not with the cocoa economy, but with the logging and oil palm industries. These were of a very different order to what Maututu had experienced to that point. While smallholders of cocoa and coconut plantings remained largely in control of the growing, processing and marketing of their crops, the industrial transformation under logging and oil palm was characterised by highly capitalised operations that were largely divorced from local aspirations and engagement, geared primarily not to the development of local peoples but to the benefit of the national and district economy, and company shareholders. While the introduction of cocoa allowed for a progressive engagement of Maututu with outside forces, the later industrial developments entangled local people, quickly stripping them of access to their soils, blunting their political representation and threatening their social structures and cultural expressions. The chapters that follow examine the dimensions of this industrial shock, the ways Maututu responded to it and the transformations of their lives and worldview as they sought to engage with it.

As the quotation above suggests, there is an anomaly at the heart of oil palm development. It promises to generate wealth for producers, both company and smallholders. However, where the search for excessive profits drives oil palm development, other values can fall by the wayside, leading to land squeeze, loss of access to gainful employment, social marginalisation, undermining of communal values, indebtedness, dependency and 'degraded ecosystems'. The argument of the following chapters is that oil palm was promoted by government administrations and companies to improve the livelihoods of smallholders, yet, from the Maututu perspective, it has tended to aid strangers to the Maututu world in ways that have threatened indigenous wellbeing. For Maututu, this industrial program instigated a period of rapacious destruction of a scale and character that must have reminded them of the Pacific War. While that war destroyed gardens and livelihoods and forced people to flee to caves deep in the forest, industrialisation has destroyed the forests and confined Maututu to their ever shrinking hamlet homes.

Logging as the precursor of oil palm development

When I re-entered the Bialla area in 1972, a massive transformation was under way. The forest interior was criss-crossed by roads and tractor trails used by timber companies to extract every piece of valuable timber from the area (Figure 4.1). Timber jinkers carried walnut, mahogany, malas, taun, calophyllum and dillenia logs to the Bialla port for export. Village hunters using these logging tracks to penetrate the forest in search of game were rarely beyond the sound of chainsaw and timber jinker, and, as a consequence, forest game was ever more difficult to find. The logged areas were an unsightly mess of muddy tracks and broken branches. Locals commented that even spirit beings had fled.

The logging industry was directed by Amplex, a subsidiary of Golden Pines Sawmilling Company, which had obtained a lease over Bialla Plantation as their logging headquarters in West New Britain. Further south the Stettin Bay Lumber Company, co-owned by government and a Japan-based company, had commenced operations in Buluma, near Central Nakanai, with access to 434,500 hectares of forest extending from the north coast around Kimbe to the south coast, and east into East New Britain (Filer, 1997b, p. 12).

In a review of the logging industry in Papua New Guinea (PNG), Filer (1997a, p. 7) drew attention to the unsustainable forms of land use caused, among other things, by:

> dislocation of forest-edge communities from traditional culture, and their purposeful or forced absorption into a cash economy in which they are not well equipped to participate, which then serves as an incentive to sell their forest resource to the highest bidder.

This, indeed, was destined to be the experience of Maututu. Very few found work in Amplex logging work. Amplex created its own labour force bubble, with the vast scale of industrial equipment, its operators, mechanics, retail and office staff largely cut off from surrounding populations. There was far less contact with these foreigners than there had been with the former Bialla Plantation manager, who had run the largest trade store in the area. There was also tragedy. A school child's life was lost when she fell from a timber jinker while catching a lift home from school. It was yet another instance of the threat of the wild to local people.

Figure 4.1: Logging roads traverse Bialla cocoa and coconut plantation, 1974
Source: Author.

In 1976, the trading company Shin Asahigawa based in Rabaul took over the logging lease of Amplex, established a sawmill at Bialla and intensified the logging of the Bialla hinterland.[1] They also brought logs from the Ulamona area north of Bialla for milling at Bialla.[2] Shin Asahigawa renamed Bialla Plantation as Ambusa. A logging conglomerate named Complex, which linked a number of independent logging outfits—Amplex (Golden Pines Sawmilling Company) at Bialla, Payne and Chjpper in Bubuu, Ulamona Sawmill Development, Buluma Logging (Hoskins) and Moimoi Sawmill (Tairobi)—used Bialla as their port to export logs and supported the sawmill there. Sawn timber was supplied from there to the wider market in PNG and beyond, but local villagers could only access scrap timber for their home construction. They often commented that the mighty trees of ancestral forests had been lost to home livelihoods.

These industrial logging operations were in stark contrast to other logging and sawmilling concerns that had engaged successfully with local villagers. The sawmill further east at the Catholic Mission at Ulamona had operated from 1898 (Saulei, 1997), providing sawn timber for the extensive settlement of the mission, initially on the Gazelle Peninsular, and, from 1928, for the mission station and local village houses among the Meramera population around Ulamona. It focused on employing local villagers in its operations. Among the Maututu, Australians Bev and Norm Payne ran a small operation from the beach alongside Bubuu village, where they built a home with their young children. Payne floated his logs to ships anchored outside the reef at Bubuu, with minimal impact on the beach surrounds. He fostered relations with local people, employing men as chainsaw operators and women in office and domestic work. Bubuu villagers enjoyed positive relations with his family, supplying them with garden produce and seeking their help in dealing with outsiders. Bev, who was a trained nurse, provided medical care to the village.

---

1   Shin Asahigawa was established in 1969 with directors Yamashida and Yoshiaki Katori, Tomaschido Ogawa, Kosi Asaoka, Farid and Fouad Wakim, Graham Francis and Lucien Edward Forbes. Lucien Forbes had interests in fishing and port operations in PNG after earlier interests in sugar in Brazil and became chair and CEO of the Forbes Group. Farid Wakim was secretary of Shin Asahigawa (1969–72) and director of Bialla Plantations Pty Ltd from 1970.

2   In 1996, Shin Asahigawa still held the Hargy Consolidated timber permit TP-14-38 (Filer, 1997b). This permit covered the period 1988–98 over an area of 25,300 hectares with an estimated timber resource of 400,000 cubic metres. The indigenous Kumo Development Corporation was also listed as holding a permit at Maututu (Hargy) TP-14-58, 1995–2005, over 14,045 hectares with an estimated resource of 613,906 cubic metres.

The logging industry was built on a distinctive ontological framework. Minnegal and Dwyer (2017, p. 262) noted that foreign capital operations were defined by commensurability ('values being measured/recalibrated against a common standard'), categorisation ('the attributes of things assuming definitional status') and anonymisation ('transactions foregoing prior relational commitment'), all exemplified in the logging industry. The forest was *recalibrated* in terms of the value of particular tree species, access to those resources was *categorised* in terms of time and labour expenditure, and the company projected their operations in *anonymous* terms by ignoring those who had for generations traversed the forest domain and related to its sacred being and ancestral sites. Such assumptions were in tension with native ontological principles. Lattas (2011, p. 90) reported that a Malaysian logging company further west along the coast of New Britain regarded local villagers as 'dumb and pigheaded; and so they were mainly employed as labour assistants'. As a consequence, he observed, logging operations created a 'law and order problem that had not existed previously', with local villagers expressing their rage through violence and theft against what they perceived as exploitative companies (Lattas, 2011, p. 88). The strangeness and unpredictability of the loggers' ways incited wild responses from villagers.

In Bialla, Amplex's disregard of village interests was highlighted in two critical events: their failure to pay debts incurred for village logs and their reluctance to furnish villagers with sawn timber for house construction. Having extensively logged the Bialla area, Amplex contracted with Meramera villagers at Lolobau, Noau and Nantambu to sell their logs to Ambusa.[3] To do this, the villagers set up a local company, the Ulevun Association, that included Pelevavu/Mengen villagers from Gigipuna and further inland to Bago village.[4] But Ambusa failed to pay the Ulevun Association for their logs. At the same time, they refused to supply Maututu villagers with sawn timber, seemingly oblivious to local resentment and opposition to their presence in the area. This resentment against the company grew, climaxing in the 1990s with the sacking of the company office and the killing of the Japanese sawmill manager by unidentified assailants; some allege the assailants were unpaid labourers, others that they were migrant settlers and *raskol* gangs, still others claim they were local villagers. The sawmill was burnt to the ground and its office looted of documents.[5] Afterwards, Shin Asahigawa withdrew permanently from Ambusa/Bialla and their

---

3   The Catholic sawmill at Ulamona was burnt to ground by its workers.
4   Ulevun (the Father volcano) is the active volcano overlooking the two villages.
5   I viewed some of these in Baikakea.

accrued debt to the Ulevun Association and its president, Denis Galea, of A$176,000 for logs supplied was repaid with the deeds to the Ambusa Plantation. Denis's son Nixon was appointed a director of Ambusa alongside the Pelevavu/Mengen oil palm mini-estate grower Leo Nantoto. However, Maututu raised objections to the Meramera Ulevun Association occupying what they still saw as Maututu soil. In response, the Ulevun Association abandoned operations on the Ambusa/Bialla site, although they made some major investments in Bialla town.[6]

Establishment of oil palm companies in West New Britain

The developments initiated by the administration's acquisition of land signalled expatriate priorities to attract foreign capital investment in the PNG export economy. Only the growth of exports would provide the finance to sustain the emerging nation-state. However, when self-government was granted in 1973 and independence in 1975, the PNG Government recognised that villagers had different ontological priorities and needed to be protected against exploitation by powerful outside interests. The Constitution of the Independent State of Papua New Guinea (1975) stated as its fifth goal:

1. a fundamental re-orientation of our attitudes and the institutions of government, commerce, education and religion towards Papua New Guinean forms of participation, consultation, and consensus, and a continuous renewal of the responsiveness of these institutions to the needs and attitudes of the People; and

2. particular emphasis in our economic development to be placed on small-scale artisan, service and business activity; and

3. recognition that the cultural, commercial and ethnic diversity of our people is a positive strength, and for the fostering of a respect for, and appreciation of, traditional ways of life and culture, including language, in all their richness and variety, as well as for a willingness to apply these ways dynamically and creatively for the tasks of development; and

4. traditional villages and communities to remain as viable units of Papua New Guinean society, and for active steps to be taken to improve their cultural, social, economic and ethical quality.

---

6   We return to this story later.

The Constitution thus recognised the fundamental tension between expatriate focus on economic growth and indigenous values of 'participation, consultation and consensus'. This safeguarding of home values against the powerful incursions of outside interests proved difficult to achieve in practice.

Logging in the Bialla area was planned from the beginning as the forerunner of an even larger industrial transformation that posed a greater threat to village interests. As domestic and international pressure grew on Australia to accede to PNG independence, the Australian administration accelerated its program to establish oil palm in West New Britain, first in Hoskins in 1967 and then Bialla in 1972 (Map 4.1).[7] In contrast to what was happening in the Indonesian and Malaysian oil palm industries, the Australian administration sought to provide for landless farmers throughout PNG by prioritising smallholder settler blocks under the guidance of nuclear estate companies. Although the administration was at the forefront of its early development, the oil palm industry in PNG was eventually dominated by just two foreign companies. In the Hoskins/Kimbe area, a British company, Harrison and Crosfield, that had extensive oil palm plantations in Malaysia and Indonesia (Jones & Wale, 1999) was selected in 1967 by the colonial administration to establish a nucleus estate with an initial target of 3,000 acres of nuclear estate at Mosa and 4,000 acres of smallholder oil palm in blocks nearby. New Britain Palm Oil (NBPOL) was formed with share capital of A$2.5 million, owned 50 per cent by Harrison and Crosfield and 50 per cent by the PNG Government. The first stage of development (1967–70) realised 1,210 hectares (2,988 acres) of nucleus estate and 1,620 hectares (4,000 acres) of smallholder plantings. The second stage (1970–75) expanded this to 4,050 hectares (10,000 acres) nucleus estate and 4,980 hectares (12,300 acres) smallholder plantings (Fleming, 1972).[8]

---

7   Preceding that, in 1963–65, soil samples from four sites in the Maututu area—Lalopo near Tiauru, Bialla plantation, Uase and Noau—were tested and research plots of oil palm planted at these sites.

8   The independent PNG Government later reduced its share and thus its capacity to control local operations. Harrison and Crosfields purchased the government share in the late 1990s, and, after that, the company passed into the hands of a succession of multinational companies before, in 2015, being acquired by Sime Darby SDN BHD, the Malaysian multinational with plantations in Pahang, Johor and Sarawak. The intense interest in oil palm expansion from international companies, particularly from Malaysia, heightened the focus of executive boards on profit margins rather than partnering local government or people in development.

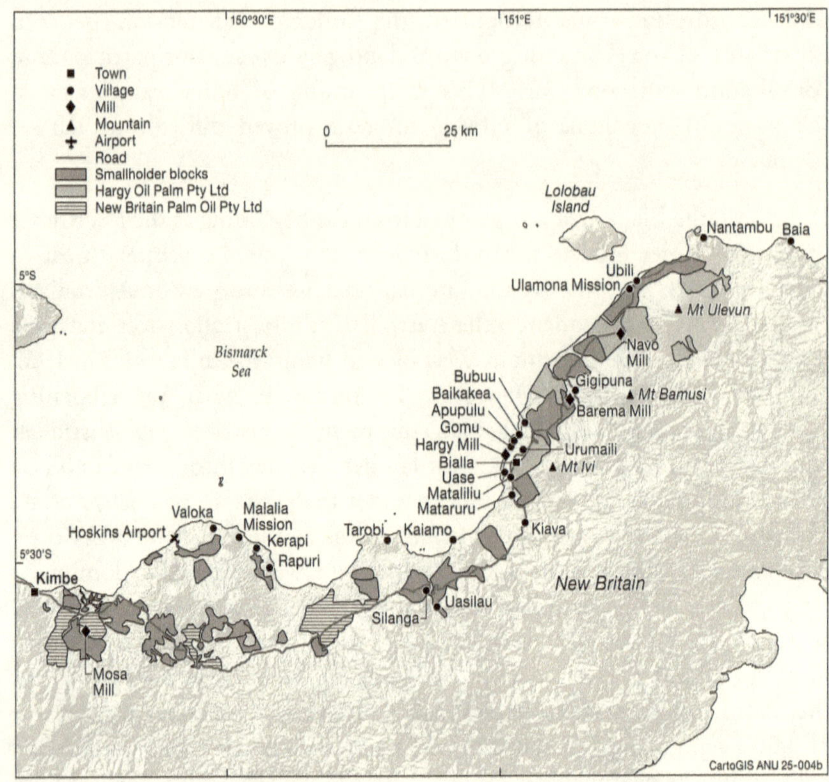

Map 4.1: West New Britain palm oil
Source: ANU CartoGIS Services.

In the Bialla area, lands department surveyors in 1965 began marking out Tiauru settler allotments at the southern border of Maututu territory. In 1969, South Pacific Palm Oil Development Pty Ltd (SPPOD) and its key shareholder, Tokai Leveller Pty Ltd, under its first chairman, Saburo Matsumoto, established a joint venture with the PNG Government to develop an oil palm nursery and a nuclear plantation adjacent to the proposed town of Bialla (Department of the Senate, 1973). SPPOD/TPPO headquarters and seedling nursery were set up at Makikiwa (Makaiwa), inland of Matililiu village, in 1972.[9] SPPOD was listed under the control of Shin Asahigawa Pty Ltd, which, in other documents, was named as a partner in the Bialla agreement. This was the same company that was a major partner in the Complex timber operations based around Bialla wharf and that had so blatantly ignored local interests.

---

9   SPPOPD set up a project company called Trans Pacific Palm Oil, named in the original 1972 Act.

The agreement signed by SPPOD with the Australian Government included the following:

- A lease for a term of 99 years over Portion 9 comprising 2980 hectares
- The Project company to erect a mill with maximum capacity to service 6500 hectares
- Settlement of 700 indigenous farmers to plant 2630 hectares of oil palm
- Encourage village farmers surrounding project company to plant 800 hectares
- Encourage farmers inland of Bangula Bay (Uasilau-Silanga) to plant 800 hectares of oil palm
- Purchase of smallholder fresh fruit bunches at a price equivalent to that paid to smallholders in Hoskins Peninsular.

(Department of the Senate, 1973, p. 9)

The company's lease included three portions within the Ambusa/Bialla Plantation, Portion 2 of 401 hectares, Portion 1 of 529 hectares, and Portion 3 of 114.5 hectares proposed for the mill, workshops, tailings pond, labour quarters and plantation nursery. Beyond this area lay the areas assigned to settlers: to the north, the Wilelo block stretching across the Lovo River as far as the Barema River; and, to the south, the Tiauru block as far as the Tiauru River (Department of the Senate, 1973, p. 19). The agreement differentiated 'indigenous' and 'village' farmers, the latter to be 'encouraged' rather than supervised. Given the company focus on establishing the nuclear plantation and settler blocks, and the poor reputation of Shin Asahigawa among Maututu, there was little chance that SPPOD would take its role of 'encouragement' very seriously.

There was little interaction of the company with villagers or local government field staff when I lived there in 1973–75. The Japanese senior staff lived in isolation in their enclave in Makikiwa, had little fluency in English or Tok Pisin, and relied on the currency of gifts to gain local cooperation. From the point of view of villagers and indigenous government officials, the company held the advantage of seemingly endless capital and powerful contacts in the capital Port Moresby. But the Japanese company managers at Makikiwa confounded local Department of Agriculture, Stock and Fisheries (DASF) staff with whom I worked because of their lack of transparency about their field operations. For example, they brought in fishing boats, fish nets and long hook lines to fish the surrounding seas, storing the catch in a huge freezer at

Makikiwa prior to export. To gain access to these fishing grounds they offered gifts of food, clothes and other goods to local big men, including a car each to the Nakanai Council president, Mapulo, and the *tahalo auru*, Mataimi, in Mataruru. They approached these big men as though they were village chiefs with final say over village resources, thus ignoring lineage and hamlet structures and 'customary' village expectations of community consultation. Indeed, these transactions were clouded in secrecy and thus encouraged these leaders to keep the windfall for themselves. This heralded a very different style of village prominence, more in the style of 'big shots' (discussed below) than 'big men' (Martin, 2007).[10] Not surprisingly given Maututu disdain of arrogant Wallaby-style behaviour, this alliance of company and 'big shots' fomented resentment among many villagers that such largesse was not more generally distributed to benefit everyone.[11] Many locals expected that these strangers, who were cultivating what were still regarded as village soils, would continue to recognise their obligations to local custodians of the soil in exchange relationships. Resentment grew to the point that Matililiu residents in 1974 barricaded access roads to prevent the company transporting the fish to their headquarters.

The Somare government was quick to act, determining that SPPOD had broken the terms of the contract signed with the Australian administration in 1972, which stated 'that their power should be restricted to those activities which were directly related to the planting, harvesting, processing and marketing of oil palm and palm oil products' (Department of the Senate, 1973, p. 3). The PNG Government revoked their oil palm license in 1976 and took full control of the company's oil palm operations. To replace SPPOD, the PNG Government invited the international palm oil producer SA SIPEF NV Belgium Group and Warren Plantation (Mount Hagen) to each take a 25 per cent interest in the Bialla operations, with the government holding the other 50 per cent. SIPEF, established in 1919, was an agribusiness group producing oil palm, rubber and tea in Indonesia, and bananas on the Ivory Coast. They renamed the company as Hargy Oil Palm Ltd (HOPL).[12] In 1984, Warren Plantation sold its 25 per cent stake to SIPEF and, in 1986, HOPL signed a 99-year lease over the land. The government left it to HOPL to manage the oil palm business and, in 2003, sold its 50 per cent stake to SIPEF, signifying their approval of HOPL operations.

---

10 This is discussed further below.

11 In 2008, the village court magistrate, recounting these earlier times, suggested to me that some villagers expected the company eventually to distribute cars to everyone as well as construct an airport (like the one at Hoskins) and a town like the district capital Kimbe.

12 Lake Hargy above Bialla was named after Fred Hargesheimer, the US pilot shot down in the interior during WWII who had subsequently established a school in Ewasse.

Table 4.1: Oil palm production in PNG, 1986

	Hoskins	Bialla	Popondetta
Nucleus estate (ha)	4,000	2,000	4,000
No. smallholders	1,500	1,000	1,400
Smallholdings (ha)	8,200	4,400	–
Type smallholder settler	1,300 settlers 200 villagers	900 settlers 100 villagers	1,000 settlers 400 villagers
Palm oil product (tonnes)	40,000	30,000	42,000
Kernel product (tonnes)	6,000	4,000	7,000
Estate employees	1,050	900	1,200

Source: Grieve (1986, p. 73).

These 1986 data indicate the large number of settler households integrated into the oil palm industry (see Table 4.1). In both Hoskins and Bialla, smallholder blocks constituted over double the nuclear estate plantings. Their total production, however, was below that of the estate, reflecting the more intensive agricultural regimes instituted on the estates. The nuclear estates in both Hoskins and Bialla hired about 1,000 employees, further encouraging migration into West New Britain, with each estate labourer assigned a specific area of the estate to manage. By 2009, HOPL estate plantings had grown to 9,906 hectares and smallholder plantings to 13,183 hectares. HOPL estate production of fresh fruit bunches (FFB) at 211,416 tonnes continued to exceed that of the smallholder (200,699 tonnes) (PN Nelson et al., 2010). No more settler blocks were assigned after that, yet the nucleus estate area continued to expand. To the original two nucleus estates of Hargy (near Bialla) and Navo (near Ulamona) were added Barema (from 2006) and Bakada Mengen (from 2010), the four estates in 2012 comprising 11,005 hectares, with total production of 244,564 tonnes, exceeding that of smallholder production of 205,798 tonnes (Thomas, 2013). The production increases necessitated two more mills at Navo east of the Lovo River and Nivani near the Barema River to process the FFB, with all produce shipped out of Bialla. By 2020, HOPL indicated that its estates had grown to 13,707 hectares merged into three estates (James et al., 2012). The national production of palm oil, concentrated in these two companies (NBPOL and HOPL), increased between 1975 and 2005 at over 10 per cent annually. By 2020, palm oil from West New Britain and Popondetta comprised PNG's second largest export earner.[13]

---

13 NBPOL also operated at Popondetta.

The rapacious growth of oil palm along the Maututu coast demanded more and more forest land be converted to the new crop. The infrastructure of mills, roads and housing continued to expand, and the companies expanded their operations even as smallholder expansion slowed. While no more settler blocks were being created, the settler population was growing rapidly through expanded households and a further migrant population attracted into Bialla searching for income opportunities. This led to the expansion of the Bialla town with further impact on the Maututu people.[14] The oil palm explosion established HOPL as the dominant agent of change in the Bialla area, with much larger resources than Bialla Rural Local-level Government (LLG). HOPL staff, particularly the general manager and community relations manager, took a keen interest in local affairs beyond the oil palm industry, taking responsibility for upkeep on major roads and intervening when local events disturbed law and order, as will be explored below. The company came to challenge the standing of the LLG because of its superior access to cash and equipment, and to the provincial government in Kimbe and the central government in Port Moresby.

Settler smallholders

The Australian administration expected that the Land Settlement Scheme (LSS) that complemented the HOPL nucleus estates would lead to an individualised land tenure system, replacing customary land tenure with something more conducive to agricultural commercialisation. According to Curry and Koczberski (2012, p. 382):

> The Australian Administration envisaged that by taking people out of the sociocultural context of village life and settling them on individualised land holdings on settlement schemes, the perceived problems of traditional communal land tenure in constraining agricultural development would be overcome.

As a result they would become 'more market-oriented and market-driven producers and consumers' (Koczberski, Curry & Bue, 2012, p. 291)—that is, their productive labour could be made legible to the global market and could contribute to national revenue. The oil palm settler smallholdings thus represented, in the capitalist logic of the administration and company, a radically different way of conducting one's life and livelihood, what Curry

---

14   Discussed below.

and Koczberski (2012, p. 382) refer to as 'an ontological transformation of the very nature of social being and identity grounded in relational identities'. By moving these families away from their home areas and settling them on separate blocks, they would become 'individuals' defined by their oil palm and food production.

In Bialla, settlers first arrived in 1975 from land-short areas in the Highlands, Sepik and the Gazelle (Curry & Koczberski, 2007) and, by 1985, there were 900 settler smallholders. This number doubled in the next two decades to 1,851 settler households as the available leasehold land was cleared and allocated. By 2005, over 2,700 LSS smallholders in Bialla were producing an annual average of 9.94 tonnes of oil palm bunches on 12,206 hectares (average 4.5 hectares per settler) (Curry & Koczberski, 2007).

LSS smallholders incurred large debts with the company for seedlings, fertiliser and block development, as well as for a two-room timber house with iron roof and corrugated iron rainwater tank. In the early years of the LSS schemes, economic studies (Emmery, 1970; Grieve, 1986) suggested that the returns on oil palm per person/day were higher than for cocoa or coffee, and, due to the larger planted area, the net income per annum was at least three times greater (Grieve, 1986). Company provision on credit of roads, transport, extension advice, seed material and fertilisers allowed smallholders to meet high set up costs. The company managed the spraying of pesticides to prevent the spread of borers. These arrangements closely bound the smallholders to the industrial regime instituted by the company. The repayment of their debts to the company was dependent on continued production and processing of oil palm bunches under supervision of the company. This was an industrial discipline with an intensity much greater than what smallholders had experienced through cocoa, coffee or copra production in their origin areas. It was particularly geared to the industrial requirements of this crop, with its strict growing and milling schedules. From the company point of view, their oversight promoted greater discipline from the grower in caring for their palms and harvesting maximum FFB fortnightly. Smallholder production was expected by the company to contribute something close to half of processed product through the mill, ensuring that the company took an active interest in smallholder production.

On the settler blocks, the nuclear family was the workforce, and the cultivation of oil palm took precedence over food production, particularly for the male blockholder. All members of the household laboured each fortnight to cut the bunches of fruit and carry them to the road where company trucks lifted each net of FFB for weighing before transporting the fruit to the company mill. The earnings on each delivery of FFB were reduced by deductions for transport to the mill, repayment of company debt and contribution to the growers' association fund, and were then paid by cheque, requiring the settler to visit town to deposit the cheque in their bank account or cash it through the town trade stores. Such arrangements further squeezed the household economy, as the store proprietors insisted that smallholders must spend K100 in the trade store when they cashed their cheques.

The experience of smallholder households did not prove as positive as government and the company had anticipated. In 1987, the government predicted that smallholders would achieve an annual income of about K1,500–2,000 from their 4 hectares of oil palm, substantially higher than the average annual income for Papua New Guineans of K440. However, in the first decade of palm production, settlers' annual average income fluctuated wildly, from K1,407 in 1976–77 to K2,463 in the peak year of 1978–79 and back to K701 in 1980–81. In 1985–86, the global price of crude palm oil dropped to 500 Malaysian ringgit (MR)[15] per tonne, and in 2001 to MR600. There were further abrupt drops in prices in 2008, with a fall from MR4,000 to MR1,500 per tonne, resulting in a fall in the oil palm farm gate price in West New Britain from K400 to K85 per tonne. At this low price, deductions for transportation of bunches to the mill constituted as much as 25 per cent of the farm gate price. At these low points, many smallholders who were able to access food gardens ceased to cut their fruit bunches, and their withdrawal of produce undercut the model of settler integration into the oil palm industry.

HOPL managers encouraged growers to put aside savings both to cover these lean times and to prepare for future replanting expenses at the end of the 20-year cycle, thus lessening their debt to the company. To encourage such savings, HOPL discontinued their replanting credit scheme during the 1990s in an effort to make smallholders take more responsibility for their own production. But settlers did not respond as expected to such directives. For the settlers, the blocks were less of a capitalist enterprise than a ready source of cash when needed. Instead of putting their savings away for later investment in replanting, they spent much of their earnings on immediate needs, such as trade store commodities, school expenses, ceremonial obligations and housing improvements. Exchange relations grew strongly

---

15 The Malaysian ringgit and PNG kina were of near equal value.

among settlers, particularly within ethnic groups, and households set aside earnings to fulfil these obligations. Indeed, smallholders were motivated to harvest more FFB when large amounts of cash were required for communal events, and they sometimes chose to contribute to a common fund to meet these costs. Thus, social obligations within the exchange system could actually spur on production. Indeed, Curry (2003, p. 417) reported that 'failure to engage in exchange can result in reduced yields of cash crops', rather than their increase as envisaged in the company model. HOPL reintroduced the credit scheme in 2001 in response to the meagre savings smallholders had made in preparation for replanting.

Oil palm production affected the gender division of labour in the settler households. The industry put the onus on men to manage the oil palm, and, although women tended the palms and participated in harvesting, men were disproportionately engaged in the cutting of the FFB from the palm as the palms grew taller, and in the transport of the heavy FFB to roadside for truck pickup. Women put more of their energies into food production on the 2 hectares initially reserved for subsistence gardens, and increasingly marketed their produce to local markets (Koczberski, Curry & Bue, 2012). In addition, the dependency on cheque transactions empowered the household husband, who held the bank account and had first call on the cash when he went to town. Similarly in West Kalimantan, Indonesia Tania Li (2015, p. 6) observed how the expansion of oil palm was undermining women's rights: the signing over of settler blocks to the man of the household meant that women lost 'their economic autonomy and decision-making power'. Many men ignored family demands, such as school costs, clothes for the family or store-bought food, to spend the cash on alcohol, to the dismay of their wives.

In West New Britain, there was increasing agitation from women for more equal access to oil palm earnings, leading the companies and PNG Government to institute the Mama Lus Frut scheme in 1997. The *lus frut* (loose fruit) referred to here were the individual fruits dislodged from the FFB when they hit the ground, which were often ignored by the men in transporting the produce to the roadside (Figure 4.2). Under the scheme, women (and children) were encouraged to collect these fruits to deposit in a separate net at the roadside weighing station, with the income from these separately calculated and paid by cheque to the female partner. In the Hoskins LSS, both men and women spoke favourably about this innovation and noted a reduction in household conflicts over oil palm income, despite the fact that the *mama lus fruit* income was only 26 per cent of total household income from oil palm (Curry et al., 2019; Koczberski, 2007).

Figure 4.2: Young oil palm with fruit bunches forming, 2017
Source: Author.

The LSS households expanded as children raised their own families on their parents' block, prompting new tensions to emerge. With little alternate land or employment available, all sought a living from the single block, leading to greater demands on oil palm income and the intensification of garden production on lands not converted to oil palm. Population density on the Hoskins LSS blocks rose from 5.9 persons per block in the early 1970s to 13.3 persons in 2000 and 14.72 in 2010. In Bialla, by 2000, there was an average of 11.1 persons per block (Koczberski & Curry, 2005; Koczberski, Curry & Anjen, 2012). In response settlers converted their 2 hectares of food gardens to oil palm, leaving themselves with only the margin around the house on which to grow food. Increasing pressure on oil palm income gave rise to a system of production known as *wok bung wantaim* where those in the extended family associated with the block would work together and even invite labour (Elahi & Michael, 2017) from adjoining blocks. Curry and Koczberski (2013, p. 338) saw this as reflecting 'alternative ways of valuing labor … labor is entwined in the relational economy and is strongly embedded in networks of obligation and reciprocity that typically extend well beyond the household'. But the *wok bung wantaim* strategy was not without its tensions as younger generations sought a larger share in the family production. This led in the mid-1990s to married sons pushing for a new form of production organisation called *markim mun* 'monthly rotation', a solution where co-resident families took it in turn, month by month, to work the block and harvest the fruit. This arrangement appealed to some as reducing the 'stresses and conflicts over work and income from the block', but it led to lower production on the block as cooperative harvesting was abandoned and the several shareholders were reluctant to expend on fertiliser and other inputs (Curry & Koczberski, 2007, p. 37). By 2001, Curry and Koczberski reported that 50 per cent of LSS smallholders in Hoskins and 32 per cent in Bialla used the *markim mun* arrangement. Although the oil palm industry was proving a boon for company and government, the smallholders were struggling to realise the dreams that had brought them from their origin areas (Elahi & Michael, 2017).

The town of Bialla and local administration

On the hills above the port and mill the provincial government developed the new town of Bialla to accommodate the headquarters of the Bialla Rural LLG (that, in 1995, replaced the Nakanai Council), high school, hospital, police headquarters, bank, post office, market and two streets of trade stores run by PNG and expatriate (South Korean, Philippine and mainland Chinese) proprietors. An expanding fleet of privately owned public transport vehicles ferried settlers and villagers to and from the town to their settlements up to 30 kilometres away. The town also attracted migrants from all over PNG seeking their fortune in the rapidly expanding economy. Many of these settled around the town in informal housing. The town became the gathering point for the diverse groups of people who came to constitute the Bialla LLG population—local peoples, migrant settlers, migrant labour force, company and business households, and government employees. This was reflected in the increase in the population of the Bialla LLG area between 2000 and 2011 of 58.4 per cent, compared to 43.1 per cent for the same period in the Hoskins LLG area. According to the 2011 census, there were 58,373 residents in the Bialla LLG area, including 2,672 in urban Bialla. A World Bank report of 2023, however, recorded the Bialla town (Figure 4.3) as 'home to more than 13,000 people' (World Bank, 2023).

Figure 4.3: Bialla town, 2017
Source: Author.

The Bialla LLG area comprises 20 rural wards, each represented by a *kansil* (ward councillor). Apart from these ward representatives, women's organisations are also represented in the LLG. The Organic Law on Provincial Governments and Local-level Governments of 1995 determined that LLGs are to enact laws, maintain the peace and provide local government and service delivery, including water and power supply, social services, housing, aid posts and clinics, community sport, recreational and cultural and industrial shows.[16] LLGs are involved in the development of roads and parks, refuse collection and disposal, environmental protection, food markets, economic promotion and tourism. This is a formidable workload for a council with only five or so staff who must contract out many of these tasks. Only a few LLGs levy fees and rates, but they can apply for grants. In 2014, each LLG received an annual budget of K500,000, with the PNG Government proposing that this eventually be increased to K2 million. Such funding proved totally inadequate to provide and support all the services required in this rapidly expanding area. Throughout PNG, LLG performance has been marred by funding shortfalls, lack of skills in management, and in project and budget planning. Commenting on the Organic Law on Provincial Governments and Local-level Governments, Curry and Koczberski (2007, p. xvi) noted:

> whilst the structures are in place, LLG activities are generally severely constrained by funding shortfalls to the extent that basic services for the community cannot be delivered. Typically, LLGs lack the resources to perform even basic administrative functions.

The heavy trucks ferrying oil palm bunches to the mills wreaked havoc on roads weakened by torrential rainfall, and the flooding of rivers in the wet season took out bridges. The Kimbe–Bialla 'national' road annually lost such bridges to floods, but the PNG Government struggled to maintain it (Slattery et al., 2018). Secondary roads were the responsibility of the provincial government in Kimbe, which was also short of funds for such maintenance. The Bialla LLG was critically short of funds to support

---

16 Provincial, district and LLG staff are salaried members of the national public service. Bialla LLG is one of six in the Talasea District, which, together with the Kandrian-Gloucester District, comprise the West New Britain Province. The provincial staff manage key areas of health, fisheries, agriculture, forestry and natural resources, trade and industry, and education, and in that capacity liaise with LLG staff when required. Districts form an open electorate represented by a member of parliament and their staff are largely focused on conducting census and demographic data. Hoskins and Bialla are included in the Nakanai District.

schools, health posts and local/village roads. Its offices were in a poor state of repair and its staff, including the president, were frequently absent from the office.

Increasingly, the PNG Government, at all three levels, surrendered construction and maintenance of facilities to key companies. When SIPEF bought the PNG Government's 50 per cent share of Hargy Oil Palm in 2003, it joined the government's tax withholding scheme, under which 60 per cent of that tax is withheld by the company to spend on building roads and other infrastructure for the government. The LLG was able to request such funds for the building of school classrooms and teachers' houses, but had little say in how the funds were managed. Because of the lack of coordination between various levels of government and the shortage of local funds to maintain and build public infrastructure, the company acted as a quasi-government body to support its objective of ensuring smooth development and the processing of oil palm. This resulted in the company employing their own labour and equipment rather than contracting the work to local businesses. This made business sense to the HOPL managers but further undermined local interests. It consolidated the company and its managers in the local Bialla area, not just as an industrial producer but as an agency maintaining roads, health posts and school buildings, running sports carnivals, and sponsoring ecotourism and health projects. In 2004, in an attempt to augment LLG funding, the LLG president arranged with HOPL to establish a 25-hectare mini-estate on government-acquired land, to be run by the company as part of its nuclear estate but with the proceeds accruing to the LLG to support its activities. Given the difficulty for the LLG in accessing funds from the provincial government, this was a practical solution to allow the LLG to maintain village roads, schools and health clinics.

HOPL, on its website, stated:

> The prime reason behind the local investment is to contribute to the economy of the region by providing employment opportunities, boosting revenue, supporting social projects and promoting more local business participation.
>
> (SIPEF, n.d.)

This was the responsibility of the HOPL general manager at Bialla, who sought improvements in the welfare of local populations by directing company resources or using political influence at higher levels. Ultimately, however, the general manager was responsible to the SIPEF Board of

Directors and shareholders based overseas, who demanded the company's commercial success. The manager commented to me that when they hosted the executive directors from Belgium twice a year in Bialla, these men and women were entirely focused on the production 'bottom line' in respect of each plantation and each mill, setting ambitious production targets per hectare. They had minimal interest in the social and political relations that the site managers needed to cultivate across the area, nor in environmental protection, even though these sectors were fundamental to the company's international reputation under RSPO (Roundtable on Sustainable Palm Oil) stipulations.[17] These concerns were left to the site managers, who had the difficult task of wedding local village and smallholder interests with the demands of their executive board.

Conclusion

The oil palm industry brought thousands of settlers to the smallholder blocks, and additional population to the town of Kimbe. Many were attracted to the area in search of opportunities and settled in informal accommodation on the outskirts of the town or with *wantok* (own ethnic group) in the settler areas. Increasing rates of landlessness and unemployment among settler children resulted in the proliferation of *raskol* (hoodlum, criminal) gangs and violence, at times escalating into clashes between settlers and local villagers, or attacks on business premises. Many of the law and order problems on the settlers' blocks were exacerbated by drunkenness (Curry & Koczberski, 2007). Gang violence increased, resulting in the kidnapping of the Bialla bank manager in December 2008 and the payment of a ransom by the bank to the gang. In January 2020, the Chinese owner of the New Town supermarket in Bialla was shot dead by a gang of eight who tried to rob the store.[18] In addition, public transport vehicles were held up regularly by *raskol* gangs on the long road south to the airport and Kimbe town and

---

17 Recognition of an oil palm producer under the Roundtable on Sustainable Palm Oil (RSPO) gives the company access to more lucrative European markets. It requires the company to protect primary forests, respect customary ways and livelihoods and care for the environment. The RSPO guarantees Certified Sustainable Palm Oil, representing about 19 per cent of global palm oil production in 2019 (RSPO, 2019).

18 The 'criminal gang' was apprehended within a few days on information from the local settler communities.

their passengers relieved of their cash, mobile phones and other valuables. Any resistance of passengers to the *raskol* could be met with violence, possibly death.

Oil palm production introduced different priorities into the lifeways of indigenous people because of its large-scale investment in plant and machinery and its constant pressures of production targets (Filer, 2007). Processing of the oil palm fruit is done ideally within 24 hours of harvest, necessitating the siting of the oil palm mill in close proximity to the plantings of the crop and the hiring of a mill workforce to operate and maintain machinery and transport vehicles 24 hours a day. This in turn requires the maintenance of roads required for the heavy trucks. The palm oil is then shipped directly to overseas markets by large tanker ships docking regularly at the port. This scale of investment places particular demands on growers and resident populations, of a kind more similar to the mining and logging industries than to copra and cocoa production. The oil palm industry ties farmers to a long-term, even multigenerational contract with the oil palm company in which the company assumes control of the industrial production as the sole supplier of seedlings, pesticide and fertiliser on credit to farmers and the sole purchaser, miller and exporter of produce.

In their review of the oil palm industry in the Asia-Pacific, Cramb and Curry (2012, p. 225) raised concerns about:

> the allocation of vast areas of public land and forests for large-scale commercial development, to the benefit of a small number of agribusiness firms and their patrons in the political and bureaucratic elite; the politico-legal undermining and overriding of customary claims to land that has often accompanied this manifestation of the so-called 'global land grab'; the often unfavourable terms on which landholders and settlers have been incorporated into large-scale development schemes; the potential for conflict within unequal local communities, between local and migrant growers, and hence between different ethnic groups; and the precarious working and living conditions of many migrant plantation workers.

In their overview of the industry, Cramb and Curry (2012, p. 228) add that 'the performance of these schemes has been highly variable, depending crucially … on the commitment and competence of the plantation company in supporting its smallholders', and on the contractual basis of that relationship. Cramb and Curry (2012, p. 224) list the 'perennial problems' facing government in the oil palm industry as:

balancing the trade-offs between subsistence and commercial farming, between commodity specialisation and diversification, between smallholder and large-scale forms of production and between private- and public-sector involvement in supporting or managing oil palm development.

One outcome noted by oil palm researchers in Indonesia was the uneven spread of benefits among indigenous populations. They drew attention to growing inequalities because the benefits of the oil palm industry were offered to local indigenous elites as well as powerful outsiders, such as government officials, teachers or politicians who brokered deals with indigenous groups for blocks of customary land (Li, 2015; McCarthy, 2010; McCarthy & Cramb, 2009). Aware of such negative outcomes, the PNG Government sought to provide better monitoring of the relations between oil palm companies and smallholders, but, as we have noted, such companies have been able to assume a dominant position in local affairs. While initially, PNG administrations had looked to oil palm to relieve land shortages across the country and enhance settler welfare, the industry was far more successful in building corporation profits than in establishing a viable livelihood for PNG smallholders. Cramb and Curry (2012, pp. 228–29) noted that 'it is unlikely there will be any further state-sponsored land settlement schemes' in PNG, as the existing schemes are 'struggling to absorb an increasing population and workforce', aggravated by the lack of off-scheme employment opportunities. Oil palm is not a labour-intensive industry. Even the large, 6-hectare blocks allocated to incoming households did not provide adequately for the multigenerational households that came to occupy them. Settlers constantly looked to augment their income for survival.

Maututu thus faced enormous challenges as the might of the company and overwhelming numbers of strange settlers invaded their soils. Particularly in the early days, when government attention focused on the development of an industry through smallholder resettlement schemes, Maututu fortunes looked gloomy. Despite the promises of the company to protect the indigenous villagers from the worst impacts of oil palm development, this was not the key concern of company managers nor of the local-level and provincial governments, whose resources were severely limited. The following chapters examine how Maututu responded to these encounters with the wild outside.

5

Village oil palm as engagement with the wild

> Examining success stories such as the West New Britain oil palm experience, where three decades of migration and settlement on customary land have occurred in a relatively peaceful fashion, might provide lessons that could be applicable elsewhere.
>
> (Allen & Monson, 2014, p. 13)

The above quotation seems overly positive as an assessment of the Bialla or Hoskins experience of oil palm. While the oil palm industry itself flourished, incorporating thousands of smallholders, the industrial expansion was not always viewed by those smallholders as a success. This chapter will focus particularly on how Maututu over the last 50 years have responded to the industry.

It is important to understand the various perspectives and aspirations that different agents—villagers, smallholders, companies, local-level government (LLG)—brought to their industrial engagement and to follow the passage of such aspirations through the realities they encountered. Building on Tsing's (2005) concept of the 'friction' in such encounters, James et al. (2012, pp. 22–23) referred to the politics arising from three different ontological 'formations of being and becoming'—tribal, traditional and modern—that can exist coterminously within a cultural setting. 'Both-ways politics' and 'both-ways learning' entailed 'a lived reconciliation' across the frictions of change, 'with all the continuing discomfort and tension that such a process entails'. In Stead's analysis, 'modern and customary forms of social relations can exist coterminously' (Stead, 2013, p. 19). Her end goal is to recognise in the 'multiplicity of entanglement' tensions and deep ambivalences as well as instances of powerful customary authority. Filer (2007, p. 145) recognises such 'customary' authority:

> the social dynamics of the 'customary' landscape are not determined by the capacity of customary landowners to resist or roll back the process of alienation, but rather by their capacity to enter into, and benefit from, the social relations of compensation which reflect and condition the process of resource development.

In a similar vein, Minnegal and Dwyer (2017) indicate that ontologies and epistemologies are always co-productive and dynamic. They point out that Kubo peoples both resist and accommodate to these contrasting perspectives, and, in doing so, their own and the company's ontological and epistemological perspectives become labile.

The political ontological approach I am exploring here reflects some of the same tensions. I have outlined in previous chapters a Maututu ontology at variance with those of colonial administrators or oil palm executives. The Maututu perspective expounded in the myths and demonstrated in their entanglements with colonial governments, Christian missions and cash crops favoured neither a retreat into *kastom* as a 'home' prison nor a radical conversion to outsider perspectives. Instead, Maututu resembled their mythological ancestors in accosting the wild and strange and seeking a beneficial engagement to bring a transformation of home life. Such pioneering seemed to be more 'on their own terms' in the earlier village and cocoa developments but their efforts faced more formidable challenges during the Pacific War and when industrialisation, with its massive logging, oil palm monocropping, settler migration and town development, got under way. The following chapters dissect this 'multiplicity of engagement'. There are signs that Maututu are finding ways to engage with these wild incursions and forge new mediations with the strange outside. Fifty years after oil palm was first introduced to the Bialla area, Maututu retain creativity in forging important partnerships with outsiders.

Early Maututu engagement with the oil palm industry

The colonial administration during the early 1970s discouraged Maututu village communities from participating in the industrial transformations taking place all around them. From the perspective of government officers, first under the Australian administration, then under PNG self-government (1973–75), the villagers were better left to farm their cocoa and copra and tend to fishing, hunting and sago processing. They had access to cash through cocoa and copra, and the administration concluded that they did not have the individual drive and discipline to make a success of oil palm blocks. The colonial administration was convinced that economic transformation had to be built on individuals rather than communities, and, thus, initially favoured land-poor families from elsewhere in PNG who were willing to leave their kin relations to forge a new life. The land settlement schemes planned by both colonial and independent governments envisaged that, by taking people away from their village subsistence farming and settling them on household blocks oriented to commercial crops, the perceived constraints on agricultural development from communal obligations could be overcome (Hulme, 1984; Koczberski, Curry & Anjen, 2012; Koczberski et al., 2009).

In my role as a Department of Agriculture, Stock and Fisheries (DASF) field officer during 1973–75, I was asked to hold village meetings to prepare Maututu for the pending transformation of the area. Although Maututu were permitted to apply as oil palm settlers, there was little interest from the administration in encouraging either that or village oil palm (VOP). Rather, during the period of self-government when expatriates still dominated the DASF, the administration encouraged Maututu to consider expanding their subsistence activities, improving their pig and fish production, and extending their gardening activities so that they could sell to the incoming population of settler farmers. These administration officers expected that the incoming settler population would marginalise Maututu economically and dominate them politically and so, to address that, they encouraged alternative financial opportunities for villagers, allowing them to remain at home with their customary pursuits and shielding them from the impact of capitalist development taking place on the slopes of their ancestral domain. The administration's effort among villagers was low-key: it left matters to the business development division, which had no officers in the area and little coordination with DASF or with oil palm companies. Such efforts demonstrated, if such was needed, that oil palm development was directed primarily towards raising national and corporate revenue and mitigating land and political pressures elsewhere in PNG, rather than improving the welfare of local populations.[1] As one Maututu leader commented later to me, 'we were dismissed at first as mere spectators of the oil palm boom'.

To Maututu villagers, the main threat of the oil palm industry lay in the thousands of settlers the administration planned to introduce into the area. They represented the wild outside far more powerfully than the crop itself. At a Nakanai Council meeting on 30 May 1969, one of the *kansil* remonstrated that the proposed settler blocks must be acquired by Maututu to prevent the entry of vast numbers of outsiders into the area. Such people would engage in fights with locals and rape local women, he said. He encouraged local girls to get married quickly to fellow Maututu in order to increase the village populations and proposed that the settler population should always be represented on council by a Nakanai. At the time, villagers told me that they feared the influx of stranger settlers because of their sorcery and their love magic. These strangers would be entering the Maututu domain, not at the behest of villagers but of the administration that villagers accused of promoting stranger interests over their own. At a later village meeting at Matililiu in May 1972, locals again urged young women to marry Maututu men and have many children to build up the local population. They expressed regret about the long-term alienation of their soil to settlers from different ethnic groups and called for all young men to take up oil palm blocks to counter the entry of vast numbers of outsiders on their soil. These objections to oil palm development were not, therefore, focused on the crop itself, but on the incursion of dangerous strangers in large numbers into the Bialla population and onto Maututu soil. The financial success of these strangers could sideline Maututu enterprise and the intermarriage of Maututu women with the strangers could produce a new generation with little commitment to 'being Maututu'. The focus of concern was to sustain relations within the 'home' community because these thousands of settlers could not be trusted to forge such relations.

The work by villagers in clearing the forest and planting diverse crops amply demonstrated their hard work, skills and knowledge, and their adaptability and enterprise were already evident in their expansive cocoa plantings. In 1969, I heard Maututu remark that young women no longer sought

---

1   At the time, the Mataungan Association in Rabaul was campaigning strongly for the return of commercial properties on the Gazelle.

a partner with shiny skin (attributed to men resisting fatty meats) but, instead, sought a man who had proven himself through his cash crops and his access to money. Thus, contrary to administration expectations, from the very beginning of the oil palm developments, Maututu indicated their interest in experimenting with the crop. In meetings I convened in 1972, Maututu were already discussing the importance of adopting oil palm, just as previously they had adopted cocoa, and were acknowledging that oil palm was about to become a key crop in their lives. When the administration finally in 1975 called for indigenous applications for settler blocks, many Maututu responded, seeing it as a means to access cash incomes and 'modern' status. Maututu demonstrated they were open to the opportunities that the oil palm crop might bring as a supplement to their production of cocoa and copra.

Maututu as settler smallholders

It was after the transition from colonial government to PNG self-government and then independence in 1975 that the incoming PNG Government took up the challenge of incorporating local villagers into the cultivation of oil palm. This reflected the different perspective that the independent PNG Government brought to the development of people and resources. At a village meeting at Bubuu in April 1975, leaders noted that government was offering loans of A$1,000 to Maututu who joined the settlement scheme and was guaranteeing high prices for fresh fruit bunches (FFB) until the loan was paid off. At the time, oil palm was promoted as a government scheme, with no mention of company interests. It was not explained how such high prices might be guaranteed. Mirroring the principles of the PNG Constitution that protected customary rights and village integrity, the new government displayed a level of understanding of the ontological perspectives of village farmers that was refreshing. It appeared to want to protect the welfare of local populations in terms of their customary priorities alongside the new economic opportunities.

Maututu interpreted the government approach as seeking a partnership with them and they responded boldly. Almost 50 Maututu applied, and, in 1977–78, were granted 6-hectare blocks in the settlement scheme. In the Hoskins Land Settlement Scheme (LSS) in 1977, fewer than 0.5 per cent of blocks were allocated to local villagers (Valentine & Valentine, 1979). In Bialla, the proportion was much higher—46 among the 700 smallholders (7 per cent). Twenty-three men from the villages of Gomu, Apupul, Baikakea,

Bubuu and Uase were granted blocks in Tiauru Section to the south, and another 23 from Gomu, Apupulu, Baikakaea and Bubuu in Wilelo Section to the north. According to Kau, who gained a block in Wilelo, other villagers declined the offer because they did not recognise it as a partnership. Instead, they imagined it as *wokman blong gavman* (government labourers).

Each blockholder paid an annual K75 lease fee to the lands department. They were required to move as a family to the block and join the population of settlers, committing their children to the settlement school. They were thus physically separated from the hamlet community that had provided their strongest sense of identity, support and inspiration, and placed in a heterogeneous collection of settlers living separately, each on their own block, and required as individual nuclear families to provide for their own welfare. This was in stark contrast to village life where so much of daily activity was done through relationships within the community. At first, men and women laboured heavily in clearing and burning the trees and undergrowth on the blocks and planting the allocated palms, 240 palms on the first 2 hectares. They also cultivated food gardens and built their houses there. There was little cooperation with settler households in these tasks, as Maututu and other ethnic groups remained wary of each other.

At 'home' in the hamlet, a site as large as 4 hectares would never be cleared as an individual project but as a cooperative task involving up to 20 'dividuals' under the leadership of a 'big man', probably with the intent of holding a *mage* feast. Together they would fell and burn the timber and then divide the block into many smaller allotments for husband and wife teams (or other partnerships) to clean the soil and plant the crops. In contrast, the clearing and planting of these large oil palm blocks entirely by the leasehold couple represented an unwelcome 'individualisation' of garden activity. It also differed from the planting of their other cash crop, cocoa, which generally occupied only half a hectare and was planted in an abandoned food garden already cleared of larger vegetation. In addition, the maintenance of oil palm was far more intensive, requiring constant pruning and removal of dead palm leaves to prevent disease, as well as the cutting of all undergrowth that impeded the growth of the palms. Such work was initially monitored closely by DASF and Oil Palm Industry Corporation (OPIC) officers and company supervisors anxious to guarantee maximum productivity and to ensure rapid repayment of debts.[2]

---

2   OPIC was established by the PNG Government in 1992 to provide field extension and development services to smallholders in the oil palm industry. It replaced DASF supervisors.

Oil palm dictated a cycle of indebtedness. The debts incurred to the government or company for planting stock, fertilisers and pesticides were paid off as instalments deducted from oil palm earnings by the company. Then, after 20 years, the debt started all over again when the block was replanted. This was in contrast to cocoa, which Maututu rarely replaced—and, when they did, used seedlings grown themselves. Ideally, oil palm smallholders could hope to pay off their primary debt to the company within 11 years, afterwards realising a surplus income for up to 10 years over and above their continued outlays on fertiliser and insecticide. This, of course, depended on stable world prices for palm oil and the continued productivity of the palms, neither of which proved predictable. The world prices for both cocoa and palm oil fluctuated quite unpredictably, at least in the eyes of smallholders with little knowledge of the world events affecting those prices. They tended, rather, to suspect the company of manipulating both mill gate prices and transportation costs to improve corporate profits.

When I returned to the area in 2009, Maututu reported to me that they had initially done well as settlers, but that most of them had since left the blocks. One of these early Maututu settler smallholders even claimed that he had received a 'top producer' award in 1990. They were helped initially by being able to access food from village gardens, to which they returned regularly. Over time this dependence declined as they established food gardens on their blocks, to the point of only gathering coconuts from the village, some of which they were able to sell to settler neighbours. However, they recounted the difficulties they faced getting their children to school, with the children having to walk from their blocks to a central school in the LSS at Wilelo or Tiauru. Concern for their children's welfare among outsiders became one of several factors motivating families to move back to the village and, by the mid-1990s, all but a few of the original Maututu settlers had returned with their families to the village. Some had missed the daily involvement in village social relations; others preferred their children to attend the village school where some teachers spoke Maututu and the children had their best friends. Even the 'top producer' mentioned above did not continue on his block but hired an outsider to manage it while he returned to village farming. Very few Maututu remained long enough on the block to pay off their initial debt to the company. A key year appears to have been 1986, when farm gate prices for oil palm bunches dropped to 'near zero' and many Maututu stopped harvesting or tending their blocks. Such poor prices would have prolonged the time it took to pay off their initial loans, delaying the longed-for income streams expected from oil palm. But the mid-1980s also generated an enthusiasm for plantings of VOP (see below), such that their withdrawal from settler blocks probably indicated their preference to grow the crop closer to home on village soil.

Their withdrawal from the settler blocks might have confirmed company perceptions of the 'lazy native'; however, as we shall see, these villagers did not abandon their blocks to escape agricultural work but to enjoy the social relations and securities of village life, while committing to grow oil palm at 'home'. These early settler smallholders appear to have rejected the assumptions of industrial growth models and made choices fashioned by their indigenous priorities. Rather than relentlessly pursuing the financial rewards of individualised farming, they opted to value their social networks and their obligations to take part in communal affairs. Their intent was to bring benefits from the wild outside into the domestic community, rather than divorce themselves from that community.

While only a few Maututu settler farmers remained in residence on their blocks, some retained their leases and appointed an outsider to manage the block, dividing the income with them as leaseholder. Lapou from Bubuu recalled planting 2 hectares of his block in Wilelo in 1980 and caring for the palms until they flowered, learning how to pollinate the flowers and later introducing the weevil *la viri* as a pollinating insect. He then planted a further 2 hectares with another 240 palms. Although he continued to manage his settler block, even he abandoned residence on the block to return to the village. Lapou narrated how he and his family had been terrorised on their block by a giant python, which they designated a *taua* spirit.[3] Lapou sub-leased the block to a Chimbu settler but was shocked in 2015 when this man sold the block without Lapou's knowledge, leading to a court case at which he sought, successfully, to reclaim the block. Despite these tensions, Lapou remained critical of his village mates. He insisted that if they had held onto their blocks, as he had, they might have had the success he had, but they were greedy, he said, choosing to realise quick cash rather than pursue a steady income that might have supported their children's future.[4] In his view, their rejection of settler production was more about short-term

---

3   As narrated above, he killed the python but a drop of its blood fell on his daughter causing her to fall sick and die.

4   Lapou built a modern, permanent materials home and acquired a car, which was maintained by his son who was a mechanic in the company workshop. For several years, he was *kansil* for Bubuu-Baiakea-Gigipuna.

financial reward than repairing social networks. This was evidenced by the fact that he had chosen to retain ownership of his settler block while returning to live with his social networks in the village.

This tension between individual pursuit of financial gain and obligations to kin and neighbours continued to challenge the blockholders, just as Chao (2020) had noted of an earlier stage of oil palm cultivation among the Marind. International oil palm companies, with government support, were seeking to exploit the land and labour of indigenous people to generate revenue, both for themselves and the national economy. In thinking about indigenous capacity for involvement, government failed to recognise that villagers, even as they engaged with the new crop, would prioritise their 'home' social identity and reciprocal exchanges over the pursuit of individualised profit-focused production.

Village oil palm

The agreement signed in 1972 by South Pacific Palm Oil Development Pty Ltd (SPPOD) and the colonial administration had included the following clauses: 'encourage village farmers surrounding the Project company and settlement scheme to plant 800 hectares to oil palm' and 'encourage the existing settlement scheme farmers located inland from Bangula Bay (Silanga-Uasilau) to plant 800 hectares to oil palm' (Department of Senate, 1973, p. 9). Local villagers, in Bialla, and in Silanga and Uasilau, were thus envisaged as contributing 38 per cent (1,600 hectares) of smallholder plantings, while the settler population contributed 62 per cent. However, initially, the colonial administration and SPPOD focused only on settler smallholders.

That changed in 1977 when the PNG Government invited members of the Nakanai Council and several big men from the Maututu villages to visit the Mosa plantation at Hoskins run by the New Britain Palm Oil (NBPOL). There, after inspecting the palm oil mill and its nuclear estate, they signed an agreement with the government to establish VOP in Bialla. Each of them returned to Maututu with an oil palm seedling for planting. In 1978, the PNG Government approved the establishment in Bialla of VOP. In doing so, they instructed Hargy Oil Palm Ltd (HOPL) to negotiate with villagers to open up village land to oil palm cultivation. This finally activated the terms of the original agreement to encourage Maututu to adopt VOP.[5] OPIC field staff were assigned to guide the village cultivation in consultation with company staff.

The situation that faced Maututu VOP growers was somewhat different from that faced by the settler smallholders. While they were dependent on company provisions and controls and entered debt arrangements like those of the settler smallholders, they retained the cooperation of their village communities and the ability to combine oil palm with other cash crops such as cocoa. Reflecting this, villagers rarely planted more than the required minimum of 2 hectares in oil palm, and, even though many replaced their cocoa with the new cash crop, much cocoa was retained. As with the earlier establishment of cocoa plantings, households did not necessarily plant on their lineage soil, but on soil where they had made food gardens. They did not, at that point, foresee a future situation in which soil was in short supply and the lineage or hamlet claimed the soil back. In addition, some lineages did not have soil contiguous with the roads used by company trucks, with the result that the company refused to support oil palm on their inaccessible soil. They were thus forced to approach other lineages to access suitably located soil.

Maututu villagers did not uniformly adopt VOP. The two villages closest to the company nursery and the Tiauru settler blocks, Mataruru and Matililiu, were the first to plant.[6] One village grower in Bubuu reported to me that, initially, there was a lot of opposition to VOP and only 30 households in the village adopted the crop. He opted to grow both oil palm and cocoa, planting 7,000 cocoa trees on 12 hectares in the late 1970s. Those who hesitated to plant oil palm included Baikakea farmers who remained committed to cocoa and did not plant VOP until 1991. Villagers' ambivalence in the early years focused on how much work was entailed in preparing the large blocks and their doubts as to whether oil palm would prove better than cocoa. As the palms grew higher and harvesting became more dangerous, some farmers began to speak favourably of communities in the island of Buka who had decided against oil palm in favour of cocoa and copra.

5   Kean (2000) indicates that it was only in the late 1980s that the West New Britain Government initiated village oil palm production among Bileki villagers of Hoskins, providing loans for the clearing and planting of 2-hectare blocks.
6   Neither of these villages were represented in those who took up settler blocks, perhaps indicating their early preference for village production.

Figure 5.1: Village oil palm, 2017

Note: The mature palms have been poisoned and are being replaced by young palms interspersed with food crops.

Source: Author.

Company and government efforts were initially directed towards establishing 'individualised' responsibility for each VOP block through registration and titling in the name of the husband. However, after the 2004 Food and Agriculture Organization of the United Nations Land in Africa Conference, there was increasing recognition in the international community that 'full individualization and registration of customary tenures has often failed to deliver the anticipated increase in agricultural investment and productivity' (Koczberski, Curry & Anjen 2012, p. 183). With that international recognition came a greater focus on an 'adaptation approach', supporting and building on existing customary tenure, something acknowledged in PNG, at least ideally, in the 1975 Constitution. But this ran counter to the commitment of the oil palm industry to individualising smallholder production and the debts it incurred, built on their assumption that maximum production was attained only through individual ownership of land (Figure 5.1).

After the slow early uptake, village plantings increased through the 1990s as oil palm revenue began to compare favourably with cocoa revenue (Curry & Koczberski, 2012). In 2005–06, there were 1,593 blocks of VOP in Bialla, covering 3,669 hectares (average 2.3 hectares).[7] This was already over double what was initially proposed by the Australian administration, and comprised 31 per cent of the total smallholder oil palm area (Curry & Koczberski, 2007, p. 14). Once established, a 2-hectare block required about eight days labour per month, four days harvesting for the fortnightly pickup and four days cleaning vegetation around the palms and pruning excessive palm fronds. This left ample time for work in gardens and other pursuits. With the alternatives of garden and cocoa production, villagers could refrain from harvesting oil palm when prices were low. Household cash income was augmented from marketing of food crops and betel nut, and off-farm work. In 2004, 13 per cent of settlers and 20 per cent of village smallholders in Bialla benefited from household members employed off-farm (Koczberski & Curry 2005, p. 331). This occasional preference for other income sources reflected home priorities but contributed to village smallholders' reputation as 'much more fickle producers' than settler smallholders (Curry & Koczberski, 2012). Yet, such 'fickleness' reflected the ways they were incorporating oil palm into their 'home' situation.

As with cocoa, oil palm production relied on the labour of the nuclear household. As in the clearing of forest for subsistence gardens, inter-household labour was only invited in the initial clearing and planting stages; afterwards, each household took responsibility for maintaining and harvesting their own block. As all produce in the village was weighed and transported the same day, it was unlikely that much inter-household cooperation could emerge. Only single men could be recruited from outside the household for the task.[8] I only observed larger groups of kin working a single block when that block was planted in the name of a widowed woman, or when the blockholder was getting too old to manage the harvest on his or her own. Thus, as Michael Dove (1983) pointed out for the swidden societies of Kalimantan, production was limited by labour rather than land availability.

---

7   Including VOP of Maututu, Mengen and Meramera villages.

8   Bileki, with its lower take-up of VOP, may have had more kin labour available. Curry and Koczberski (2012) observed in Hoskins that 'the lineage and often other members of the broader kinship group contribute labour' in these blocks, and that oil palm became 'central to reproducing intra- and inter-household relationships'.

In village garden and cocoa plots, both men and women cooperated in cultivation, harvesting and consumption. This gender partnership was threatened under VOP arrangements where blocks were formally registered in the husband's name. In the initial years of oil palm production, the company accounted the income by cheque to the husband who might cash the cheque and spend the money without his wife's knowledge, even though she had laboured with him on the block. In some cases, husbands purchased cartons of beer to drink and were inebriated by the time they returned home. The Mama Lus Frut scheme introduced in 1997 acknowledged this imbalance, although the 'loose fruit' comprised only a small portion of the total harvest, usually one of six or seven nets harvested on each block. Overall, loose fruits constituted only 14 per cent of the total harvest (Curry et al., 2021). Recognising this continued imbalance, many Maututu men topped up their wife's net with FFB, recognising these earnings as hers to spend as she wanted. They still acknowledged that the 'mama' earned at best half what the 'papa' earned. A further benefit of the Mama Lus Frut initiative was that the names of both the woman and man were written on a wooden sign nailed to a tree where the weighing of the nets occurred. This informed the truck driver of the names of both accounts to be credited, but it publicly announced their partnership in working the block.

In 2007, approximately 46 per cent of the total area of smallholder oil palm (in Hoskins, Bialla and Popondetta) was classified as VOP plantings (Curry & Koczberski, 2007). After the mid-1990s, there was no further release of land for settler smallholdings but VOP continued to expand, although their production levels fell short of nuclear plantation and settler outputs. Curry and Koczberski (2007) reported that, in 2006 in the Hoskins scheme, LSS smallholders achieved only 60 per cent of nuclear plantation levels of production, while VOP growers achieved a paltry 38 per cent. It was this poorer productivity that the new HOPL manager sought to address on his appointment in 2008. At the time, world prices were fluctuating wildly. The world market price reached 4,000 Malaysian ringgit (MR) at the beginning of the year, only to fall to MR1,500 at the end of 2008. In the first week of December 2008, the market price of palm oil dropped to K530. At the time, the mill gate price for bunches was K154.39

a tonne, but at the farm gate farmers were receiving only K103.21 a tonne.[9] In such circumstances it was difficult to persuade villagers to harvest FFB when they had other, easier sources of livelihood, such as cocoa, fishing and food gardens.

One VOP smallholder's fortnightly receipts (Table 5.1) indicate the unpredictable fluctuations in income that producers experienced. These receipts indicate that, with loan repayments to the company reducing the farm gate price by a further 30 per cent, the grower was left on 7 December 2008 with just over K70 a tonne. By January 2010, the mill gate price had almost doubled while transportation costs had fallen by a third, making the returns from oil palm much more attractive. In February 2013, the mill gate price had fallen again, to only K133 tonne, and Maututu were comparing this unfavourably to the price of a bag of dry cocoa beans at K400 or a tonne of copra at K500.

Table 5.1: Village oil palm smallholder's receipts for a fortnight's production (kina per tonne)

	December 2008	January 2010
Mill gate price	147.26	269.00
Transport	44.05	28.00
Farm gate price	103.21	241.00
Cheque deduction	0.50	–
Less BOPGA contribution	2.00	2.00
Loan repayments 30%	30.00	71.70
Cash received	70.71	167.30

Notes: BOPGA (Bialla Oil Palm Growers Association) represented smallholders in consultations with company and government.

Source: Author's research, based on village oil palm growers' fortnightly dockets.

---

9   The mill gate price of K154.39 was improved by a value added tax (VAT) of 1.43, and reduced by an OPRA levy of 1.77, a sexava pesticide levy of 2.50, and OPIC levy of 4.00, and a 10 per cent VAT on OPIC of 0.40, leaving a mill gate price of K147.26, and, once a transport cost of K44.05 was deducted, a farm gate price of K103.21. From this, a further deduction was made from the total amount for the cheque K0.50 and a BOPGA (Bialla Oil Palm Growers' Association) fortnightly levy of K2.00 was made. After this, a further deduction was made of 30 per cent for repayment of any outstanding loans to the company. In one case, the husband was repaying a loan of K11,189 and his wife from her account a loan of K1,091. Thus, the farmer received about K70 a tonne, when some months previous to this he/she had received K400 a tonne.

Maututu were troubled by two aspects of oil palm production. The first was the wild fluctuations in the prices they received, interpreted by many smallholders as driven by the arrogance of the company. When prices fell, many Maututu chose not to harvest, demonstrating their relative autonomy from the industry. Second, they questioned the many deductions made by the company from their farm gate earnings. There were deductions for transport, for loan repayments (for seedlings, fertiliser, pesticide and other inputs), and for the services of BOPGA, OPIC and OPRA (Oil Palm Research Association) (Curry & Koczberski, 2012).[10] Their suspicions about the company were enhanced by a lack of information on world market prices. Neither HOPL nor OPIC made these available and farmers had no internet access to monitor world market prices. As a consequence, village discussions concluded that either the company was exploiting them for its own profit or the truck driver who weighed the produce of each block was under-reporting the weight and then booking an additional weight under his own or a relative's name. Villagers also noted that, while the company insisted they cut the stork off the bunches, the bunches from the nuclear estate were delivered with long stalks; on the basis of that observation, they suspected that the stork contained oil content that they were not allowed to claim. There was also resentment that everyone was charged for a set delivery of fertiliser even though many did not apply all of it in their blocks.

The wild fluctuations in farm gate prices thus generated distrust of the industrial partners and undermined partnership benefits. In November 2017, villagers remarked to me that the company 'had them by the nose' (*ubi la maisumiteu*).[11] At the time, the farm gate price of bunches was K278 a tonne, before deductions for fertiliser, pesticides and nets reduced that further. In comparison, they claimed, NBPOL at Hoskins was paying K280 a tonne at the farm gate and making no further deductions for fertiliser and pesticide. On one occasion, Bialla VOP producers petitioned NBPOL to purchase oil palm bunches from Bialla, because they had lost trust in HOPL, but HOPL successfully took NBPOL to court to stop such purchases out of their allocated crop area. Better-informed farmers at this point were calling for the release of the growers' fund, a contribution deducted from each grower's fortnightly

---

10 OPRA is a not-for-profit research arm of the oil palm industry, under the direction of the two PNG milling companies (NBPOL and HOPL) and OPIC as a representative of smallholders. All oil palm producers pay a volume related levy, calculated through the milling companies.
11 Some domesticated pigs had string inserted in their noses to enable their control.

income to cover such emergencies.[12] Neither the company nor government provided information about the use of this revenue, and many growers were unaware it was being deducted. The call was unsuccessful, as neither the company nor OPIC supported the suggestion to release the funds.

VOP growers regretted that they had no leaders capable of standing up to the might of the company. In 1982, five Maututu village producers sat on the Oil Palm Central Committee under the Department of Primary Industry (later Department of Agriculture and Livestock), alongside representatives of the Tiauru and Wilelo Division settlers. The Central Committee later became the Bialla Oil Palm Growers Association (BOPGA). Although nominally included in oil palm deliberations, these BOPGA representatives often lacked the knowledge to pursue village concerns. Communication with OPIC field officers was poor and BOPGA's representation of growers' interests was later undermined by the inclusion of officers from HOPL and OPIC. Distrust of OPIC and BOPGA grew. For example, when OPIC conducted a village survey in Baikakea in December 2008, few villagers were present to respond to the survey, and even the village BOPGA representative was absent.

As a result of the oil palm industry, Maututu became a minority on their own 'soil'. Only 4 of the 20 wards in the Bialla LLG included Maututu villages. Although a Maututu from Urumaili village, John Ilisi, son of Mapulo Gaa, was LLG president for the first four terms (1995–2015), his leadership of the council led to few improvements in village facilities. After the 2015 elections, a settler replaced him as president; as a minority, Maututu may not gain the presidency again. Indigenous villages have not fared well under the LLG administration or HOPL management of tax funds. Up to 2018, there was no piped water to village populations and only Uase, Matililiu and Mataruru had access to electricity, despite the fact that the hydro-electricity turbines on the Lovo River were located on Maututu land. The village health posts were in poor condition, without supplies and unstaffed, with no indication of strategies to deal with this and regain community confidence. Needless deaths occurred within the village from illnesses such as malaria and diabetes. Maututu raised a variety of issues with their LLG representatives. These included the indigenous claim on the Ambusa/Bialla land, management of the Bialla airstrip, repair of local roads, maintenance of local school buildings and health posts, the negotiation of electricity

---

12 Initially each grower had K1 per tonne deducted from their fortnightly cheque, and this amount increased to K5 in 2004. In August 2002 the fund totalled K240,000.

supply to all villages, and the increasing pollution of local streams and marine environments. Village dissatisfaction led to accusations that LLG presidents were self-seeking, reflecting a general distrust of LLG processes.[13]

Conclusion

Despite their distrust of both the company and LLG, Maututu village production continued to grow. Some smallholders in Gomu village in 2010 were harvesting up to 13 tonnes a fortnight, the largest fortnightly cheque received being K3,000, with the average receipt for FFB around K300 per producer. A local schoolteacher compared this to her salary of K200 a fortnight, which she said was barely enough to cover the cost of food and other necessities for her family. VOP farmers were also able to negotiate a bank loan, with repayments deducted from their fortnightly produce cheque at the rate of 20–30 per cent of the total income received. A company executive informed me in 2017 that a VOP blockholder with 2 hectares of oil palm could expect to earn K15,000 a year, an average of over A$500 a fortnight. In 2017, there were 1,963 VOP blocks supplying the HOPL mills, an increase of 23 per cent over the decade. Those years saw a large number of village houses improved with sawn planks and corrugated iron roofing sheets and an increase in the villages of consumer goods such as mobile phones, footwear and fashion clothes. Oil palm had contributed to a material improvement in village life.

Maututu responses to oil palm suggested that the capitalist priorities of the company were secondary to the 'home' ontological priorities of relationality. They incorporated oil palm within 'home' regimes that continued to promote cooperation, exchange, and kin and neighbour relations as the fundamentals of a dividual's way of knowing and being. However, oil palm put pressure on these core values. People raised particular concerns with me about the new crop. First, oil palm took up more land because the blocks demanded of each grower needed to be larger to meet the requirements set by the company. Second, oil palm required growers to become dependent on the company for materials and finance and, because of the debt incurred, to become compliant with company directives on how they managed their

---

13 One example was a 2003 PNG Government grant of K300,000 to the 'Maututu Corporation' to purchase shares in HOPL. Only the LLG president and one other director were said to know what had happened to these funds. Another accusation mentioned A$50,000 given to the Maututu LLG president from Chico University for access to Lake Hargy that was never distributed.

blocks. Third, oil palm was demanding on their labour because of the need to clean and trim the much larger blocks, and, perhaps more importantly, such labour was more demanding on men and tended to exclude women, except in tidying up the loose fruit. Fourth, this encouraged unequal financial benefits for men and women. While cocoa income was paid in cash to whomever delivered the wet beans, oil palm income was disproportionately paid to the male blockholder. Fifth, they evaluated oil palm in terms of their own priorities rather than the production targets and quality issues emphasised by the company. For them, the oil palm block was one part of their being in which they were focused on meeting the social obligations of ritual, exchange and family livelihood rather than profit-making.

There was a sense of anger and disillusionment as Maututu pointed out to me that they could neither fly on planes nor travel to Australia, and that they had no electricity supply to their homes or sealed roads to their villages; nor did they have access to jobs and schooling. Their collective disappointment led them to a sense of inferiority, which increased their low political standing in the LLG. A key conclusion of a social report commissioned by the PNG Centre of Environmental Law and Community Rights (Anderson, 2006) was that oil palm had not provided the improvement in lifestyle that was expected in the discourse of industrial expansion and resettlement of land-short populations. Many village homes remained of bush material; electricity and piped water was yet to reach many villages; and farmers struggled to repay their oil palm debts over many years, only to face the prospect of further huge debts when replanting took place. In 2010, I discussed at length the developments of the last four decades with one elder who had been *kansil* for Bubuu and Baikakea, held a settler block and had extensive VOP. He was highly critical of the Australian land purchase of the 1960s and categorised oil palm as 'extraction', not 'development'. There had been little development in the Bialla area, he said, despite the wealth that oil palm had created, by which he referred to the lack of true progress for Maututu in the terms in which they evaluated progress.

Curry (2003, p. 406) explored in his research among village and settler oil palm producers in West New Britain how their engagement with the new crop:

> can be transformed or recast by place-based practices to create an
> alternative modernity that, in practice, bears little resemblance to
> the idealised notions of market economic relationships and the
> economically rational, utility-maximizing individual.

Curry (2005, p. 130) concluded that 'indigenous communities are able to shape how capitalist development is to be embedded in their communities to accord with indigenous sociocultural values and practices'. He challenged development planners to seek, rather, the enhancement of oil palm production in terms of how it becomes 'embedded in local place-based practices of exchange', and, thus, to enable the flexibility of the industry to better accommodate local priorities (Curry, 2003, p. 420). The next chapters explore how villagers articulated their priorities with the demands of industrialisation (Figure 5.2).

Figure 5.2: Village food garden under poisoned oil palm, 2017
Source: Author.

6

Home and outside: Ontological points of tension for village oil palm

The demands of oil palm production raised critical issues for the local smallholder that were quite different from those envisaged by the company. The company and government tended to see the key challenges for smallholders in terms of how they adjusted to the work and skill requirements of planting, maintaining and harvesting their blocks. The neoliberal focus was to engage the smallholder efficiently in the production requirements of the new crop. Such an objective had more traction among the migrant smallholders who had left their village and kin to invest their future in oil palm. But even for land-poor highlanders, just having access to what would become their own piece of land was incentive enough and their commitment to oil palm was secondary to that. Many turned to vegetable gardens not just for household consumption but also market access to cash, particularly as they continued to prioritise exchange relations, both within the settler community and with kin in their origin place.

Village oil palm was a different proposition. The village block of 2 hectares was not seen as, by itself, sufficient to support a household. This block was only feasible in conjunction with the food gardens, cocoa blocks, and forest and marine resources that sustained village life. But while Maututu held strongly to priorities of relationality, the incursions of oil palm required transformations of home values.

Shortage of soil and the incorporation of lineages

A future in which indigenous villages no longer have access to sufficient soil for their needs was not foreseen by the administration in the days when the government acquired the vast areas of land in the hinterland, or even when settlers first moved in. Was the administration so intent on agricultural transformation through oil palm that it ignored local village welfare? My own experience at the time suggests that the colonial administration never expected villagers to adopt oil palm within the village, in which case the village soil remaining to them may have sufficed for Maututu cocoa and food gardens. But such a view seriously underestimated Maututu interest in the new crop and the revenue it would generate.

Unlike cocoa development in Sulawesi (Li, 2016), among the Maututu cocoa was introduced on former garden plots without raising alarm about future availability of garden space. Soil was plentiful and livelihoods were guaranteed by subsistence gardens. However, when Maututu engaged with village oil palm, their view of soil began to change. Particularly in the villages bordering Bialla town (Uase, Gomu, Matililiu) the loss of hinterland forest areas and the expansion of village oil palm alerted them to the finite limits of the soil still available to them. Other villages gradually became aware of the situation facing these inner communities and access to soil increasingly became a focus of community concern.

All village oil palm (VOP) growers faced decisions as to how much soil they committed to oil palm resources. When food gardens were converted to cocoa or oil palm in the 1980s, it was a matter of experimenting with the new crop rather than alienating that block of soil for what might be more than 20 years. As a result, Maututu planted oil palm on soil that they shared within the *karakara* close to their hamlet settlement. Yet, as they converted their food gardens into oil palm, they were forced to make gardens further and further away from their homes, increasing the burden particularly on women who transported the heavy garden tubers home for cooking. In the early years of VOP, if the food garden was sited adjacent to access roads it was almost inevitably replaced by oil palm. Yet growers came to realise the decision to plant oil palm had long-term consequences. Unlike with subsistence gardens that were abandoned after several years, or cocoa blocks that incurred few household debts, with oil palm, farmers were not able to reverse the decision due to the level of debt they incurred with the company.

VOP required major investment of capital in planting materials. This was realised in loans the villagers took with the company to be repaid over the production life of the block. For the company, land was the surest asset on which to commit a loan, but that had to be guaranteed by legal lease or land title. This was the pattern they established for the migrant smallholder, whose rights to their block were contingent on them paying off the loan to the company. In contrast, the Maututu villager did not see their soil as a physical asset; it was not defined under government law and the company could not legally take control over the VOP block if the grower failed to repay the loan. The company voiced concern that a blockholder could be forced off his block by lineage custodians of the soil, leaving the company debt unpaid. This led to government and the company attempting to convince Maututu that 'land' was—or had become—a material asset with clear boundaries and defined 'owners' who could be held responsible for loans incurred on the blocks. This was an ontological shift that was not readily acceptable to villagers.

In their 'purchase' of soils in West New Britain, the Australian colonial administration presumed, on the basis of its ontological definition of 'land', that the blocks were owned by exclusive kin groups. During my time as a field officer for the Department of Agriculture, Stock and Fisheries (1973–75) I was asked to investigate 'land' ownership and customary boundaries defining access to that 'land'. But Maututu who accompanied me on surveys of the area were clear that their 'soil' was defined by its centre rather than by its boundaries. That is, areas were associated with former *karakara* comprising affiliated lineages who had farmed soils centred on that hamlet or with ancestral spirits who resided there.

The administration concern to establish clans as 'landowners' was formalised under the Land Groups Incorporation Act 1974, which, in its wording, gave substantial recognition of local customary contexts. The Preamble to the Act declared that its aim was to 'recognise the corporate nature of customary groups and to allow them to hold, manage and deal with land in their customary names' (Fingleton, 2007, p. 27). The Act facilitated customary groups to hold title to their land through the legal incorporation of the group as a corporation with 'perpetual succession'—that is, the group continued to exist after the death of any of its members and the sale of its assets. 'Once legally incorporated the group can sue and be sued, enter into contracts and do other things a corporation can do' (Power, 2008, p. 8). The incorporation legally required the group to formulate a constitution that set out the composition and manner of appointment of the controlling body of the group, the way in which the group acted and the way its actions were recorded, and the details of the group's dispute settlement authority (Fingleton, 2007). It was thus strongly driven by the ontological premises of the expatriate administration. Rather than recognise customary practices, this refashioned them in ways that suited capitalist interests.

The Act generated local ontological friction around soil beyond the comprehension of the administration officials who presumed these 'customary' rights. Golub (2007, p. 45) makes a similar observation, concluding from his study of the mining industry that 'landowner groups have been entified out of a preexisting cultural milieu which lacked preexisting social forms enduring and durable enough to be institutions which structure life around resource developments'. Weiner (2002, p. 6) warned that the architects of the Land Group Incorporation Act took sociality 'as evidence of communal, corporatist ownership and decision-making', and insisted that the Act had instead instigated a process whereby novel corporate groups were being formed. This was because the administration, through the Act, insisted on its ontological understanding of land, land ownership and exclusive corporate kin groups. In his study of Papua New Guinea (PNG) coffee cultivation, Weiner (2013, p. 103) concluded that 'it is the customary organization of labour, not of land per se, that underpins smallholder coffee production in PNG'.

Government was aware of the crisis over access to land that had arisen among the Tolai of East New Britain, a matrilineal society with whom Maututu had decades of close contact. Tensions had arisen among the Tolai cocoa growers because large areas had been alienated under the colonial administrations of Germany and Australia for expatriate plantations. The enthusiasm with which Tolai adopted village cocoa only exacerbated those tensions. In his analysis of disputes among the Tolai, Keir Martin (2006, p. 40) documented a:

> tendency to attempt to constitute the *vunatarai* ['clan/lineage group'] as a local land based descent group, as a discrete owner of land and to minimise claims made on the basis of reciprocal interdependence that threaten that identity.

He noted:

> the development of tendencies to assert clan identities in a manner that seems much more fixed and descriptive than the fluidity that has traditionally been associated with Melanesian sociality … [As] land holding units, clan identities have perhaps become more unitary and fixed over the years.
>
> (Martin 2006, pp. 96–97)

The Tolai appeared to have defined their *vunatarai* in increasingly exclusive ways in the context of land claims, as land became scarce under a cash crop regime. In wider terms, Martin (2006, p. 40) suggested that there was strong individualisation, by which he meant both of the singular nuclear family and of the exclusive corporate group, through their deliberate rejection of reciprocal interdependence.

The oil palm industry among the Nakanai had different dynamics to both cocoa production on the Gazelle and coffee production in the PNG Highlands. Oil palm blocks made less demand on labour but they incurred large debts to the company. In the oil palm industrial process protected under the incorporated land group (ILG) Act, 'customary' kin groups were essential less for their labour than for the security of land tenure that was vital to the financial arrangements the company entered into with smallholders. It was on the basis of such guarantees of 'land ownership' provided by the corporate group to the grower that the company could go ahead with providing the large loans that smallholders incurred for their planting materials.

As with other 'wild' intrusions into their world, Maututu attempted to engage with these new demands. They first had to identify fixed tracts of soil that had significance to themselves as a kin group and then to define who among their *karakara* had rights to plant permanent crops there. Later, following government guidance, they 'incorporated' groups by listing lineage members, sometimes including more distant clan mates. Each ILG then created its own board consisting of chair, secretary and treasurer. These Maututu ILGs, largely confined to a single lineage, assumed increasingly exclusive management of the soil under their legally constituted leadership. Tension among those who had long shared in those soils was inevitable. The 'wild' threatened chaos at 'home'.

In particular, lineages with strong historical affiliation with soil near their hamlet judged it to their advantage to form an ILG that could effectively deny soil access to those from other lineages who may have customarily lived with them in a hamlet and shared custodianship over surrounding soil. As observed in Bialla, Hoskins and, particularly, Popondetta over a 20-year period between 1986 and 2006:

> the distribution of landholdings that occurred when oil palm was introduced is increasingly being questioned by the present generation of the primary landowning groups … members of many customary landowning groups are becoming more resistant to non-clan/subclan villagers developing new blocks on their customary land.
>
> (Curry & Koczberski, 2007, p. 16)

In an extreme example, some Maututu began to question the customary claims of even Mapulo Gaa and his son John Ilisi, elected by them as president of the Nakanai Council and president of the Bialla Local-level Government (LLG), respectively, and both lifelong residents of Urumaili village. Both of Mapulo's parents were from Rapuri in Bileki territory, and, according to these revisionist views, Mapulo could only claim rights in Maututu land through his wife, whose rights to Maututu soil stemmed from her father rather than her mother.[1] This allowed the rights of Mapulo and Ilisi to be more readily questioned when access to soil became critical.

Increasingly over these years the Village Court had to deal with conflicts arising as members of a lineage or clan residing in other villages attempted to access soil and timber. For example, a land dispute arose in Baikakea over the soil of the Vorega lineage being cleared by an Apupulu resident. Kubaki took the dispute to the Village Court. Kubaki is not a Vorega member but was considered the guardian of this soil, because the sole remaining Vorega members from Baikakea were living south of the Tiauru River at Kiava, and he guarded the soil in their name. The Village Court decided in Kubaki's favour but determined he would have to compensate the Apupulu man K3,000 for his labour in clearing the land.[2] Kubaki then invited a Baikakea couple, also not Vorega, to plant the block in oil palm and take responsibility for paying the compensation. None of this challenged the primary claim of the Vorega lineage to the soil but it allowed a non-affiliated farmer to settle on the soil and introduced a monetary evaluation of labour expended on the block.

The Village Court magistrate reported to me in 2013 that shortages of soil in Gomu, Apupulu, Uase and Matililiu were a frequent cause of disputes among them.[3] Under customary practice, house sites had never been contested, as big men frequently invited 'strangers'—that is, dividuals outside the core affiliated lineages—to settle there. In these villages, however, lineage members were increasingly preventing these non-lineage persons from building a house on lineage land within the village settlement, even taking them to the Village Court when village discussions failed to resolve the issue. Even the Village Court decision became unsatisfactory to some, who then took disputes to the Lands Court. In one Gomu case in the 1990s,

---

1   Mapulo's wife's father was from Urumaili, but her mother from Apogo near Uasilau in Loso Nakanai territory.

2   Village Courts are limited to maximum fines of A$1,000, so this appears an anomaly (Houghton, 2017).

3   Village Court magistrates are 'respected' persons formally recognised by government to conduct Village Courts. Lawyers are specifically banned from Village Courts, in distinction to District and National Courts (Houghton, 2017).

the son of a Kabulu man persuaded his father's lineage to set up a jointly managed oil palm estate, but he then registered the block in the names of his sisters and his daughter, not as an estate, but as a VOP block. Two decades later when he attempted to replace those palms, his father's lineage took the matter to the District Court. This was a desperate decision, as it submitted authority in the matter to lawyers and an outside legal system. The usual village dispute settlement enabled multiple parties to state their views in a public forum and, through that process, seek a village consensus, but the District Court silenced these voices and submitted proceedings to outside lawyers and judges. To many Maututu, these District Court challenges by key lineage members aimed arrogantly to exclude non-lineage from using the soil and were contrary to communal priorities. Their appeal to 'outside' courts and laws was a threat to the integrity of the *karakara* and village.

'Wild' actions of ILG Boards

The ILG Act had another consequence for community relationships. The individuals nominated for the ILG Boards were given an authority over lineage affairs that was no longer contingent on the group's endorsement. Holznecht (1997, pp. 551–52) describes the land 'companies' set up under the Land Groups Incorporation Act as typically formed around a leading figure and members of his in-group. This group held the executive management positions and controlled the board of directors. They were able to 'put themselves forward as being truly representative of all resource owners in an area'. Among Maututu, it was often the case that the negotiations of ILG Boards with outsiders were not transparent to lineage members, increasing the possibility of them ignoring relational priorities. Communal life had always been marked by debate in men's house or village common spaces, but the appointment of ILG directors marginalised community consultation. Golub (2007, p. 43) suggested that disputes that frequently erupted over land in mining sites were not 'a corrupt deviation from normal practice, but an example of it'. Communities relied on such debates to generate consensus. However, such discussion in Maututu communities was silenced when ILG Board directors acted unilaterally by reaching secret agreements with outsiders. Like the 'big man' Wallaby, these directors lost the respect of their neighbours and kin.

The danger in the ILG arrangements was that it gave individuals as ILG directors much greater authority than that earned by a respected 'big man'. It was these men (few were women) of the ILG Board who signed off on contracts and managed bank accounts. The formation of the ILG brought new privileges to those who were able to assert their seniority in the lineage group. Their authority was constituted on the basis of the Act rather than on their capacity to lead their lineage and *karakara* to foster exchange relationships and to accumulate and redistribute wealth. It was, thus, an authority constituted through their recognition by outsiders rather than their exchanges with *karakara* members. This outsider recognition tended to stem from their communication skills in Tok Pisin and their familiarity with outsider modes of conducting social relations (e.g. through meetings in hotels over a 'drink or two'). Increasingly, these ILG leaders usurped the formal village leaders, *komiti* and *kansil* as the most active in dealing with outsiders over developments on village soil. This was because they could bypass group consultation and negotiate directly with the Department of Lands or with other outsiders over matters to do with 'land', without such agreements coming to the notice of ILG members.

These ILG leaders thus assumed a position of 'big shot' (Martin, 2006). Martin defined the 'big shot' as an individual claiming prestige on the basis of wealth and outside success rather than on community terms. Dividuals became ILG Board members because they were seniors in their lineage, but their standing as ILG office holders—particularly as head—allowed them to ignore the interests of fellow lineage members to acquire status and wealth as 'individuals'. This incurred resentment from lineage and hamlet members when they appeared to prioritise individual accumulation over distribution to ILG members. Lineage members in these cases came to resent the privileges of the board members, including their access to finances intended for the group. Some of these ILG heads, through their proprietorship over the soil, became wealthy, purchasing equipment such as chainsaws, sawmills and vehicles, taking plane trips to major urban centres, financing their children's education, and enjoying the comforts of iron-rooved and sawn timber houses or power generators. Others, it should be said, managed ILGs with more consultation, ensuring that all those with a link to the soil were recorded as part of the ILG. They recognised that ILG registration of all members of the lineage was security over future moves government or private corporations might make to alienate the soil from villagers.

The logging industry was beset with the same wild action. Holznecht (1997, p. 552) noted that the newly authorised ILG directors 'invariably sided with the logging company in any kind of dispute or action because their current income was derived from the company'. He added:

what does seem to have changed is the scale and the ability of customary constraints and social control mechanisms to keep community leaders and their followers operating within particular socially acceptable structural and cultural parameters.

(Holznecht, 1997, p. 560)

In his analysis of logging in West New Britain, Lattas (2011, p. 105) concluded that:

neoliberal privatization policies, a crisis in state funding and a nationalist emphasis on local business ventures gave rise to local landowner companies [in which] … local power brokers are able to take control of modern corporate structures and appropriate their resources away from local communities.

Government and the company continued to push for firmer guarantees of land ownership. In 1979, government introduced provisions for 'lease-lease back'. Filer (2014, p. 87) describes this process thus:

the idea was that a group of customary landowners would be able to lease a portion of customary land to the state, so that the state could then register a title over it and lease it back to that same group, thus allowing them to grant subleases to the nucleus estate operators on terms negotiated between the parties.

In Hoskins, New Britain Palm Oil Limited extended nuclear plantings through these lease-lease back arrangements by paying to the ILG the land rental fees and royalties on production, and by allocating to the ILG shares in the company. The offer provided shareholder dividends for the ILG (Cramb & Curry, 2012). Hargy Oil Palm Ltd (HOPL) managers were also keen to benefit from these lease-lease back arrangements. In Urumaili, Ilisi, as ILG head, negotiated a lease-lease back arrangement with HOPL over a block of 30 hectares adjacent to the hamlet, which the company then planted in oil palm.[4] Under this lease, at the end of 20 years the block would return to the custody of the lineage. Such an agreement reaffirmed the lineage as the interested party and the ILG and its board as the legal

---

4   Filer and Lowe (2011) describes this arrangement whereby the state leases land from landowners and then leases that land to a third party, thus circumventing the illegality of commercial interests gaining direct control over customary land. Cramb and Curry (2012) explain that the Land Act in PNG prohibits customary landowners from leasing land directly to outsiders. Instead, landowners within an ILG lease their land to the national government that then subleases it back to the ILG, which, in turn, can sublease it to the private company, usually for a 22 or 44 year period.

agent under the Act. At the same time, it enhanced the prominence of 'big shots' like Ilisi who were able to commandeer resources to gain individual wealth without being answerable to lineage members.

There was an unwillingness or incapacity to challenge the actions of lineage leaders in these dealings with outsiders. One Maututu elder who had been PNG's land commissioner voiced his impatience with his fellow Maututu as being 'too nice'. He explained that, instead of confronting each other in debate or physical violence, as highlanders might do, Maututu say nothing and so let individual leaders act alone without consulting the group. He despaired of the transformation of leadership in recent years into a pattern focused on control of external funds and networks rather than community consensus. For example, Tomare, as a Baikakea ILG head, negotiated with loggers to exploit an area of forest on the rim of the Hargy volcano. Tomare and Ruru, 'big men' of Lolo lineage and Kumo Development Corporation, were proposing to sell the area between the Lovo and the Barema rivers to migrant settlers, and it appeared the rest of the lineage and other lineages with interests in the soil could not find the means to challenge them. The LLG president, Ilisi, was also highly critical of such 'sales' of soil. Yet neither as a Maututu leader nor as LLG president did he openly oppose them but relied instead on hoped-for intervention from the district government. Within the ILG arrangements there were no channels of formal or informal consultation by which decisions made by individual elders could be challenged by the wider community. The village *komiti*, ward *kansil* and LLG president did not have the 'outside' authority to challenge lineage decisions because of the legal primacy of the ILG, and lineage members were seldom aware enough of what negotiations were being made by the directors to challenge them.

Under these conditions of opaque agreements by ILG directors with outsiders, the leadership of 'big men' and council/LLG representatives was undermined. They seemed unable at times to achieve cooperation across lineages, hamlets and villages. Disputes between groups became more difficult to resolve and this situation affected Maututu effectiveness in dealing with *lain ologala* (outside groups) such as HOPL (Houghton, 2017, p. 282). Houghton documented a dispute that Uase villagers had with HOPL. It had been going on for more than 17 years over the location of the HOPL mill and labour barracks on what were still seen by villagers as Uase soils, though acquired by the Bialla Plantation in 1912. This dispute was aggravated by various new incidents. In 1998, Uase villages demanded compensation from HOPL for land and sea damage, particularly the erosion of the coastline and damage to reefs due to the palm oil jetty extensions. When HOPL, through its lawyers, insisted on the case being held in the National Court in Port Moresby, Uase villagers did not have the finance to continue the case. In 2005, Misiel, a Uase leader with tertiary education, persuaded Uase villagers to donate funds to renew their compensation claims against HOPL, but again they could not sustain legal proceedings in the national capital.[5]

Legal proceedings such as these prioritised capitalist ontological assumptions over village frames of reference, but this did not have to be the way. In 2010, HOPL waste dumps overflowed, flooding Uase gardens, and an oil spill from a palm oil tanker devastated a local reef. Angered by the lack of coherent leadership from their elders, Uase youth reacted by damming waste collection outlets, flooding the mill. This forced a different approach from a group of lineage leaders who, instead of going to the courts, invited HOPL managers to attend a village feast and discuss the deteriorating situation between the company and villagers (Houghton, 2017). This had the potential for a partnership between 'outside' and 'home' agents. Both *lain* (parties) agreed to regular consultation in the future, a signal that effective cooperation among lineage leaders could continue to provide leadership.

Not only were lineage big men distrusted in these new arrangements, but also the massive amounts of cash made available through logging and oil palm industrialisation challenged patterns of leadership between hamlets and villages. By 2003, timber purchase rights and the Log Export Development Levy fund, which had accumulated from the government levy on logs exported through Bialla, had reached a total of K700,000.[6] This trust fund was reportedly released to the three villages of Gomu, Uase and Urumaili but with no transparency about where the funds were deposited. According to Boas Malilige, a Matililiu elder who worked in the LLG office, the LLG president, of Gomu, signed a deed of release for K300,000 of those funds into a bank account under the name of an unknown 'Maututu Corporation'. The funds were never distributed to local villagers and there was no public record of what became of them. Boas formed the Nakanai Welfare Association to claim what remained of the trust funds but his claim was unsuccessful. In 2017, Misiel of Uase announced he would establish the Maututu Resource Owners' Association to claim the funds. Before he could

---

5   Misiel was pastor of an independent church in Uase who spent five years as a missionary in the Philippines.

6   Meramera villagers had already claimed K5.5 million from this fund.

advance this claim, Misiel himself was voted out of his chairmanship of the association because he had accepted a payment of K325,000 from HOPL without discussion in the village. The payment was compensation for the 26 hectares of the former Ambusa/Bialla Plantation on which HOPL had constructed labour barracks. Misiel acknowledged to me that he had been voted out because fellow villagers accused him of selling the village stake in the Ambusa/Bialla Plantation without their knowledge. Although Misiel was one of those Maututu who declared that villagers have a problem because they do not stand together, he himself was accused of neglecting kin networks and furthering his own leadership position because of his dealings with outsiders.

Individualised business enterprise

The rise of 'big shots' was witnessed not only in ILG and village leadership but also in the emergence of oil palm mini-estates. In the Bialla area by 2012 approximately 6,500 hectares were under 'community-managed oil palm plantations' (Koczberski, Curry & Anjen, 2012). However, little of this was in the Maututu area, but among the Meramera villagers further north, where one villager, Nixon from Noau village, was earning K1 million a year from his estate. His business enterprise had benefited from earlier logging contracts with Amplex and he had expanded his business to include a petrol station, tyre repair workshop, accommodation lodge and café within Bialla town. He was one of the directors of the Ulevun Association that held the freehold title over the former Bialla Plantation.

On a lesser scale, there were a few Maututu who expanded their plantings into mini-estates. Lapou, who held 6 hectares on a settler block managed by outsiders, planted three 2-hectare blocks in Bubuu village with 720 palms and employed family members to harvest the fruit and care for the blocks. Lapou remained a respected elder in the village, a former *komiti* for Bubuu, then *kansil* for Baikakea-Bubuu-Gigipuna, and the head of a lineage that had claims to substantial areas of soil around the village. He capitalised his oil palm enterprise by paying wages to his labour force of K20–50 a day. He was later able to buy his own truck, which his mechanic son maintained.

In Mataruru there were two mini-estates. The Babex enterprise owned by Sira controlled about 40 hectares of oil palm. Sira, who was employed by the education department for 21 years, was the boss of Babex and his son supervised a labour force of 20 Uwoli people from Pomio on the south coast. The workers harvested 40 tonnes a fortnight of fresh fruit bunches, which, in times of high prices, brought in A$18,000 a fortnight. Using their own 4-tonne Isuzu truck, they transported the bunches to the mill, thus earning the higher mill gate price. The other mini-estate of over 30 hectares at Mataruru was established by Mataimi, who had been first to receive help from South Pacific Palm Oil Development Pty Ltd in 1974 when they established the nucleus estate not far from Mataruru. Both these men were leaders of their lineages and able to commandeer sizeable areas of soil. They challenged home patterns of exchange relations by relying on outsiders, 'wild men', as plantation labourers rather than looking to village kin.

John Ilisi from Urumaili (as mentioned above) had, while LLG president, negotiated a lease-lease back on a mini-estate of 30 hectares of oil palm. His earnings allowed him to invest in a house in town where he lived. He also used his own truck to transport bunches from his estate to the mill. For a time Ilisi used a labour force of mountain Mamusi people, but when they quit because of the low pay he employed company labour in their spare time to harvest the crop. His increasing absence from hamlet affairs and kin relations led to some criticism of 'big shot' behaviour. Nearby in Gomu, Ben Irima also established a business enterprise. He had three oil palm blocks in Gomu and another large block inland from Matililiu and had acquired a block overlooking the Ivi caldera, which he was logging in 2017–18. Two cars and two tipper trucks were parked near his home at Gomu. His neglect of kin relations in his management of the caldera block was to generate heated criticism in the northern villages (detailed below).

The emergence of these entrepreneurs introduced inequalities in cash wealth unknown in the earlier cocoa era. These mini-estate entrepreneurs not only pioneered much larger plantations but also invested in trucks that enabled them to economise on the costs of getting the bunches to the mill. They also employed 'outsiders' as their workforce rather than invite their kin and neighbours to share in the labour and proceeds of the enterprise. They were, in these ways, ignoring their 'big man' exchange obligations. Big men depended on attracting the contributions of large numbers of men and women towards *mage* presentations; however, they also needed to support members of their own *karakara* in their household enterprises. Ilisi's father, Mapulo, for example, was recognised in his time as a 'big man' and the cocoa plantation and fermentary he had established at that time had only enhanced that reputation because he continued to share resources with others. The 'big shots' of the oil palm era manipulated lineage holdings to their private advantage, then employed an outside labour force to extend their oil palm. That allowed them to invest in capital assets, such as trucks and cars, that they owned as individuals and to build impressive homes out of permanent materials. In doing so, they paid less attention to distributing their wealth through exchange networks. For these entrepreneurs, norms of social reciprocity weakened and they became increasingly individualistic in their enterprises.

The objection to business enterprises on Maututu soil in some cases focused on the investment of capital alienating the soil for the long term from *karakara* and lineage members with an interest in farming or building there. Minson ToPidik built a permanent materials piggery in Bubuu in 2017, with a concrete floor and walls, iron roof and water tanks. ToPidik and his son were planning to acquire a breeding pair from the agricultural station at Moramora near Kimbe, supported by a loan from the National Development Bank. He intended this to be a commercial enterprise, selling pigs to settler and Maututu households. At the time he encouraged his *karakara* and lineage affiliates to join with him in sustaining the venture, particularly by providing root crops for the pigs. However, before the breeder pigs could be delivered, his claim to the use of this soil came under dispute from kin who questioned the planned distribution of business profits. This tension around long-term occupation of lineage soil to generate 'individualised' wealth through business enterprise was also pertinent to oil palm blocks.

Trend towards individualised block ownership

VOP arrangements enabled loans to individuals strengthening their household's claim to 'own' their block. It also heightened their awareness of these tracts of soil as a physical asset that could enable the generation of wealth through oil palm or other commercial business. This consolidated a sense of a permanent association of that household, usually a husband–wife partnership, with that block of soil, enhanced by a sign on every block naming the couple who 'owned' the block. The formally demarcated block, registered to a named individual or couple, confirmed their right to use the soil for the life of the crop, acknowledged by government, company and lineage. In one sense, this was a continuation of Maututu acknowledgement of the grower's ownership of crops and trees they had planted, but the administration's stress on ownership of 'land' challenged home assumptions.

While the oil palm industry pushed towards individual ownership of 'land', the village interpretation of this process indicated that such tenure of blocks was by no means permanent, nor had it led to any transformation of Maututu assumptions that 'soil' remained in the custodianship of lineages. For most Maututu, the VOP farmer had been granted access to soil, and for a defined period. This led sometimes to questioning of the credentials of those working the block. For example, Koasiro of the Abeabe lineage in Bubuu planted his oil palm on soil affiliated with the Keakea lineage. After about 15 years, Keakea members asserted their claim to the soil and stopped Koasiro from harvesting the bunches for four years, by which time the palms had become too high to harvest. They were thus challenging his rights to replant the block. In many cases, replanting proved to be the moment when lineages asserted their right to divest a grower who was not of their lineage and assign the block to a lineage member. In another case, the Garua lineage in Baikakea allowed their clan mates in Bubuu to plant oil palm on Garua land in Baikakea because the lineage's soil in Bubuu was not accessible to company trucks. But, at the same time, they expected to reclaim these blocks when they came up for replanting. This would force their Bubuu clan mates to look to their own soil quite remote from their village for replacement of their oil palm blocks.

Such tension between individual entrepreneurship and community custodianship of the soil prompted further measures from government and the company to ensure the security of loans to the VOP grower. Government instituted the Community Land Use Agreement (CLUA) that served as a practical measure whereby lineage elders could guarantee the use of soil for the individual enterprise. In 2013, I witnessed an OPIC fieldworker coordinating the signing of a form that would guarantee an individual lineage member the right to convert 2 hectares to oil palm. The form required the signature of three lineage elders, including at least one woman and one man. The signatures were witnessed by an OPIC officer, local government land mediator, ward councillor, local church leader and a clan leader from a neighbouring landowning group (cf. Koczberski, Curry & Anjen 2012; Koczberski et al., 2009). In addition, problems of transparency were addressed by insisting that the signing of the agreement be publicly observed by members of the landowning group. This cumbersome arrangement was intended to give the company, or other loan agency, confidence in advancing credit to the VOP planter or to the entrepreneur to invest in their business. It also recognised the elders who retained the right of the lineage to turn that block over to someone else if the original individual failed to plant all of the block. In such a case the lineage would be responsible for bearing the debt of the inputs that had been incurred by that individual. The agreement thus clearly recognised the lineage as the ultimate custodian of the soil and guarantor of the loans. However, with its formal procedures focused on the production of signed documents rather than community consultation, the CLUA clearly favoured the advance of capital investment priorities. Government extended such arrangements to agreements between landowners and any other outside group wanting to establish a plantation or other business on lineage land. While the CLUA arrangement could advantage the lineage through the monthly rents payable on the block, it was a highly bureaucratised procedure requiring the cooperation and co-presence of multiple parties under the guidance of overstretched and ineffective OPIC fieldworkers (Kapia-Mendano, 2012). As such, it was rarely used during the years of my research. Instead, it was common for lineage ILG leaders to prefer an informal agreement with the outside party, often leaving other lineage members unaware of what had been agreed. The former PNG land commissioner commented to me that these land use agreements were unsatisfactory in that they did not recognise the perpetual belongingness of a lineage to the soil, over and against any individual claims of access.

These attempts to acknowledge both 'home' priorities of lineage 'soil' and capitalist demand for legal guarantees on investment demonstrated again the ontological tensions that the oil palm industry fuelled. Indigenous processes that confirm an individual's long-term access to soil for the cultivation of oil palm, or for some other enterprise, are based on exchange of food and valuables witnessed by the larger community, whereas administrative processes are focused on the collection of signatures to seal an agreement that cannot be challenged further within the community. Koczberski, Curry and Anjen (2012, p. 192) pointed out that such arrangements dramatise the difference between indigenous and capitalist systems. Ironically, officials acknowledged that the CLUA agreements had no standing in the law courts. Given the chronic soil shortages in many Nakanai villages, it is increasingly unlikely that such agreements will gain the approval of all signatories, and there will be more incentive to side-step the process. Insisting on a formal document as the basis for such agreements favours outsiders' ontological premises and ignores indigenous systems of legitimating land use through communal feasting and gift giving. From their contrary ontological viewpoint, the company and government were reluctant to trust the social networks and lineage affiliation with soil at the core of the indigenous ways of knowing and being.

Settler expansion onto Maututu soil

As settler households grew in size and number these outsiders sought to expand their plantings. In the 1980s and 1990s, some settlers were able to obtain access to settler blocks that Maututu were abandoning. But such transactions were not free from misunderstandings. In the case mentioned in Chapter 5, Kau from Urumaili worked his settler block in Wilelo until 1996, when the palms must have been about 16 years old and then sold the block to a Morobe migrant for K9,000.[7] In 2018, he estimated the block to be worth around K40,000 and, on that basis, took the settler to court to claim the rest of what he considered a fair price.[8] For Kau, his association with the block had not been severed when the migrant took over the block.

In later years outsiders were emboldened to use fallow or forested Maututu soils. They were able to acquire access to the soil from lineage leaders without the completion of a land survey and without any written formal agreement that stipulated the agreed 'sale' price of the land, the amount and timing of payment instalments, or the specific rights and obligations of the migrant or the landowners. 'Seldom was there any written evidence that the land transaction had the approval of the clan' (Koczberski et al., 2009, p. 187).[9] The outsiders acquiring land in this way believed that the cash payments made to the lineage leaders gave them ownership of the 'land', but this was rarely the understanding of the customary landowners. Instead:

> [the] landowners drew on customary principles that viewed land as an inalienable resource held by the kinship group … As customary landowners they believed they had the right to determine what livelihood activities migrants could pursue on the land.
>
> (Koczberski, Curry & Anjen, 2012, pp. 187–88)

The outsiders envisaged passing on to their sons the right to cultivate the soil or to operate a small business enterprise there without needing to consult further with the customary landowners, but, legally, the soil remained under customary ownership and, according to 'home' assumptions, could be repossessed by the landowners on the death of the 'purchaser' or the replanting of the block (Curry & Koczberski, 2009). For 'landowners',

---

7   In 2002, several blocks at Hoskins were sold for K15,000–30,000 (Curry & Koczberski, 2007; Koczberski & Curry, 2005).

8   The outcome is unknown. Kau died in 2019.

9   Koczberski and Curry use the term 'land' under indigenous ownership, whereas I prefer to call this 'soil'.

the soil remained an inalienable resource. As Curry and Koczberski (2009, p. 100) explained, 'land tenure on customary land remain[ed] deeply embedded in social relationships', which needed to be carefully maintained by the outsider through gift exchanges, such as contributions to the bridewealth and mortuary payments of their customary landowning hosts. These 'purchasers' were expected to share some of their oil palm income and to contribute to lineage and village events—that is, to assume customary obligations to the custodians. On the death of either the clan leader who granted access to the soil or the outsider who took possession of the soil the agreement had to be renegotiated as between new partners and the previous agreement could be annulled (Curry & Koczberski, 2009).

In Matililiu, a large area of soil was 'sold' to settlers from Sepik by a lineage head, Boeboe, without any written signed documents. Boeboe reportedly made no attempt to consult other members of his lineage or other affiliated lineages with an interest in this soil. As a consequence, even the LLG president refused to recognise the transaction. However, a number of Sepik families settled on the block and established businesses there, including a thriving truck fleet and mechanical workshop. This left villagers very uneasy as to whether they would ever be able to reclaim their soil. If they were to do so, they realised, they would have to pay the Sepik families for their *vogarila* (strength, labour) invested in the block. Villagers were highly critical of Boeboe for allowing this to happen. In another case in Baikakea, Kubaki accepted cash from a Sepik settler to settle on village land by the upper road. Village mates were furious and threatened to burn the settler's house down. This forced Kubaki to warn the settler that 2018 would be their last year on the village plot, or they would face violence from the village young men.[10] At that point the settler abandoned the block.

By 2009, 200 hectares of village customary land in Bialla, and 2,721 hectares of customary land in Hoskins, had been 'sold' to 'outsiders' for oil palm development, 'typically as two- or four-hectare blocks', often to the children of settlers or to company or government employees' (Koczberski et al., 2009, p. 34). These authors estimated in 2009 that 30 per cent of smallholder oil palm on customary land in the Hoskins area was planted by 'outsiders'. Maututu proved much less willing to part with their soil in this way, and, when they did, insisted that such payments were for access to the

---

10 The 'West for West' campaign in the Hoskins area at the time of the 1993 provincial elections saw 173 settler households evicted from customary land, although, in some villages, such as Gaungo, there was still a large migrant population of LSS blockholders (Curry & Koczberski, 2007, p. 20).

soil rather than ownership of the land. Koczberski Curry and Anjen (2012, p. 189) reported that in any more formal land use agreement, customary landowners insisted that it:

> should state explicitly that the outsider acquiring the land was not purchasing the land outright as freehold title, but rather obtaining usufruct rights to the land for defined purposes … and for a specified period of time … If the migrant tried to on-sell or sub-lease the land landowners insisted they had the right to repossess the land and return it to common property.

Recognising such difficulties, particularly when an outsider sought access to the soil, Koczberski, Curry and Anjen (2012, p. 191) proposed that the 'migrant should make regular payments to the landowning group to retain long-term access to the land … based on the value of production from the oil palm holding', and, to be transparent, that such payments should be made through deductions from the growers' payments. The increasing concern of lineage custodians about their long-term affiliation with the soils reflected this ontological friction between industrial and indigenous views of land/soil.

Conclusion: Ontological friction

This chapter has noted the frictions generated by the industrial expansion of oil palm. These affected village soil use, the local ecology, leadership patterns, lineage structures and cooperative labour. Under industrial development, it became much more difficult for village populations to assert their ontological priorities and they were frequently dismayed at how these could be dismissed as irrelevant by outsiders. Government regulations to suit industrial expansion undermined community management of soils. Community consensus came under pressure from government insistence on lineage exclusivism. Privileged big men took advantage of their familiarity with outsiders to gain financial advantages over their settlement neighbours and were less inclined to share their wealth with community others.

The industrialisation of land and lineage thus posed critical questions for Maututu, but it did not result in the capitalist logic of production replacing the ontological priorities of the village growers. Curry (2003) contended that the commercial priorities of oil palm production were considered by Nakanai as secondary to the kin priorities of managing the land. He challenged development planners to see village oil palm production in terms of how it becomes 'embedded in local place-based practices of exchange', and noted 'an efflorescence of gift exchange in tandem with a greater participation in oil palm production' (Curry, 2003, p. 407). Rituals and ceremonial exchanges among settler and village smallholders in Hoskins were timed to occur when participants received their oil palm income, which could then be contributed to customary practices, and this in turn triggered substantial increases in harvests of fruit. The pooling of oil palm income strengthened group identity and furthered indigenously defined goals and objectives. Lattas (1998, p. xxxvi), in commenting on West New Britain societies, noted that:

> through the world of ceremonial exchange the world of commodities comes to be not so much negated as familiarised. Its alienating relationships of money and wage labor give way to a world of kinship.[11]

This is an alternate modernity facilitated by oil palm revenue, which, however, has not led to a rejection of the relational values at the core of Maututu ontology. How these distinct values came to be articulated in Maututu ways of knowing and being is explored in the final three chapters.

---

11 Curry (2003, p. 409) compares this to a similar trend in Wenzhou Province in China (Yang, 2000), noting that in the rural areas of China and of West New Britain 'large-scale industrial development, using foreign capital, has facilitated a resurgence and expansion of nonmarket logics', such as in ritual exchange that reflects 'the resilience of indigenous cultural values'.

7

Accommodating the wild and transforming the domestic

In negotiating with the industrial forces of oil palm production, population expansion and commercial enterprise, Maututu transformed their own home life and relations, ensuring that community and identity was sustained. This chapter focuses on those elements central to Maututu worldviews, the transformations in their kinship relations and residential patterns.

Matrilineal principles and access to soil

A key quandary that faces a Maututu man today is the tension between his responsibilities towards his children and his responsibilities towards his sister's children, to whom he is elder in the *maratatila*. A man has always retained close links with his sisters' children as lineage mates, passing onto them his knowledge and some of his property. But this is balanced by his relationship with his own children to whom he also divides his knowledge and property. Maututu elders may also pass on knowledge and property to 'adopted' kin. Among the Maututu in the 1960s, such tension was minimal. Men would suggest to me that they cared for both their own and their sisters' children: they contributed to the bridewealth of sons and sisters' sons and received portions of bridewealth of daughters and sisters' daughters. They would pass on their personal possessions, such as betel nut and coconut palms, spears, shields, wristbands and the like to both sets of offspring. In recent times, material possessions such as cash crops have acquired greater significance and, with that, their inheritance poses a greater dilemma.

Martin (2006, p. 124) suggests the same for the Tolai:

> The situation faced by Tolai today is one in which they have
> competing moral obligations ... to balance the needs of his children,
> who are of another clan, with those of his clan.

It is useful to raise again the comparison with the Tolai people of East New Britain, because they too are a matrilineal society and have had a long association with Maututu through exchange, schooling and mission activity. Many Maututu are fluent in the Tolai language, Kuanua. The Tolai preceded the Maututu in experiencing the colonial incursions on their land and subsequent land shortages brought about by expatriate cocoa plantations. Under these pressures, the Tolai, since the 1950s, have debated whether they should replace their system of landholdings vested in the matrilineage with one based on the patrilineage or on individuated holdings, so as to accommodate the desire of men to pass on their holdings to their children (TS Epstein, 1968; Martin, 2006, p. 31, citing AL Epstein [1969]). Tolai children were able to stake a claim to their father's land by aiding his lineage in amassing and distributing large amounts of *tambu* shell valuables at mortuary feasts. More recently Martin (2006, p. 36–37) describes the 'increasing tendency for Tolai men to buy land in order to secure the rights of their children to inherit land'; he suggests that Tolai 'increasingly prioritise claims made on the basis of exclusive individual ownership over inclusive overlapping claims'.[1] On the Gazelle Peninsula, the pressure on land came with the expansion, not of oil palm, but of cocoa.

It is interesting, therefore, to see how the large number of Tolai settlers in West New Britain on oil palm blocks visualise the future for their children. Curry and Koczberski (2007, p. 15) observed that, among both Tolai and Nakanai smallholders in Hoskins, 'alienation of land for cash cropping is leading people to claim exclusive rights of access to, and inheritance of, these resources of their fathers'. Tolai settler smallholders recognised that sisters' sons of the leaseholder had a claim to the Land Settlement Scheme block but that the blockholder could pay compensation to his sisters' sons to validate inheritance rights for his own children (Curry & Koczberski, 2007, p. 9). Tolai thus recognised the tension in matrilineal society between the rights of their own and of sister's children, and attempted to resolve it through financial compensation. Yet, even then, they accepted the

---

1 Here, Martin (2006, p. 37) refers to the characterisation made by Lea (1997, p. 12) of Melanesian land tenure systems as emphasising inclusive rights 'where one does not inherit land (and hence cannot be disinherited), but one "acquires rights on recruitment to a descent line"'.

likelihood that once settler blocks were inherited by the son they would be subject to the claims of the son's lineage—that is, the matrilineal principle would prevail in the next generation.

Unlike the Tolai, there was no suggestion among Maututu that matrilineal principles were at risk of replacement by patrilineal principles, despite the preference of Maututu parents to pass their block to their children. As with cocoa, there was generally no objection to them doing that; however, if the village oil palm (VOP) block was at the end of its productive life, there tended to be greater scrutiny of its status, as replacement of the palms incurred new debts and locked the tenancy of the block for another 20 or so years. The inheritance of cocoa in the 1970s was not about soil, but about stands of trees from which heirs could derive revenue and sustenance. Oil palm challenged these patterns because it required much larger areas of cultivation and represented greater financial and labour investment. Given the tendency of outsiders—both company and government—to assume that the block smallholder also 'owned' the block as 'land', Maututu became very wary when the smallholder was not of the lineage affiliated with the soil. Particularly where the mother was from another village, the block was likely to be on the father's lineage soil or on the soil of a lineage to which he was closely affiliated. In these cases, there was incipient tension, because, by the father passing on his block to his children, tenancy was passing into the hands of a person of another lineage—that is, of the mother. Fathers, therefore, sought a secure way to allow at least one of their children to inherit the oil palm smallholding.

This tension led to a unique solution among the Maututu, the *posolagu* arrangement. A man's first child, either son or daughter, *la posolagu* (*lagu* meaning forward/in front), was allowed privileges within his/her father's lineage, becoming in a sense the child of both lineages. Maututu say *la posolagu te tamala* (the firstborn follows their father), as distinct from the other children who follow their mother. This does not mean that the *posolagu* is not of their mother's lineage, but the firstborn is acknowledged by their father's lineage as also of their group. The gift to the *posolagu* of access to the father's lineage soil is seen as *mapa la vuluti*—that is, another instalment of bridewealth passed from the husband's group to the wife's group. This special relationship of father with *posolagu* is also celebrated in the father bestowing various property, such as betel or coconut palms, ritual shields or even forest knowledge, on the firstborn. The *posolagu* revered the *ruvu* and *olu* of both their mother's and father's lineages. As a child of both lineages, the *posolagu* avoided marriage with a cross-cousin who was seen as a clan mate. Indeed, the elaborate rituals that marked the life crisis events of the *posolagu* increased their attractiveness to partners beyond close kin, and so new exchange relations resulted. Thus, in principle, the *posolagu* would in marriage extend home relations to more remote, 'wild' kin.

I was told by elders that, in the past, they had celebrated their *posolagu* in distinct ways throughout their lives: when the child was born; when he or she was about seven years old and their ears were pierced and the lobes extended (until, ideally, they hung to the shoulders and were decorated with dogs' teeth);[2] when the mother's brother or parents were invited to pierce the child's nose; in their early teens or younger, when the child was celebrated *tagu la ivula* (adorn their hair) with a headdress of bird feathers placed on their head (*ubi la sapepe/vuo te masegi*[3]), and a large *mage* feast was presented to the mother's lineage and her origin *karakara*. Some ceremonies were only carried out for the *posolagu*, and other ceremonies were celebrated in more elaborate ways depending on whether the *posolagu* was male or female (Figure 7.1).[4] The father's reputation was enhanced through such ceremonies in which he consolidated important exchange relations with his wife's kin, the same group to whom he made bridewealth payments.

The key ritual in the *posolagu*'s life was *ubi la sapepe*; however, in my 40-month stay during 1968–75, I only witnessed one such ritual, sponsored by the most prestigious leader in the area, Mapulo. Following the advent of oil palm, there have been many such rituals, as parents have been able to access cash through oil palm to purchase the required pigs and have persuaded their kin to plant the gardens necessary for the food distribution. Chris Gregory (1982) pointed out how ceremonial exchange can be exaggerated in the context of market expansion. Among the Maututu, access to more cash allowed the ritual presentation to include store-bought goods, such as bags of rice and tinned fish.

---

2   Elders were describing an immediate past, as some in 1968–69 still had these extended lobes.

3   The *sapepe* was reserved for the male *posolagu*. A female *posolagu* had a similar ceremony called *vuo te masegi*, when a vine was tied across the girl's forehead to the back of her head, a line of lime powder painted down the middle of her head front to back, and white cockatoo feathers were stuck in the hair.

4   These included the emergence of the baby and mother from the 30 days of confinement within the house; the first acquaintance of the child with lineage sites or prominent village sites; the initiation ceremony of later childhood; and, for girls, their first menstruation, when the headdress was placed on the youth's head and pigs and food exchanged (*tagu la-ivula*, decorate the hair with headdress).

Figure 7.1: Ilisi, *posolagu* of Mapulo, being prepared for coming out ceremony, 1974
Source: Author.

In contemporary Maututu society, this ritual efflorescence reflects the desire of parents to celebrate their firstborn in this public way and to consolidate the *posolagu*'s claims as a future leader of a *karakara*. The father announces ritually that the *posolagu* (firstborn) has claims on his father's lineage and *karakara*, including access to soil. The ritual primarily states the right of the firstborn to identify with their father's group. This recognition of the *posolagu* in both mother's and father's lineage is another challenge to government prescriptions of exclusive lineage membership, as in the incorporated land group (ILG) model. In contradistinction, Maututu see it as a consolidation of exchange relations between lineage groups, particularly those represented within the same *karakara*. As an instalment of the marriage exchange, the offer to the *posolagu* of access to soil is a further recognition of relations between the *karakara* of the father where the family probably reside and the origin *karakara* of the mother, to whom her other children look for support. Later-born children can only access soil from their lineage elders, such as their mother's brothers, and so, for this reason, particularly in the past, spent time in their mother's brother's *karakara*.

This allocation to the *posolagu* of a man's plantings on his own lineage soil does not raise objections from the father's lineage group. Villagers generally accept the allocation of cash crops in this way as a way for a father to pass on the product of his industry to his *posolagu* son or daughter.[5] The arrangement *posolagu te tamala* does not prevent the *posolagu* also planting on the soil of their own lineage, —that is, of their mother, but it is likely that they leave that to their siblings who have no access to soil through their father.

However, there were various views as to whether this was a permanent alienation of these soils from the father's lineage to the mother's lineage through the *posolagu*, and whether the *posolagu* could then pass these plantings onto their first-born, which would further obscure the affiliation of the original lineage with that block. Some assured me that the first born could not dispose of the block without agreement of the lineage of their father and that such permission was unlikely to be granted when soil was scarce. There was a case before the District Court in 2018 of a man who arranged for his *posolagu*, his son, to plant oil palm on soil affiliated with the father's lineage. The son then attempted to register the block in the name of his *posolagu*, his daughter. His father's lineage took the case to court asserting their continued custodianship of the soil. In another case, a non-Maututu (Tolai) pastor paid the Biso lineage in Baikakea for access to soil on which he built his home. His *posolagu* son then married a Maututu woman, not of the Biso lineage, and planted oil palm on the soil and he intended to pass that oil palm on to his first born. I was told by other Maututu that the *posolagu* of neither generation had a claim on the soil itself. They explained that, in this case, the *posolagu* were inheriting crops and that the soil could still be resumed by the Biso lineage when the crop was replaced.

Due to the growing shortage of soil, Maututu have had to strategise long-term access to oil palm blocks. Men whose best access to soil is through their own lineage rather than their wife's thus endeavour to use that soil for oil palm for their *posolagu*, while other fathers whose lineage is short of soil look after their children through plantings on the mother's lineage soil. In the current times, all villagers know that claims of the *posolagu* to long-term use of the soil are likely to be contested in later years by lineage members who respect the *posolagu* continuing to farm that soil, but plan to take back custodianship once the *posolagu* dies. It is access for cultivation that they allow—not ownership of the soil.

---

5   The father may be referred to publicly not by his own name but as the 'father of …' (name of *posolagu*).

This transformation of inheritance principles is by no means complete, nor is the direction of change necessarily consistent. Social relations and group membership are always under negotiation. While there are the outside pressures to determine exclusive membership of the social group 'owning' the soil and to see the soil as individuated 'land' when planted in oil palm, there is an equally strong tendency among Maututu to extend the relationships that are deemed to constitute the *karakara* and lineage through a range of other means. Lineage membership remains porous. For example, in contemporary Maututu villages, more and more 'stranger' (*ologala*) women from outside Maututu have married Maututu men. When such women come from matrilineal societies they are quickly integrated into the matrilineal system of the Maututu by recognising their home lineage's affinity to a local lineage.[6] In contrast, women from patrilineal societies on the mainland have not been accepted into a Maututu lineage, which means that their children also have no lineage affiliation. In such marriages, it becomes critical for the Maututu father to insist on his *posolagu*'s claims to his lineage soil.

Realignment of residential patterns

As lineage exclusivity has increased residential patterns have changed. Most oil palm blocks today belong to farming couples planting on soil associated with their lineage, that of the wife or the husband, and this has affected residence choices. In Gomu, for example, oil palm cultivation on what was seen as lineage soil led to the re-siting of hamlets close to where the lineage had their oil palm blocks. In all villages, settlement has become more differentiated into distinct hamlets, each with clear lineage identification. In these cases, other lineages and kin co-resident there are seen as more marginal. A woman in Gomu, for example, was in a dispute with her husband stemming from his inability to contribute to household livelihood. She blamed her parents for marrying her to a man for whom she had no feelings and who had failed to contribute to the household economy. She was of the Kabulu Buleha lineage based in Bubuu but had followed her divorced father to Gomu where she married. She planted oil palm on Kabulu clan land in Gomu but the lineage there was Kabulu Balogo and she was informed that she would lose the land when it came time to replace

---

6   These include women from Meramera, Bileki and Tolai language groups. Affinity may be claimed because of common totems or historical partnerships.

the palms. Although they had poles and corrugated iron prepared for a new house, she was not willing to rebuild where they were currently living, on her husband's lineage land, because, in the event of divorce, she would no longer be permitted by the lineage to live there. In the past, residents relied on their affiliation to the big man rather than the lineage for their house site. More recently, hamlet soil is more pointedly under the lineage, who may insist on their right to determine what is done on that soil.

With access to oil palm revenue, Maututu have resumed holding large *mage*, but whereas in the past these were occasions to invite 'strangers' from outside villages, in more recent times participation has been limited to separate hamlets from the one village, the feasts presented by one lineage group or hamlet to another lineage or hamlet group in the same village. Persons from other villages attend not as members of a village or *karakara* but as kin of the hosts.[7] This reflects not just the larger populations now found in each village but also the sharper delineation of lineages within separate hamlets. For example, in 2010, the *karakara* centred on the lineage Kabuliala in Baikakea celebrated the initiation of seven *posolagu*, all but one the children of men or women of the Kabuliala lineage (the one exception was the son's son of Kabuliala). These youths were, then, not all members of Kabuliala, but it was their Kabuliala parents who organised the planting of gardens and procuring of pigs. The feast was presented to the children of two brothers in Baikakea, Taloloku and Ulupita of the Vauvatu lineage and the lineages of their wives, both Kabulu, who comprised another *karakara* within the village. These Kabulu lineages and their *karakara* partners returned this presentation in late 2018 when seven male and three female descendants of Ulupita and Tololoku were crowned with the *sapepe* headdress and three younger boys had white feathers stuck in their hair as a preliminary to their *sapepe*. The feast that accompanied this ceremony was termed the 'feast of Mololoa', the *posolagu* daughter of Ulupita and member of the Kabulu lineage. It was she who invited kin from other villages to contribute store-bought cloth and rice to the presentations. The feast therefore enhanced the lineage and hamlet of the hosts by strengthening their exchange relationship with other significant lineages and *karakara* within the village (Figure 7.2).

---

7   Villagers challenged my recollection of former times as holding very few of such *mage*, saying that they had always carried out such initiations, but they did agree that *mage* feasts where other villages attend as distinct *karakara* and dance *e rae* are no longer held.

Figure 7.2: Dismantling a display of betel nut at a *mage* feast, 2017
Source: Author.

Negotiating commercial enterprise in the outside world

The establishment of 'outsider' oil palm thus led to major transformations in 'home' relations in regard to soil, lineage and *karakara*. Despite the focus of industrialisation on 'individuals', Maututu farmers remained as 'dividuals', building networks of relations through lineage and karakara. This also marked commercial enterprises in the village. While most directed oil palm revenue into communal activities, such as the holding of life crisis ceremonies or church celebrations, a few focused on the establishment of small enterprises, such as pig breeding, trade stores, cocoa fermentaries or trucking. Many of these new enterprises envisaged their market to extend beyond fellow Maututu to the stranger world of settlers and town residents.

Some came to rely on these stranger relations to the point of neglecting their relations with kin and *karakara*, the so-called big shot pattern, but many others strengthened their home relations in order to succeed in the outside world. As their enterprises required substantial financial investment, they built on networks within their *karakara* and lineage, inviting affiliates to contribute cash towards the venture. In general, they did not see these enterprises as primarily financial investments. The material assets could prove to be ephemeral, but the name of the lineage or *karakara* who made the investment would continue despite deterioration in the assets. The cars that lie in every village, abandoned and rusting due to the expense of keeping them on the road or the lack of local mechanical skills and spare parts, nevertheless bear witness to the success of the group in originally acquiring the asset.

In Baikakea and Bubuu, a family grouping of Kabulu-Kabuliala-Uge lineages, calling themselves Baibu, aggregated their oil palm income to purchase a Toyota utility in the early 2000s for use as a public transport vehicle taking people to the town for market, hospital, high school and trade stores.[8] They gained a contract from Hargy Oil Palm Ltd (HOPL) to bring children from the uphill settler community of Area 8 into Baikakea Primary School each day, and they hired the vehicle out to settlers and other villages when needed. They were supported by one of the family who was

---

8   Baibu included the hamlet *karakara* focused on the Kabuliala lineage in Baikakea, plus the half-sister through their common father and her husband and married children in Bubuu. She and children were of the Uge lineage and her husband from the Kabulu clan.

a vehicle mechanic at the New Britain Palm Oil (NBPOL) nuclear estate. He advised the Toyota driver, his mother's brother, in conducting periodic repairs, and would himself carry out regular maintenance. In 2009, Baibu purchased a flat-tray truck to replace the Toyota utility. The Isuzu truck had a price tag of K109,000. With a deposit of K21,000 accumulated from their Toyota business, they negotiated a bank loan, repaid at K5,000 a month over 36 months—a total repayment of K180,000. The huge cost of the investment demonstrated the commitment of the families to working together. To run this business, diesel fuel had to be fetched in 44-gallon drums from Kimbe over 100 kilometres away, where spare parts also had to be sourced. The truck operated with one licensed driver and a conductor who sat at the back and collected fares.[9] In 2009, diesel for the truck was costing them K550 a week, and wages K700 a week, and on any day of a six-day week they would take in between K180 and K500 in fares. Clearly this put an onus on the group to invest in the truck from their other revenue, principally oil palm, in order to continue the truck operations. This meant that when they needed extra cash for the monthly loan repayments the family had to harvest oil palm on all their blocks and put the revenue towards the truck. They also recognised the need to grow their investment savings account to cover the replacement of the truck after the loan was paid off, and it required firm financial management on the part of the group leaders to ensure that earnings were put away into savings rather than shared out among kin who had contributed to the original purchase.

It was thus a major achievement when the group purchased a second Isuzu truck in 2017, with a deposit of K44,000 and a loan of K75,000, which they paid back at K3,537 a month over 24 months (total cost K128,888). They resolved to pay off the loan more quickly by using their oil palm earnings and by seeking contract work for the trucks to augment the regular services. At the time of my visit in 2017, both trucks were hired out in Kimbe to transport people to the Kimbe Games, enabling the group to increase their debt repayments. They later expanded their business by buying a house in Bialla town, which they rented out for K600 a fortnight. They also ran a village trade store. The Baibu group in 2017 was discussing further investments, such as procuring a loan from the National Development Bank to purchase a 30-foot motorised boat that could be used for fishing beyond the reefs and for passenger transport to Rabaul, and establishing a fuel

---

9   With few exceptions, all passengers paid their fares, though many were kin and village mates of the truck crew.

station on the district road. Like the other enterprises, these were envisaged as promoting the lineage grouping. Baibu members put their labour and oil palm revenue into an enterprise that raised their group's reputation across Maututu villages. Their enterprise demonstrates the importance of kin groupings resembling the big man's *karakara* of former times rather than the ILG of industrial arrangements. Such contemporary kin alliances are not limited to a single lineage but to a grouping built through inter-lineage marriages.

The indigenous principle of business investment exemplified here is not based on capital profitability but on social sustainability. The business is important to the group, not primarily as a profit-making venture but as a symbol of the group's socio-political standing and 'to achieve social objectives' (Curry & Koczberski, 2013, p. 345), particularly building on exchange among kin and neighbours that brings prestige to the whole *karakara* and lineage. It extends their political influence within and beyond the village and consolidates the social exchange relations that constitute their lives. For example, from a capital investment perspective, trade stores are not a good business proposition as the stock can become depleted when the store managers provide goods free to kin or on credit to others. Every Maututu trade store faces enormous challenges in limiting the amount of credit allowed to its customers, most of whom are kin or village mates. I described in a previous chapter how the operation of the Maututu Cooperative Society's trade store was frequently undermined by what business development officers called 'mismanagement'. When the credit is not repaid, the trade store languishes. But the affiliated kin group or *karakara* then invest more revenue from elsewhere to restock it. Curry (1999) concluded that village trade stores and village-based transport businesses are unsustainable due to the difficulties of preserving enough revenue to maintain the asset. It is therefore noteworthy that the Baibu trade store and transport business continued to operate because of the willingness of Baibu members to contribute labour and resources towards the enterprise. The qualified mechanic volunteered his time to maintain the vehicles. Senior members of the group kept a close check on the drivers and conductors to ensure they continued to provide good service throughout the day and to hand over all takings to the Baibu treasurer. This encouraged them to continue to plan further ventures.

It was also a *karakara* of linked lineages that purchased the Lucas mobile sawmill in Baikakea. The Lamo Auru Development Corporation (LADC) was established in 2006 by Ben Masori, formerly a teacher and then personnel manager at HOPL. He was advised by FORCERT (Forests for Certain, Forests for Life), a non-government organisation based in Kimbe focused on working with remote communities, 'to take the lead in their change, balancing their environmental, economic, social and cultural interest'.[10] LADC represented three different lineages within the village. Some villagers even claimed that the project belonged to the whole village of Baikakea. By 2008, the project had erected a steel frame to accommodate a small office building in Ben's hamlet. In 2012, they obtained a bank loan to purchase a second-hand utility truck, a Lucas mobile sawmill, and a buffalo and jinker trailer to drag logs from the forest. Initially the plan had been to drag whole logs to the beach at Gomu (Baikakea was located behind mangrove forest), where they could export either whole logs or sawn timber. But the venture ran into difficulties. No-one had experience in handling buffalo and they were never able to persuade the animal to drag the trailer. Ironically, for villagers and outsider alike, the 'wild' buffalo never left the settlement, spending its days grazing by the stream. The jinker proved not sturdy enough for the transportation of whole logs and was also abandoned, and Gomu villagers opposed the shipment of harvested logs from their beach. In 2013, the sawmill was cutting planks in the hills high above Baikakea to fulfill a contract for an Apupulu client when Gomu villagers raided the camp and took all the planks, claiming the soil and timber as that of their ancestors who had originated in Baikakea. The local-level government (LLG) backed these claims, imposed a fine on the sawmill operators and, until the fine was paid, embargoed the sawmill. Without a source of revenue to repay the loan the bank threatened to repossess the sawmill. Their enterprise faced collapse as a consequence of inter-village hostility (Figures 7.3 and 7.4). At this time, HOPL was seeking timber for its own house construction program and the company paid the fine, enabling the return of the Lucas sawmill to the LADC so that it could provide the company with timber. After this initial help, LADC was able to rebuild the enterprise. In 2017, the mobile saw was again in full use, under the control of the Lamo Auru Community Conservation Authority (the renamed LADC), with its small group of operators paid on a fortnightly basis. After fulfilling the HOPL contract, the sawmill was transported around the village gardens to process felled trees into planks for local housing in the villages and settlements. The success of this enterprise was built not only on the LADC members but also on the partnerships they developed with outsiders, both company and householders.

---

10   See FORCERT, [Homepage], forcertpng.org.

Figure 7.3: Planks sawn for village use from tree within poisoned village oil palm block, 2017
Source: Author.

Previous chapters demonstrated the opportunism of ILG leaders to gain benefit from oil palm expansion by exploiting lineage relations as 'big shots'. But as the discussion on *posolagu*, hamlet consolidation and *karakara* investments has demonstrated, lineages and *karakara* have also worked together to take advantage of new opportunities, in the process ignoring the ontological premises of capitalist industry to remodel 'home' priorities. Curry and Koczberski (2013, p. 345) observed of the oil palm area that:

> initiatives that are most likely to be sustainable on a long-term basis are those able to accommodate a high proportion of the revenue generated being redirected to the indigenous exchange economy without causing the enterprise to become insolvent.

Figure 7.4: Mobile saw in operation in village garden, 2017
Source: Author.

Holznecht (1997, p. 46) drew attention to this 'dynamism of local organization … that aims to be adaptive rather than maladaptive' to new opportunities, and concluded that 'the identities of landowners must be refined and transformed—on their own terms and in their own ways'. Such business ventures may become insolvent in a capitalist sense, but they are far from insolvent in a social sense because the supporting lineage and *karakara* are prepared repeatedly to reinvest in the business. In doing so, they recognise the risk of their big man assuming 'ownership' of the enterprise. The tension between the priorities of relational and industrial worlds was the reality in which they built their enterprises.

The company as partner?

As described in a Chapter 4, industrialisation enabled the company to become the dominant influence in the affairs of the Bialla LLG region, bringing alternate viewpoints to bear on both settler and village populations. Maututu activists like Boas Malilige, who was LLG staff, pointed out that its increased community role enabled the company to grow its own business rather than distributing opportunities to local businesses or promoting local enterprises. For example, in its maintenance of roads and other community assets, the company preferred to employ its own labour force and equipment rather than contract the work to local businesses that might have enhanced community benefits from the projects. Similarly, the company promoted individual entrepreneurs with whom managers had a long relationship, but this only encouraged these individuals to act as 'big shots' with disdain for customary patterns of partnership. The company managers preferred local leaders who advocated for change or controls desired by the company and, in consequence, local politicians and administrators and local elites became dependent on their partnership with the company. Maututu working in the company were also able to use that position to gain personal advantage. For example, one man from Gomu who had worked for the lands department and then joined HOPL intervened over soil claimed by Bubuu lineages at the Barema River. Claiming expertise as a former lands department staff member, he determined that the soil lay within the area acquired by government. This allowed HOPL to lease the land for their Nova mill.

My village interlocutors pointed out that the quasi-governmental role played by company managers undermined local Maututu interests. Several Maututu who had become lawyers practising outside the area were willing to lead challenges to the company when they perceived it to be acting against community concerns. In 2017, a recently formed Lands Committee in Baikakea took HOPL to court for extending their nuclear estate plantings onto lineage soil. To do this they had to employ two land surveyors to mark the boundaries to the disputed site and faced the challenge of raising K20,000 for legal fees. But they succeeded in having the company pay compensation and respect indigenous soil. In the 2010 legal challenge (described in Chapter 6), Uase village took HOPL to court for polluting local seas with factory effluent, demanding K1 million in compensation. In this case, HOPL managers referred the case to their lawyers at the national level, and ultimately protested that only the Belgian head office could be answerable to such a large claim.

Villagers asserted that the company often misled them (*visigolo*, tells lies). When such cases were heard at Bialla, villagers became perturbed because the judges sent from Port Moresby or Kimbe were accommodated at the HOPL guesthouse, under the influence of the HOPL managers. Conversely, if the cases were heard in Port Moresby, villagers incurred large costs in travel and accommodation to attend. Tension between Maututu and the company could lead to threats of violence. Villagers boasted to me that when the son of the SIPEF managing director visited Bialla, they threatened him and the next day he fled the area by plane. On another occasion, I accompanied a delegation of villagers demanding a meeting with the company's Community Development Branch. We were received by the branch staff and a useful discussion took place, but I was directly accused, mistakenly, by HOPL staff of inciting the dispute. They apparently did not think it conceivable that Maututu could take such action on their own.

In November 2018, John Ilisi, ex-president of the LLG and a resident of Urumaili, claimed that the road that accessed the company senior managers' quarters at Likiliki was built on village soil. Urumaili villagers demanded the company construct a new access road on government land and compensate villagers for the use of village soil over the previous four decades. To promote their cause they attempted to close the road with boulders and banana trunks. At this point the HOPL general manager called Maututu leaders, including John Ilisi, to a meeting at company headquarters. Ilisi declined to attend the meeting because it was convened on company premises. Thus, many villagers were critical of the claims the company made of 'community development', seeing it as largely in accord with an agenda driven by company priorities.

All these incidents demonstrated a willingness to form larger groups to take action when they faced the might of the company. In Uase, such action was organised through a village committee representing 12 lineages (Houghton, 2017). Baikakea villagers formed the Baikakea Lands Committee, and, in Urumaili, the former LLG president united his hamlet in defiant action over the Likiliki access road. Maututu challenged the power of the company in order to negotiate more beneficial outcomes for home communities. Those Maututu who had gained experience among outsiders as lawyers, public servants or entrepreneurs brought that experience to bear in negotiating with the company. Together with many of the village elders, they insisted that Maututu priorities be given prominence in these negotiations, thus resisting the attempts by the company to base negotiations on outsider ontological principles. In these cases the disputants were unable to establish mutual respect under which partnership could be attained. However, the LADC–HOPL arrangement detailed above describes a more positive relationship in which the interests of both parties were met.

In contrast to their normal dealings with the company, Baikakea leaders told of their partnership with a large construction company, Nivani Ltd. Its general manager, David Stein, an Australian expatriate, had hired Maututu for local operations ever since he founded the company in 1988. He respected their diligence and trustworthiness, a far cry from the common expatriate view at the time. He even asked Maututu friends to negotiate his marriage to a woman from Ulamona when he was constructing the HOPL Sova mill there in the 1990s. Maututu proudly claimed that they had stood by him in establishing his company, even when he did not pay good wages, and, in reciprocation, Nivani constructed a road direct to Baikakea from the upland highway, and laid the concrete floor for the village church and an adjacent meeting hall. According to them, their relationship with his company had not been built on financial incentives but on the reciprocal relationship between them. As one village elder recalled, when he suggested that David provide the concrete to the church for free, despite knowing David was not a churchgoer, he added 'God will bless your company if you help us', and David did help them.

Such a partnership for Maututu relied on building mutual respect. Villagers sought a semblance of kinship or affiliation with government or company staff with whom they engaged, but, instead, HOPL expatriate staff would restrict their involvement to 'business-like' conduct. That made trust difficult and cooperation superficial. In the Maututu myths, the hunter's survival is only possible by creating or recognising a kinship bond with the powers of the outside world. The *taua* turns out to be an ancestral spirit who invites the hunter into a partnership that releases creative energies and transforms community life. Maututu, through their partnership with Nivani, realised benefits that enhanced their agency and their priorities:

> Being cast in the realm of indigenous exchange means that the relationship with landowners has social value and implies respect for the host group—respect for their authority as landowner … respect for their culture, and respect for their behavioural mores.
>
> (Koczberski et al., 2017, p. 160)

Maututu sought similar outcomes from their dealing with HOPL, but with little success. The priorities of the company, demanded by the remote SIPEF, saw local concerns and wellbeing as merely a road to company prosperity. Their worlds, though bound materially through oil palm, could not be woven into a creative partnership.

The reassertion of rights in soil, not land

As the oil palm plantings expanded and 'wild' outsiders flooded into the area, Maututu realised the gravity of government's assertion that the 'land' had been purchased, and they began to voice their disagreement. As more local men and women have gained qualifications and standing nationally as lawyers, health professionals, teachers, academics and administrators, they have increasingly questioned the validity of the original acquisition of 'land' by the Australian administration, asserting that their forebears had no comprehension of the contents of the written documents. In 2008, Maututu recounted to me how their leaders had, in about the year 2000, visited Port Moresby to view the original documents of land acquisition. The Department of Lands had no documents to show them and sent them to the forestry department who produced a timber agreement signed in 1966 to pay A\$272,000 for timber rights over the whole Hargy area. In 2009, a Maututu lawyer pursuing the case asserted to me that the A\$64,000 paid to villagers in 1964 was also for timber rights, because no documents existed that indicated that it was for the sale of the soil. In 2017, the former LLG president also insisted that these moneys paid in the 1960s were for timber rights. Maututu lawyers mounted cases against the Department of Lands, challenging it to produce relevant documents. Their counterclaim stated that government should distribute to villagers the lease money paid over many years by the company for use of the soil and commit to returning the area eventually to the rightful lineages. These disputes vividly contrasted the freehold land principles pursued by government and the company, and the customary understanding of soil central to Maututu ontology (Cooter, 1991). Koczberski et al. (2017, p. 158) concluded that, 'under customary land tenure regimes, relational concepts of land tenure are therefore dominant'; however, for an administration focused on freehold title (and the growth of capital-intensive industry), exclusive and permanent property rights are guaranteed by the payment of a 'purchase' price.

The actions of these 'educated' and 'qualified' (in outsider terms) leaders to challenge the foundation of the oil palm industry represented a new dynamic in the ongoing relations of Maututu to outsiders. They were not demanding to control the oil palm revenues but to have the soil acknowledged as theirs, and to be able to determine the long-term use of the soil. Villagers have become aware of how industrial developments are affecting communal life and exchange relations; they know that their resilience as a home community depends on their capacity to organise politically—that is, to take their concerns outside the village arena into negotiations and, hopefully, partnerships with outside forces.

This increased agitation among Maututu for return of their soils also turned to the Bialla Plantation itself, which after years as a cocoa plantation became Ambusa, headquarters for the logging company Amplex. On the demise of Amplex, its plantation was ceded to the Meramera Ulevun Association, as detailed in Chapter 4. Because of the assertion among Maututu of their affiliation with Bialla soil, the Ulevun directors made no attempt to develop the plantation. With no-one harvesting the cocoa or the 'wild' self-propagating stands of oil palm in the disused plantation, villagers from Gomu, Urumaili and Uase felled some of the cocoa and coconut and planted vegetable gardens. They were responding to shortage of garden area within their villages but were also laying claim to affiliation with the soil. In 2018, Ilisi applied for the Bialla Plantation to be registered in the names of the three villages, Gomu, Urumaili and Uase, on the basis that their ancestors had built their hamlets and worked their food gardens there at the time the Germans acquired the plantation. Ilisi also proposed that the government compensate the Ulevun Association for the plantation. That this was even contemplated seems to indicate the growing boldness and influence of key leaders.

HOPL managers were not sympathetic to these local demands, as the area lay immediately adjacent to the mill. The company had already persuaded the chairman of the Maututu Resources Owners' Association in Uase to allow them to occupy 26 hectares of the plantation to construct housing for mill workers. This was in an area of the plantation adjacent to Uase that, according to local consensus, Uase ancestors had originally occupied. A Gomu man derided the Uase lineages: 'what will they eat if they continue to pursue money? Can they eat their oil palm? They have no gardening land left.' Indeed, when Uase villagers became aware of the HOPL arrangement, they forced the chairman of the Maututu Resource Owners' Association to resign.

HOPL then approached Ulevun with a proposal to plant the former plantation in oil palm under a contract between Ulevun and the company, resembling those already negotiated in Meramera villages. But in Bialla, the Ulevun directors knew they had been ceded soils of Maututu lineages and that an acknowledgement of this was needed. This galvanised leaders in the three Maututu villages to form a special committee to further their claim for the return of the soil. Finally, in 2021, government compensated the Ulevun Association and returned the Bialla Plantation to the three villages. The village communities saw this as a significant recognition of their ongoing affiliation with ancestral soils, and welcomed the partnership with the Ulevun Association and the government that had made it possible. It further distanced the company in their reckoning. The recovery of Ambusa by the descendants of the original *karakara* lineages restored an area that had been under outsider control for a century. The lineages had never accepted that the German purchase, nor the later transfer of the plantation to the Ulevun Association, negated their affiliation with the soils. They were not for sale.

The airport between Uase and Matililiu became another alienated tract of soil over which Maututu asserted their rights. The airstrip was created originally by the Nakanai Council to coincide with the opening of the council headquarters in 1968. From 1973, commercial flights from Hoskins and Rabaul provided weekly services. Initially, the council maintained the airstrip by requiring village workers on Mondays, the council workday, to cut the grass with sarib knives. However, council maintenance deteriorated in the 1980s and the weekly service was discontinued, replaced in part by regular bus services between Bialla and Kimbe when the road was constructed. HOPL took over maintenance of the airstrip, using a tractor to mow the grass.[11] The airstrip allowed the Department of Education to fly in schoolbooks once or twice a year and HOPL executives and managers to charter flights to Bialla. Eventually even HOPL stopped their maintenance of the strip and reverted to driving to the Hoskins airport. This led, in 2008, to Uase and Matililiu villagers seeking to reclaim the airstrip soil and convert it to cultivation. They placed obstacles on the airstrip to insist on its closure and demanded that the land be returned to them. Faced with growing shortage of soil on which to garden, villagers activated their claims to ancestral affiliation with an area that the Nakanai Council and then LLG had long controlled. At the time of writing, the claim had not been resolved.

Conclusion

The last four chapters have examined the establishment of the oil palm industry on Maututu soils and the impact that industry had on village communities. Logging, then oil palm, like the forest *buata* of the myths, threatened Maututu ways of life, confining communities to their isolated hamlets. Maututu challenged these restrictions, electing to take up settler blocks and then planting VOP blocks. They explored relations with incoming settlers, even extending to marriage and the loan of soil for gardens. A few families were able to send their children through high school and then onto tertiary education. Throughout these decades they continued to assume the essential terms of their existence, based in dividualism through exchange networks, lineage and kin affiliations, distinct language and rites of passage, *karakara* communities, and ancestral affiliations to forest and marine resources, especially soil and fishing grounds.

Most Maututu have benefited from oil palm income. Improved homes in permanent materials, cars and trucks for transportation, specialist items such as football boots and sporting clothes, mobile phones, and greater mobility by mini-bus to Kimbe and by plane further afield. Some have achieved esteemed positions in the outside world, as lawyers, teachers, administrators, etc. Some of these benefits would no doubt have emerged without oil palm but oil palm blocks have provided the means for those resident in the village to access larger amounts of cash. Locally owned sawmills process timber for the improvement of village houses and village churches have been rebuilt in

---

11   In 2002, Mount Pago in Hoskins erupted, closing the Hoskins airport, and Ewasse became essential for air travel into West New Britain, with daily commercial flights to Rabaul for two months.

permanent materials. Lineage groups have sustained commercial enterprises in which they express pride. In these respects, the Maututu 'home' has been strengthened through its engagement with outside forces.

However, Maututu existence has remained perilous in the face of an unresponsive company and an expanding settler population. The LLG presidency passed to an outsider. Maututu children struggled to compete against settler children in winning places to senior high school and, from there, to tertiary education and training. Some Maututu, more comfortable in their dealings with outsiders, were tempted into becoming 'big shots' rather than 'big men'. Overshadowing all this was the shrinking of the Maututu domain as outsiders occupied surrounding soil and forest areas receded. More radical responses, partnerships with outside forces, such as those with Nivani or the Ulevun Association, were required if Maututu were to retain their 'sense of being' in this rapidly changing world.

8

Spirit partnerships in industrial times

The preceding chapters have explored the ontological frictions that colonialism and industrialisation brought to the Maututu world. These were reflected in distinct ways of viewing soil/land, clans and lineages, hamlet and village membership, resource investment, enterprise management and consultation practices. Such ontological frictions were also experienced in Maututu spiritual relations as they accommodated to the changes brought about by missionisation and industrialisation.

De la Cadena (2010, pp. 334–35), in discussing indigenous cosmopolitics in the Andes, cites a letter written to Pope Benedict XVI in 2007 by Humberto Cholango, an indigenous leader in Ecuador, in which he says 'our religions NEVER DIED, we learned how to merge our beliefs and symbols with the ones of the invaders and oppressors'. De la Cadena (2010, pp. 334–35) suggests that this:

> letter changes the problem by lifting religious practices from an exclusive concern with the sacred or spiritual, and placing them within historical, earthly, and political concerns of cohabitation between Catholic and non-Catholic, indigenous and nonindigenous institutions.

Western ontologies have increasingly positioned the spiritual as distinct from the material, enabling a discussion of religious beliefs and practices as though they occupy a delimited space of social being. The consolidation of Christianity in Papua New Guinea (PNG) only furthered such a view by designating a particular building as the church and Sunday as the 'holy' day, complete with congregations sitting in neat rows in their best dress, following holy books written in an outsiders' language, singing a distinct set of songs, listening to sermons, then retiring to a Sunday meal, and refraining from work in the gardens for the day. These were all at odds with 'tribal' ways of dealing with the spirit world. This chapter explores what kind of ontological transformation these practices initiated, and to what extent industrialisation furthered such transformations.

Early church and *la masori*

As described in a previous chapter, Maututu tell of their ancestors bringing powerful books back from their visit to the Gazelle and then inviting missionaries from the outside to introduce Methodist ways to the hamlet populations. The resultant 'church', both as a physical structure and congregation, played a key role in the colonial administration's program of aggregating scattered hamlets into villages. The Christian message of peace spoke out against earlier patterns of *la gata* (spear) and helped to ensure that hamlet populations settled peacefully together under *luluai* and *tultul*. The Methodist pastors ran the early village schools. I attended the village Methodist Church with all my neighbours in 1968–75.[1] The bush materials church had rough hewn logs and lengths of bamboo for seats and a slightly raised platform and pulpit at the front for the preacher. Its palm thatch half-walls allowed cool breezes and, occasionally, rain to blow through. Each Sunday, adults and children in their very best clothes gathered in the building, children at the front, adult women behind them on the left and men on the right. We sang hymns in the Kuanua language of the Duke of York Islands and listened to a sermon from mostly local pastors in Maututu language. Garden work, hunting and fishing on the Sunday were discouraged and Maututu instead spent the day relaxing in the hamlet. Barely two decades since the disruptions of the Pacific War, Maututu had settled in centralised villages decreed by the colonial administration, and enthusiastically adopted the patterns of behaviour espoused by the mission church and the colonial administration (Figure 8.1).

---

1   In 1968, the Methodist Church in PNG merged with the Papua Eklesia (formerly London Missionary Society) and the Kwato Mission to form the United Church, but this had very little impact at the time on the way villagers conducted their church life.

Figure 8.1: Tauvere, Koma and children dressed for church, 1969
Source: Author.

The myth-teller Boia, in discussions with me, made a distinction between the *la masori* (darkness), in which he located the traditional stories he told, and *la matagaga* (bright and clear) of more recent knowledge gained through schooling and Christianity. For him, this distinction was not between bad and good, backward and civilised, but between the world of the ancestors and the contemporary world. The ancestors themselves, as ancestral spirits, were located in the dark forest, and recognising their presence through the accurate telling of their stories was seen by Boia as essential to contemporary wellbeing. Paige West (2016, p. 126) suggests that narratives (she is writing of the Gimi people of PNG) craft:

> both ontology, or a set of propositions about what is in the world, and epistemology, as the story is then used … to understand what is happening in the present. A tale some might have discounted as 'myth' is actually a clear set of propositions that help people understand and be in the worlds they create and in the worlds that they are cast into with outside interventions of all kinds.

The analysis that follows in this chapter suggests that *la masori* and *la matagaga* are distinct 'worldings' that are interlocked, sliding in and out of each other. As LiPuma (2001, pp. 5–6) suggests of the Maring of the Bismarck Mountains, PNG, '[their] conception of Jesus, his miracles, and his place in the social cosmology has been inseparable from Maring conceptions of ancestors, magic and clansmen'. Maututu worldings are articulations between 'wild' and 'home', of both the 'dark' and the 'light' spaces, and inseparable from the influence of colonialism, Methodism, nationalism, commerce and industrialisation.

In their discussion with me in 1968, Maututu also referred to *la masori* as the 'time of the spear', marked by inter- and intra-hamlet fighting. They were glad to have found 'the light' (*la matagaga*) when they joined the Methodist Church. The mission pastors taught the adult population to read and write in Kuanua.[2] The pastors preached about the Christian God and his son Jesus. In their language, Maututu referred to God as *La Suara* or *La Taua* or by the Fijian term *La Kalou* (this last term the one used in the Kuanua Bible).[3] *La Suara* recognised the Christian God's power and authority, as held by the Maututu big man (*suara*). In contrast, *La Taua* indicated the Christian God's affiliation with all the *taua* (spirits) of the forest—*la masori* (the dark wild place) that remained a vivid part of local worlding. One night in 1973 I was asked by the hamlet leader to ride my motor bike with lights blazing out beyond the hamlet boundary into the overgrown gardens in order to chase away some dangerous agents (spirits, sorcerers, outsiders) that he sensed were threatening the hamlet. As Strathern (1980) remarked of the Hagen spirit world, danger lay in this uncontrolled, unpredictable and unregulated space, but it was in this 'dark' space that Maututu looked for creative partnerships.

Shame and confession in the early church

In contrast to Maututu understandings of unpredictable encounters with forest spirits, the Methodist teachings were explicit about the requirements of human behaviour in engaging with the Christian spirits. Sunday practices were only a part of this. In addition there was teaching about 'sin' as personal behaviour that displeased *La Kalou*. The missionary teaching was that the individual sinned when he/she disobeyed God's command. The Maututu used the term *la iruru* as their translation of this Christian

---

2   These pastors received two years of training at theological schools in Rabaul. It was not until the 1980s that local pastors were invited to undertake a further three years of training to graduate as *talatala* (ministers) themselves.

3   As described in an earlier chapter, *suara* was the holder of a wristband of immense spirit power. The last man to hold the *suara* in the Maututu area died in 1946.

teaching, meaning 'go astray' or 'get lost' as a man might experience in the forest when he became vulnerable to wild spirits. This local view focused on the 'dividual' cut off from home, while the church view focused on the 'individual' being cut off from God, inciting divine anger and potentially misfortune, illness or death that, in *la masori*, were attributed to sorcery or wild spirits.

As such, *la iruru* was particularly perceived as behaviour that affected community and kin relations. When, in June 1969, Kukuva died in Baikakea, his death did not attract the usual outpouring of community grief. Kukuva was widely known to steal things, such as money, betel nut, tobacco and food, and his death was accepted as deserved because he did not respect others in the hamlet. 'God killed him for stealing', one person told me. In *la masori*, stealing betel nut from another could result in illness due to the protective spell the owner had placed on their palm or their basket where they kept their betel nut, and only admission of guilt and a plea for mercy from the owner could remove the spell on the thief. But Kukuva was never one to admit his guilt. Men and women foretold his death, even Kukuva was said to have foretold his own death, and, on the day of his death, neighbours and kin did not show him the normal respect due to the deceased, continuing to go to the gardens and to the sea, failing to offer the requisite gift of cloth as a final mortuary present, and declining to wail. People joked about his death, with no evident fear of the wandering spirit. His death was God's just punishment.

Another resident, Vuloloa, allegedly used sorcery to kill a married woman who rejected his sexual advances. Pastors and missionaries spent much energy condemning sexual promiscuity as a 'sin', so Vuloloa was publicly condemned for both his initial demand on the woman and his subsequent sorcery. After the woman's death, her son-in-law, who was described as a 'very good man', read aloud from the Bible and called out the name of the sorcerised woman, and, as a consequence, I was told, Vuloloa became sick and died.[4] He had called down God's judgement on the ungodly. The Christian God was said by Methodist pastors to punish wrongdoing, even down the generations, the greatest 'sin' being adultery by either man or woman. But, just as in the case of sorcery spells in *la masori*, in *la matagaga* sickness as the consequence of sin could be healed if the person confessed their sin to God. In these situations the pastors became the main channels

---

4   I did not record which verses were read.

of God's powers. In 1969, I was told that many went to church because of their fear of what the pastor might do to those who did not attend. He was an agent of the powers of the Christian spirit.

But in regard to adultery, church teachings were at odds with local moral understandings. Sexual promiscuity was commonly vaunted by Maututu men and women in the 1960–70s as an expression of their vitality. Such sexual liaisons commonly occurred on the margins of the gardens, at the meeting point of domestic and wild zones. Many of the myths told of such meetings between the hero of wild origins and a woman of the village open to new experiences from the wild. In the 1980s, Ann Chowning (1989, p. 27) observed that the missionary teachings of both Catholic and Methodist churches at Hoskins had not been successful:

> in their attempts to influence extramarital sexual behaviour. Some men insisted to us that God would not have created sex and then forbidden people to enjoy it. The missionaries could and did, however, forbid public activities that led to sexual license [such as the *vakakuala*].[5]

Likewise, Maututu had to deal with the tension that there were behaviours disapproved in formal church teachings that were quite acceptable in village affairs. Community meetings regularly raised the cases of married men or women who were in extra marital affairs, seeing these as injurious to the betrayed marriage partners. But there was no attention paid to youth who were enjoying pre-marital sex, although elders would pressure the couple to set up home together in the event of pregnancy. Maututu myths clearly extolled the beneficial outcome of 'wild' liaisons, as the new partnership brought benefits to the community.

In the village meetings that focused on immoral behaviour, defined by either church teachings or community norms, the accused's misbehaviour was already public knowledge so that the finding of guilt was not the principal goal of the discussion. The public discussion focused on the fine to be paid to the injured person, an exchange between the 'guilty' and offended parties that brought peace to the community. However, in church teachings, it became important for the sinner to publicly confess guilt and thus restore relations with God. A striking event of the church calendar was the service held on New Year's Eve when members of the congregation confessed 'sins' of the previous year. During the service, almost all adult congregants, men

---

5   Described in Chapter 1.

and women, and some older children one by one walked to the front of the church and publicly confessed their sins of the year. These might be relatively harmless to others, such as angry or hostile thoughts, but many would confess to outbursts of anger, particularly towards their spouse, stealing another's betel nuts, spreading gossip against their neighbour, even seducing another's husband or wife, or practising sorcery. In many of these cases, village justice had already been pronounced by the elders. As far as I could ascertain at the time, the confessions did not surprise anyone nor stir any further discussion of the behaviour. Rather, they seemed to relieve the confessor of shame and to clean the village of sin and immorality—that is, of 'wild' behaviour—before they welcomed the New Year. But such behaviour was also prone to arrogance. I attended another confession service held on a Sunday afternoon in May 1969 when, after 10 men and women 'confessed', a young man remarked to me that 'most of it was talk. They never change their behaviour but bask in their holy words.'

His remarks reflected Maututu recognition of two key personality types demonstrated most strikingly in myth in the personalities of Wallaby and Orphan Dog. Arrogant boasting was seen as behaviour that eventually drew community rejection. Shame, in both its indigenous understandings of social isolation (as of the Orphan Dog sitting in the ashes) and its Christian teachings of separation from God, was seen as a condition engendering physical, social and spiritual death. The understandings of both *la masori* and *la matagaga* were that it could be healed through community rehabilitation in partnership with ancestral spirits or the Christian God. The New Year's Eve service provided an opportunity for both the arrogant and the shamed to seek community reinstatement.

Robbins's (2004) account of Christianity among the Urapmin of the Mountain Ok region in the PNG Highlands—a group who only adopted Christianity in the 1970s—identified confession as a distinctly exogenous element that fostered Western notions of individuality as distinct from the local focus on 'dividuality'. Robbins claimed that the paramount innovation brought from the outside with Christianity was the emphasis on the 'individual' as sinner, a state of shame from which he or she found escape impossible. In the initial period of Christianisation among the Urapmin, public confession of sin triggered suicidal behaviour out of shame for what had been said in the confession. Eventually, to avoid such public shaming, the church instituted a highly ritualistic institution of confession whereby each person met privately with the pastor or deacon each month to confess their sins, such confessions never divulged by the pastor to the rest of the community. Robbins (2004, p. 3) concluded that the Christianity practised by the Urapmin was an innovation rather than transformation:

> That is to say, change in Urapmin was not a matter, as so much contemporary anthropology expects, of a traditional culture assimilating a new one and constructing in the process a hybrid entity that is either still largely traditional or else different from both of its starting points. It was, instead, a case in which people seemed to grasp a new culture whole.

In his account of the Urapmin conversion, Robbins (2005, p. 47) drew attention to the power of humiliation in instigating a rejection of traditionally oriented structures by those courting the dream of 'develop-man', adding that: 'once people have reified their culture it is but a short step for them to begin making conscious efforts to discard it and replace it with something new'.[6]

However, Rumsey (2004) indicated that among the Urapmin, as more generally in Melanesia, there were traditional practices of confessing acts of wilfulness when they were seen as immoral behaviour. Rumsey (2008, p. 464) later suggested that the majority of Urapmin confessions were 'to do with feelings of anger against other Urapmin', and, to this extent, their Christian confessions were transformations of pre-Christian community norms rather than a whole new culture, as Robbins contended. Rumsey (2008, p. 467) concluded that there was 'a great potential for practices of confession to serve as points of articulation between endogenous and exogenous socio-cultural orders and forms of personhood'. His argument was not just that the new Christian practices bore marked continuity with traditional practices (even as Urapmin may emphasise their novelty), but that it was misleading to represent the old and the new as distinctive standalone 'cultures'. 'Urapmin may be seen as having already been hybrid long before Christianity came on the scene' (Rumsey, 2004, p. 591). As an alternative to this, Mere Roberts (2013, p. 112), in her work among Māori, proposes the possibility of multiple ontologies, in which the *whakapapa* 'way of seeing and understanding the world is open to change and interpretation according to the narrator's experience, knowledge and/or circumstances'.

---

6   The term 'develop-man' describes a traditional construction of progress:
     To 'modernize' the people must first learn to hate what they already have, what they have always considered their well-being. Beyond that they have to despise what they are, to hold their own existence in contempt—and want, then, to be someone else.
                                                                              (Sahlins, 2005, p. 38)

As Christians, the Maututu did not hide away their 'wild' behaviours, as the Urapmin may have done, but brought them into the public discourse through village meetings and then confessed them at the annual church service. The sin was dealt with only by restoring the relational 'dividual' through the public exposure of *la iruru*. In this way, the endogenous focus on the risk that extreme acts of anger or shame brought to the community was extended to the person's relationship with God. Anger towards another, causing harm through stealing or swearing, disrespecting others through immoral sexual activity—these were all added to the list of 'wild' behaviour that separated the person from the community and from God. Through confession at village meetings, the unpredictable danger lurking outside the community and threatening both human and spiritual relationships was dealt with. In *la masori* if a sorcerer was identified through a séance following an unexpected death he was asked to confess (but rarely did). In *la matagaga* he could confess at the annual service, and often did, promising that his wayward behaviour was at an end. But Maututu rarely accepted such promises of sorcerer reform, noting that his solitary and surly behaviour indicated an inclination to sorcery. Although sorcery was addressed through Christian confession, its wildness remained a danger to the community.

The threat posed by the wild, central to the ontology of *la masori*, became central also in the Methodist ontology of *la matagaga*. Epistemologically similar behaviours were noted in both as *la iruru* (lost, sinful) with their potential to disrupt relationships within the community and with the spirits, including *La Taua*. The pastor, like the big man and the healer, became a spirit medium in restoring community through the public exposure of damaged relationships.

Initial impact of industrialisation on relations with the spirit world

Industrialisation put new pressure on the expression of 'dividual' within relationships. The pressure for individualisation in economic enterprises threatened communal priorities that included church and spirit relations. I have little information on church life through the 1980s, but some accounts suggest that the authority of the church was shaken. One woman recalled returning from George Brown High School in the school holidays in the early 1980s to find the local church moribund. The congregations, she recalled, would dust off the Bible and hymn books for the Sunday service and sing 'stale' hymns, and for the rest of the week 'forget about God'. Another account suggested that the arrival of the oil palm introduced a population who were not attending church and seemingly showing no interest in the Christian God. These outsiders threatened to draw villagers away from home community, including church practices. As they drifted away from the 'law of the church', according to a *kansil* at that time, locals were losing the ability to discriminate between good and evil and, as a consequence, lived increasingly sinful lives, stealing, swearing, lying, getting drunk, talking loosely and indulging in casual sex. Paul Koasiro, who was an ordained minister (*talatala*) through the 1980s, recalled that local communal and spiritual awareness declined and people drifted away from Christian principles. According to him, Maututu villagers became 'long mouth' Christians—churchgoers but not 'alive' as believers. A key characteristic of this period, as several reported to me, was a moral backsliding, when people ignored the spirits of both *la matagaga* and *la masori*. As a consequence, the New Year's Eve confession lapsed and the standing of pastors and church elders diminished. Jebens (2000, p. 185) recorded that, in the Bileki Nakanai village of Koimumu in the 1990s, people deplored the loss of traditional culture. They asserted that the resulting transgression of customary laws was responsible not only for physical deterioration of the environment and loss of fertility in the gardens. 'Big Men are no longer respected and parents no longer obeyed, which reputedly has led not only to an increase of individualism, jealousy, and egotism but also to a general loss of shame' (Jebens, 2000, p. 185). The aggressive intrusion of the outside threatened to undermine village and church ways of being.

The Christian revival

The Christian revival of 1995 took place as the oil palm industry in the area was expanding rapidly. Many Maututu by this stage had established oil palm blocks and were enjoying regular, though not high, incomes. The company was contemplating the replanting of the original palms within the nuclear estate, and many settlers had paid off their initial debts and were able to spend more, a situation very visible to Maututu in the town where settlers and villagers shopped. However, these livelihood improvements were not yet enjoyed by village oil palm (VOP) smallholders who had planted later than the settlers.

Paul Koasiro became a pioneer of the revival among Maututu. He was convinced that moral and communal renewal lay in the revival of their engagement with the Christian God. A member of Bubuu village, he had become a pastor in 1970 and from 1973 to 1976 attended theological colleges at Keravat and Raronga on the Gazelle Peninsula. In 1976, he was invited to Australia, where, in both Sydney and Melbourne, he encountered mid-week fellowship groups who were 'experiencing the Holy Spirit'. On his return he was posted as pastor to Mendi villages in the Southern Highlands when they were experiencing the 'revival'. Later, after ordination in 1982, he served in Uase village where he recalled that churchgoers were not expectant of a 'revival' of the Holy Spirit. In 1994, he raised K35,000 from villagers to complete the church building in Bubuu as a way to inspire renewal, even gaining the help of the Sacred Heart Catholic priest at Ulamona who provided carpenters and transport.

Koasiro wanted to bring the industrial transformations in the area into dialogue with spiritual realities, as the transformations associated with cash cropping or tertiary education or formal sector employment were, in his view, not sufficient in themselves if not accompanied by a resurgence in Maututu identity and spirituality. In 1995, Koasiro was *talatala* (ordained minister) among the Baining people in Totovel village in the north-west hinterland of the Gazelle Peninsular.[7] He brought what he had experienced of the revival in Australia and the Mendi Highlands to this remote parish.[8] He then invited the youth of Bubuu and Baikakea to visit his church community. Living conditions there were so poor that he needed to ask the local council for the delivery of a tank of water for the visitors' needs. He recounted that these Maututu youth were only nominal Christians. At the time, he was praying that God would *lapu la valua* (pull the people) —that is, offer them a relationship. He challenged his visitors: 'Have you seen Jesus?' The revival that he envisaged clearly focused on a partnership with the spirit Jesus and the Holy Spirit, an intimacy that contrasted with the 'stale' church worship of the time.[9]

---

7   Eves (1998) links the 'revival' among the Lelet United Church in New Ireland with an evangelistic 'crusade' in Rabaul, East New Britain, in 1972 conducted by the Billy Graham crusade, but suggests that the Pentecostal impetus was much more recent.

8   One account traces the revival to the village of Lumi in Sandaun Province in 1982. Baining people were mountain people of the Gazelle Peninsular, often portrayed as unsophisticated compared to their immediate neighbours, the Tolai.

9   Maututu used two terms for the Holy Spirit, using the term *kalulu* (ancestral spirit): *Kalulula Maroka* (clean/smooth spirit) and *Kalulula Maroto* (partner spirit).

As the Maututu visitors and their hosts worshipped together in Totovel, the Maututu youth were 'slain in the Spirit', falling to the floor, prophesying and shaking violently. Some experienced healing, and 'poison men' among them 'submitted to God's will'—they confessed *la iruru*. The visitors spent several days in study and prayer, with a growing confidence in their 'rebirth' as 'new beings'. But it also gave rise to some anxiety among them about how they would be welcomed back in their home villages. Koasiro prophesied that they would be met at the wharf in Bialla by their village pastor and a group of the village congregation. He was right. They arrived home at the Bialla wharf to a waiting group of pastors and leading women and men of the Apupul circuit, and soon after were able to start Bible study groups in home villages.[10] This, like the initial coming of Methodism, was described as a power-filled transformation of village life. The 'wildness' of the Holy Spirit became incorporated as a partner (*maroto*), bringing a transformation of the community, a reawakening of *la matagaga*.

The revival began in Bubuu and Baikakea, and then was preached by the youth and their pastors to other villages of Apupulu, Gomu and Uase. Only Matililiu villagers stood firm in their older forms of church service, rejecting the guitar music and 'coming of the Holy Spirit'. The revival became marked by fiery sermons, long periods of congregational prayer, enthusiastic singing led by string bands with new songs in Maututu language and Tok Pisin, and acclaimed healings and prophesies. It was this that I encountered on my return to Maututu in 2008 and in subsequent years.

Extract from field journal

> *On December 14 2008 the parishioners of the Apupul United Church circuit gathered in Apupulu for a significant service bringing together the congregations of four village churches. The service exhibited a strong sense of the authority of church leaders under the circuit talatala and his wife. Leaders and pastors from the several village church congregations were called forward to testify about God's plan for their life, and the talatala then called forward one of the village pastors who had been stood down in the past year because of immorality—his sin (la iruru) being illicit sexual relations with a parishioner. After he had publicly apologized to the circuit for his sin, the Reverend and other pastors stood around him and prayed for him.*

---

10 The United Church combined village church congregations and pastors within a circuit under an ordained minister, the *talatala* (reverend). The Apupulu circuit consisted of Gomu, Apupulu, Baikakea and Bubuu villages.

After a few hymns, the Reverend preached from John 15: I am the vine
and you are the branches. Branches that do not provide fruit, of love,
joy, peace, kindness, faithfulness, will be cut away and burned by the
vine-grower God, while those who live in Christ will produce much
fruit. *Pointing assertively and with a loud shout to himself and the
congregation he declared that they all were guilty of not producing fruit.
Again and again he repeated this same point. As he continued to preach,
the congregation, led by his wife, broke into hymns until the volume of
their singing drowned out his sermon. But the Reverend continued to
berate the congregation with raised voice and pointing finger, seemingly
unconcerned that they could no longer distinguish his words.*

*During this performance, a woman from Bubuu walked to the front
of the gathering just near the preacher and with arms held high began
to shake powerfully. She stood for some time shaking like this and
then began to move about the congregation, embracing some men and
women and pushing some to the front with a TSK-TSK sound. One
young man from her own village whom she pushed forward also shook
strongly and began shouting the name of 'Jesus'.*[11] *Others came forward
less demonstratively, some to turn to the congregation and quietly and
inaudibly (the congregation were singing loudly) confess their sins before
turning to face the preacher in a long line while he continued to preach.
He finally concluded the sermon and stood in turn before each penitent,
holding their hand and praying over them before they each returned to
their seat. As one of the pastors closed the service with prayer, many of the
congregation spoke aloud their personal prayers, in a cacophony of voices.*

Revival-style services incited strong emotions. In one Sunday service
I attended in 2013, the singing of revival hymns was accompanied by
clapping and spontaneous dancing, with hands raised in praise to God.
The sermon delivered by a lay preacher focused on the faithfulness of
Daniel whose habit of praying three times a day to the Jewish God rather
than worshipping the Babylonian king resulted in him being thrown into
the lions' den where he was protected by angels. As the preacher continued
to expound on this story, women came spontaneously to the front to
add messages of instruction and prophesy, and men shouted out their
confirmation of the message. Men, including former and current pastors,
were in tears, and there were seemingly waves of emotion that greeted

---

11 Valentine (1965, p. 187) records that a Nakanai medium communicating with the god Sumua
would tremble as he relayed the words of the god. These direct communications with the god ceased
after the Pago volcano became dormant around 1918. Valentine suspects that Sumua became known
among Lakalai either as a result of these eruptions or due to Christian teachings about God. I heard of
no similar god or medium among the Maututu.

these spontaneous verbal expressions. Tears are not a common occurrence in Maututu life, but sermons and the confessions that often accompanied them regularly led to tears, spontaneous song and prayer.[12] The hymns engaged the whole congregation, children and adults, relieving sleepiness and confirming community. The revival worship focused on joy rather than remorse, acknowledging the power of the Holy Spirit. They became key events in rebuilding community.

In addition to the Sunday village service, residents of each hamlet met at other times of the week in a hamlet home or the open space of the hamlet to sing and hear teaching from the Bible. Prayer meetings were a key innovation of the revival held three times a week at sunset in the church building. Though all villagers were encouraged to attend, it was generally the leaders of the revival who participated. The meetings began with one or two songs before the song leader, a lay member of the church, started the prayer. As his or her prayer continued, the rest of the group began their prayers, each praying aloud. For all of them, their prayers were between them and God, audible to others around them but not intended for their hearing. Eventually, after 30 or so minutes, their voices quietened and the leader brought the session to a conclusion. According to one sermon, at such a gathering, prayer releases the power of the Holy Spirit among the community of 'prayer warriors'.[13] They declared that as they put their trust in prayer to the Christian God 'people's eyes have been opened'.

With this renewed confidence in spirit partnership, revivalists felt empowered to take their message to outside peoples. Those from Baikakea and Bubuu began holding street meetings in Bialla town and in settler communities. Baikakea formed a 'singing ministry' whose recordings of songs in Pidgin and Maututu languages became popular throughout PNG. They also built a mission team among the youth who travelled to other Maututu villages to sing and preach and heal. Villagers were adamant about the dramatic impact of the revival, seen at its strongest in Baikakea and Bubuu. As a close friend from the 1970s who became a pastor said to me:

> When you were here before the church was not alive, people did not
> understand Christianity, it was not strong. Now it is strong, people
> have stopped drinking, smoking and chewing betel due to church
> teachings. Forest spirits no longer trouble people as they did in the

---

12 On the death of a neighbour, stylised wailing is part of public response, and men may be reduced to tears when drunk.

13 They used the English term, which occurred in literature they had read from the US.

1970s. Today we hold 'prayer warrior' meetings where we pray for physical healing, marriages and travel. From Baikakea we go to other villages, because we are strong and they do not yet follow the new teachings of the church. Baikakea Christians have revelations, they prophesy and speak in tongues.

Among the Maututu, the adopted term 'prayer warrior' endorsed their understanding of a bold pioneer engaging with spiritual powers to enliven and empower the home community. In December 2008, the Baikakea community sent off a young family as pastors to a church in Mendi, Southern Highlands, with a spontaneous collection of A$359, crockery and clothes. The same week they sent a mission team to Vilelo settlers for a one-week crusade and were preparing to send another team to Matililiu to support the church there.

One of the recorded songs of the Baikakea band demonstrated the new focus of the revival. Jesus is referred to by the Maututu term *La (A)uru* (The Mighty). They sang:

Iesu taku eme, la Uru tegaku	Jesus you are mine, my Mighty One
Eau ge igo mave eau ge tilimuli eme	What can I do but follow you
Eau pou te la kilisi	I remain in prison
Eme ge eme ge gomai	Come to me, come
Gomai taku me abiagu la mahulila	Come and give me the life

The song's message in their own language expressed an intimacy with Jesus, where He is 'mine' and 'I follow' Him. As the 'Mighty One', Jesus will deliver from bondage, using the Tok Pisin word *kilisi* for the police cell, referring to an outside and unpredictable justice system. Jesus will restore to kin and village. This is 'life', at other times referred to as *pigo halaba* (fresh birth) or *sibitala halaba* (fresh appearance).[14] Being in the Maututu language and yet available through cassette recordings to the rest of PNG, the song also expresses Maututu pride in their own spirit-linked revival. Baikakea preacher Mesaki expressed this intimacy with God in a 2014 sermon based on Revelation Chapter 7. The 'touch of God' prepares us as we communicate with Him through reading the Bible and prayer. 'Listen for his direction, feel his touch. Be led everyday by his Holy Spirit, be filled with His knowledge and wisdom, His love, power and strength.' Mesaki concluded: 'Do not be anxious but rather ensure communication with God does not break down.'

---

14   One preacher in 2008 pointed to 2 Corinthians 5:17: 'If anyone is in Christ he is a new creation'.

At a community worship one evening under the village mango tree, the preacher Tegia spoke on prayer. The spirit of God, he said, guided prayer such that the prayer can channel the will and understanding of God. Thus, we should live in prayer, praying from morning to night, as that would be living in relationship with God. He portrayed prayer as an exchange with God through God's spirit. Worshippers responded with spontaneous prayer acknowledging their intimacy with God, crying out to *Jesu Karisto, Papa God, e Uma* (Father), and *La Uru* (the Mighty One). This intimacy with the Christian spirits had been absent from the 1968–75 church gatherings I had experienced. They reminded me of the partnerships with spirits that were central to many Maututu myths and formed the power of the *suara*, *valipoi* and healers of *la masori*.

Shame and confession in the revival church

The revival focused on 'sin' less as a moral failure than as a breakdown of a spiritual relationship. Men's drunken and violent behaviour was due to their neglect of the 'Holy Spirit'. Although most dedicated revivalists continued to regard the world around them, and particularly the jungle surrounds, as inhabited by a range of spirits, some of them dangerous and evil, they dismissed the ultimate power of *buata* and *savei*, or of ginger spells and sacred stones. The threat of the spirit world, for revivalists, persisted in the figure of Satan. One church elder told the story of a school in Rabaul where Satan so ruled that boys were beating up girls for even talking to anyone outside their grade. The chaplain spent several days praying about this before he addressed the school assembly. As he did, the whole assembly was 'slain in the Spirit' and fell to the floor. The chaplain then spent several assemblies guiding the school in correct spiritual practices. One outcome was that the girls were able to pursue their studies freely without restriction.

'Sin' thus demonstrated that Satan had taken control, destroying the dividual's relationship with the Holy Spirit. In the revival, confessions that had once been an annual event became a weekly feature of the Sunday service. As the sermon proceeded, a handful of congregants walked to the front to confess their sins and receive absolution from the preacher. It made no difference whether the preacher was the *talatala*, the village pastor or any one of the lay preachers, men or women. Because the confessions of those who walked to the front were rarely audible over the noise of sermon and spontaneous singing, they were a display of personal contrition directed to God. But, to the community, the dividual signalled their desire to restore social relations damaged by *la iruru*. Thus, the shame that in Maututu myths drove the Orphan to withdraw from community relations was transformed in the weekly confessions of the revival into a public confession intent on rebuilding relationships with God and with the home community.

New burial practices and the ever-presence of spirit worlds

The revival took away the fear of ancestral spirits, transforming burial practices. In 1969, Maututu informed me that when a person died their spirit wandered around the hamlet before departing to the sacred site (*la olu*) of the clan, then on to the bright blue *raunwara* (lake) of Sova near the Barema River, in whose waters each clan or lineage has a separate hamlet where they keep their pigs and gardens. In the 1960s, the dead were buried in graveyards at a distance from the settlement, partly out of concern that the ghost of the newly dead might, in its wandering, disturb the living.[15] In contrast, under the revival Maututu farmed over the graveyards of *la masori* and no longer performed the séances to contact the spirit of the newly dead. The revival church encouraged the burial of the dead next to their family's home or in a gravesite inside the hamlet compound. While in *la masori* the grave remained unmarked and the graveyard eventually reverted to forest, in *la matagaga* villagers sacralised the gravesite. This took the form of a major new ritual some months after the death when distribution of pigs and other foods celebrated the encasing of the new grave in cement and the writing on the cement of the deceased's name and dates of birth and death. In this way the ancestors were no longer distanced from the village as dangerous others, but instead were commemorated by exchange between kin and hamlets.

However, this transformation did not overlook the spirit powers that death unlocked. Even revivalist leaders feared that in the weeks immediately following a death 'strangers' could dig up the grave and rob the vital substances of the corpse to use in sorcery. In one burial that I witnessed, the grave of the *talatala*'s wife, who had been a leader with him in the revival, was barricaded with sheets of corrugated iron to prevent the thieves' entry until the grave could be covered with cement. Facing this threat from

---

15 The distanced location of the graveyard in these years may have been on the urging of mission and colonial authorities concerned about health conditions in the villages. The evidence from myths is that in earlier times the dead may have been buried under the house.

outside sorcerers, the revivalists declared that the power of God's spirit enabled them to host the spirit of their recent dead close to their homes and enjoy their company.

The threat of sorcery was enhanced by the presence of thousands of outsiders in the region. The risks were particularly great when they passed through areas of forest where sorcerers from the settler population could be lurking. Tika and Kau, for example, visited the Samarai area of Milne Bay Province to obtain spirit-water said to provide protection from sorcery. However, they were attacked by sorcerers in the years after they returned. Tika was diagnosed with both bowel cancer and tuberculosis, explained locally as the curse of sorcery. Some blamed his sickness on sorcerers in Apupulu where he had been pastor and where another pastor had contracted cancer of the mouth and died. Kau died from what was diagnosed medically as diabetes, but he attributed his sickness to stepping on lime powder left in his way by a sorcerer.

Outsiders, whether human or spirit, remained a constant threat. A young girl with a speech disability disappeared from Apupulu village for five days in 2014. People suspected that she had been taken by Kol/Arowe people from the mountains, who had been working on VOP blocks. When villagers found her five days later wandering in the oil palm blocks, they diagnosed instead that she had been abducted by *savei* spirits living in a *saiogi* tree by the stream. They burnt away the vines and ferns growing up the trunk of the *saiogi* to drive the *savei* away and assigned revivalist 'prayer warriors' to guard the girl. When Hargy Oil Palm Ltd built its second palm oil mill at Navo by Sova lake, Maututu warned that it was dangerously located adjacent to the spiritual domain. On its completion, a giant spirit snake (*la taua*) took up residence in the rafters of the mill. Its appearance signalled to locals a disturbance of the spirit realm through the neglect of relationships with the spirits. Their anxieties were eventually acknowledged by the company managers who sponsored the Maututu rituals to coax the *taua* snake to leave.

While continuing to acknowledge the spirit world of *la masori*, the revival generated new ways to counter the sorcerers and spirits of the wild domain. In 2013, a healer told me how he had prayed to God for refreshment of his healing powers. One night in his dreams an old man and a child appeared to him at the Tiauru River (where the riverbed has smooth gravel stones) and gave him two tiny stones to use in healing. His spiritually inspired practice used the stones to travel through the victim's body seeking out the *taua* that was causing the sickness and to capture it in a bottle. The victim then dispelled the bottle in their faeces and, as a result, recovered their health. The healer described the stones as live beings with eyes and nose marked on their surface, and tiny charging wires, like an electric current. Another healer referred to these stones as 'children', with the power to steer the healer's travel in dreams, even to distant places like the Sepik River or Port Moresby, in order to discover the cause of illness. This was a practice that emerged in revivalist times, and its origin was attributed to the Christian God. It vividly demonstrates the ongoing entanglement of *la masori* and *la matagaga*.

Industrialisation and the revival

Industrialisation in West New Britain both enabled and drove the revival. For Koasiro, industrial development allowed the revival to flourish through, for example, the financial capacity to purchase overseas books and tapes, and for Christian leaders like himself to travel throughout PNG and even overseas. The United Church circuit under the revival thrived in membership and its finances increased substantially. The annual revenue for the Apupul circuit of the United Church increased from K4,000 to K60,000 over only a few years. Koasiro suggested that oil palm revenues had enabled the financing of 'modern' church buildings in cement, sawn planks and iron roofs. However, he added that the revival was built not just on financial capability but also spiritual experience. An increase in village finances, he said, would only lead to conflicts among individuals, but the revival brought progress based on community values. He was implying here that industrialisation had earlier disrupted communities by encouraging individualism. It was out of this sense of 'being lost' (*la iruru*), that the youth who visited the Baining church recognised the importance of pioneering a new relationship with the spiritual world and with each other. The new connection with the 'Holy Spirit' provided strong community leadership on their return.

The revival also introduced leaders of the village churches to a global phenomenon. Several of those who studied theology in Rabaul or other urban centres brought home the writings and audio tapes of Benny Hinn, a North American Pentecostal televangelist, and the Kenneth Copeland

Ministries.[16] These materials were being disseminated into many corners of the Pacific, including Australia, Indonesia and PNG. In PNG this literature was read by those who were literate in English and formed a text for their contemplative study and prayer. The term 'prayer warrior', for example, was found in the teachings of Benny Hinn, who emphasised faith healing as a battle against the powers of evil and Satan. Benny Hinn preached to huge gatherings in Port Moresby in April 1999, and he inspired many local PNG preachers to take his call for repentance across the country.[17] In Maututu homes, I read copies of *Victory*, the monthly magazine of Texas Eagle Mountains International Church of the Kenneth Copeland Ministries. The images in these magazines, promoted as the rewards for a believer, were of a material 'prosperity' unimaginable in a PNG village.[18] But for the Maututu, it was not material prosperity that fired their enthusiasm. I was never aware of 'prosperity' as the goal of the revival preaching. Instead, they preached the strengthening of a relationship with *La Uru* through the 'Holy Spirit'. The revival was firmly focused on community revival through spiritual partnership.

Industrialisation brought increasing contact with outsiders and, with that, the emergence of alternate Christian teachings. In Maututu villages, the United Church (born out of the 1968 merger of the Methodist Mission and London Missionary Society) had long provided the sole Christian focus.[19] In Uase village, the Christian Revival Crusade (CRC) was established in 1987 by Misiel, a local who completed theological college in Port Moresby and then spent years in the Philippines on 'revival ministry'.[20] He did not limit his role to spiritual revival but included developments in agriculture and sanitation. After establishing the CRC in Uase, he encouraged fellow congregants to donate money to support CRC missions in India. In 2017, for example, they held a fundraising dinner for mission work in India, with

16 Kenneth Copeland Ministries (KCM) is based in Texas and is often associated with the preaching of the 'prosperity gospel'. Kenneth Copeland himself amassed huge wealth through his ministries, which also featured his wife, son and two daughters in key leadership roles. Benny Hinn is identified with a prosperity gospel message and faith healing.

17 The then prime minister, Bill Skate, declared publicly that Jesus Christ was the prime minister of PNG, as he sought Jesus' intervention in national affairs (Bariasi, 2020).

18 Several villagers had joined Kenneth Copeland 'Partners in Blessing' and were using its daily devotions and another study book from the KCM. This literature was also promoted by the Christian Life Movement, based in Apupulu.

19 In the 1970s, only Uase village included an alternative to the United Church, a smaller Catholic Church associated with outsiders working as health clinic nurses, council employees and primary school teachers. The Catholic Church predominated in neighbouring Silanga highland and Meramera peoples.

20 The Uase leader referred to in earlier chapters.

adults charged K20 and youth K10. Unlike the United Church, which used Maututu, Tok Pisin and Kuanua languages in their services, the CRC conducted their services in English, emphasising their familiarity with global movements. Similarly, the Christian Life Church (CLC) in Apupulu used English language. These alternate churches were not built around the village community but brought together a more diverse congregation of both Maututu and settler outsiders marked by their greater access to education, literature and travel, all correlates of industrial-era contact with outsiders.

Such alternate churches could pose a threat to home community. In Baikakea, for example, a Seventh Day Adventist (SDA) Church was established in the 1990s by a single family, one of whose sons had married an outsider SDA member and become a pastor in her church. As the only SDA Church in the Bialla area, they were joined by a few SDA adherents from the settler communities and Bialla town. Their services were conducted on Saturdays in Tok Pisin. They alarmed revival neighbours by viewing *kastom* as the counter to everything a real Christian should be (Jebens, 2010, p. 93). They advocated strongly against tribal healers who still practised in the village; outlawed the eating of pork and red fish, smoking and chewing betel nuit, all central to the home community; and advocated the close reading of the Bible by the individual over the emotional communalism of revival meetings. The father of the SDA family in Baikakea admitted to leaving the United Church when it 'became less Methodist' under the charismatic revival. Christian prayer would only work, SDAs taught, if a believer rejected tribal practices: as a warning, they instanced a key United Church leader who died in the village with a swollen stomach because he had relied on tribal healers.

Revivalists regretted that the SDA Church was engendering division rather than extending Christian love. They understood the revival to include recognition of tribal *kastom*, including the spiritual forces of the 'wild' that marked *la masori*. By recognising *La Uru* and *Kalulula Maroto* as more powerful spirits than those of *la masori*, revivalists recognised a spiritual domain that included *buata, taua* and ancestral beings. Many attested to the power of sorcery and forest spirits even as they affirmed the superior powers of the Christian spirits. Several key Maututu described *la masori* and *la matagaga* as realms existing side by side. In the 'light' of the revival, healing skills were attributed to both the power of the Holy Spirit and the potency of ginger spells. Maututu, they said, lived with one foot in *kastom* and the other in Christianity.

The tension that existed between revival and alternate Christian groups was, for the most part, accommodated within a transforming home environment. Maututu members of the CLC, CRC and SDA took part in events run by the United Church within their home village. In Baikakea, the SDA family members were respected participants in village affairs. The three children of this family had all gained tertiary education and professional employment that kept them away from the village, but they continued to have a strong influence on community affairs. Despite SDA doctrines, they continued to invest in exchange relations between lineages through sponsoring *mage* feasts, including pigs, and encouraging *e rae* dance and song. One of the family, Lydia, a professional social worker, introduced programs into Baikakea to improve the skills and welfare of local women. Home relationships remained critical to them, whether SDA or revival members, even as they were transformed by industrial-era developments.

Conclusion

In 2017, some church leaders suggested to me that the revival had lost momentum. One church elder in Apupulu remarked that people had lost touch with the revival. According to him, their earlier rejection of swearing, jealousy, theft, fighting and gossip was waning. People were turning to *no gut tok* (bad talk) and had lost their faith and their moral values. Increasingly, youth, he said, only had eyes for their mobile phones, were constantly on the move rather than helping their kin, and were influenced by stranger settlers and urban unemployed. Rather than working their own gardens, they relied on store food or stealing from others' gardens. The increased supply of cash through oil palm was seen as enticing youth to alcohol and other store goods and away from spiritual pursuits. They were rejecting the community relationships that formed 'dividuals'. They needed a new revival, he suggested. With such remarks, he was admitting to the continuing disruptions of home society by industrialisation.

His assessment may have been overly gloomy. In 2017, I attended 'fellowship' meetings held on Wednesdays in different hamlets that were well attended by families and youth—about 100 dividuals in total—who participated with fervour in singing and prayer. Revival activities remained strong at the end of 2018. There was a healing ritual in November 2018 at the home of a villager with serious back and stomach complaints. Sixty or so people sat outside his house, where the night before I had witnessed his family conducting prayer.

The next night the pastor's wife preached about the power of God over sickness brought by Satan, including even bringing the dead back to life. This was followed by a session of spontaneous prayer that lasted over half an hour, dominated by women of the community, praising God, prophesying, speaking in tongues, screaming at Satan and drawing down the power of God in the name of Jesus. As everyone prayed at once, the name of 'Jesus' was constantly uttered.

The revival church was centred on the 'power of the Holy Spirit'. Through the building of a partnership with the Christian spirit, other wildness, such as forest spirits, sorcerers and strangers, could be mitigated, and the full enlightenment of *la matagaga* brought into community life. According to Foster (2005, p. 207), the questioning of *kastom* through 'modernization entails for the peoples not only a political, economic, and/or cultural crisis, but also an ontological one'. This is not resolved, he suggested, through 'the outright abandonment or replacement of Tradition', but, rather, through local cultures becoming 'a constitutive part of modern life' (Foster, 2005, p. 208). Gewertz and Errington (2016, p. 376) refer to this as 'ontological bricolage', in which villagers (in their case study, the Chambri of the Sepik area) have a 'grab bag of possibilities', both 'traditional' and 'modern' and find satisfaction in making it work. James et al. (2012, p. 44) wrote of 'walking knowingly in more than one world' in a 'lived reconciliation between ontologically different ways of doing things'. They suggest that the 'extraordinary power' of Pentecostalism in PNG lies in its syncretic synthesis of 'tribal, traditional and modern forms of practice and subjectivity … Contemporary Pentecostalism is a profoundly modern recursion … associated with the dominance of the capitalist production' (James et al., 2012, pp. 44–45). Capitalism, such as is found in the industrial development of oil palm, does not necessarily erase indigenous ways of knowing, seeing, narrating and being.

The Maututu revival strengthened indigenous ways even as it reached out for information and knowledge within the global charismatic church. The revival thus constituted a powerful partnership with the outside world that reinvigorated their communities. Community continued to be the driving focus of church activities, yet in transformed ways. For example, in 2017, the churches of Baikakea and Gomu collaborated in an exchange of food baskets. Each of 129 households in Gomu prepared a basket of food, including fish, chicken and taro, and exchanged it for a K50 donation from their Baikakea partner, the cash going towards the Gomu church fund.

At a later date, Baikakea responded in the same way for their Gomu partners, thus raising substantial funds (K6,450) for the church. Bubuu village at the same time was planning a similar exchange with Matililiu. The scale of these exchanges reflected the strength of community participation under the revival, particularly in the hands of the women, and their openness to new forms of cooperation both within and outside the village. The healing event mentioned above was another vivid demonstration of women's role and authority that had increased in the revival. On that night, it was they who passionately dominated the prayers, bringing the power of the 'wild' into 'home' restoration.

The revival also illustrated a theme central to Maututu mythology and ontology. As industrialisation surged in Bialla, Maututu hamlets became oppressed by the dominant activities of the company and settlers. The church became moribund, increasingly under the gloom of hostile spirits. The revival was marked by a burst of pioneering energy as youthful Maututu sought to engage positively with spirit power. The outcome of this partnership of village and Holy Spirit emboldened communities to take their message of healing, prayer and charismatic worship to distant settlements, even into the industrial centre of Bialla town. Their recordings of songs sung in both Maututu and Tok Pisin were played in churches across PNG, bringing recognition to the village and Maututu in general. Traditional priorities (*la masori*) were not ignored. Congregations emphasised their responsibility for the physical and spiritual welfare of each other and reasserted the centrality of the 'traditional' United Church. At the same time, they sought to modernise the church, not just through the revival but through church structures that would allow greater freedom for the revival. In 2019, Maututu called for greater autonomy for the Nakanai/West New Britain churches by proposing that the assistant bishop, who was at the time a Maututu and located in Hoskins, be made bishop of a new synod of West New Britain. The outside world represented in the various traditions of the United Church in West New Britain was increasingly being seen as part of a home church (Figures 8.2 and 8.3).

Figure 8.2: Men dance *e rae* at ordination of ministers, 2024
Source: Patrick Temi.

Figure 8.3: Women dance *e rae* at ordination of ministers, 2024
Source: Patrick Temi.

9

Restoring the wild as partner

The previous chapter explored the Christian revival that changed the way Maututu communities expressed their 'home' communities and how they related to the spirit world in the expanding world of outsiders. The revival emerged at a time when Maututu were overwhelmed by the industrial developments that had stripped them of soil, regimented their oil palm plantings and attracted thousands of strangers to the formerly quiet outpost of Bialla. The Christian revival was a reassertion of spirit power that enabled Maututu to reshape relationships with the outside.

This chapter examines another industrial-era transformation in Maututu relations with the wild, in this case the forest itself. Maututu view the forest as a resource, but a resource only made beneficial to them through partnership with the beings who inhabit its dark spaces. Their stories portray *buata*, *taua*, frog, spider, birds and the like as beings interacting with humans as kin or partners or enemies. They are wild in their location outside the domestic world of the hamlet, and unpredictable in their interactions with humans, but they are also potential partners. Maututu stories suggest that wild plants and animals 'are endowed with agency, volition and the capacity to form mutual relations within and beyond their own species' (West, 2016, p. 517).

Industrialisation initially marginalised Maututu to 'the shadow of the palms' (Chao, 2022). The vast expanse of oil palms distanced them from the forest realms of the hinterland and, like the industrial companies that had devastated the area, many Maututu began to see the remaining forest and their village domains as a mere capital asset to be exploited. This chapter maps that degeneration and the subsequent revival of respect for the wild.

Negotiating wild waters

As industrialisation boomed, Maututu hamlet residents were isolated further and further from the forest domain. Oil palm stretched from Bialla northward beyond both the Lovo and the Barema rivers to the villages of the Meramera and Gigipuna peoples. To the south, it stretched 100 kilometres to the Hoskins Peninsular and beyond to Kimbe town. Inland, it stretched onto the slopes of the Nakanai Mountains. What remained of ancestral forests was restricted to the soils surrounding the villages on the coastal strip and a mountainous hinterland area above the oil palm where the major rivers formed. The Lovo River, particularly, was sacred in Maututu mythology. The foundation myth told of Kalakala and Koi who emerged from the domestic and wild betel nuts and, in their efforts to free their sister from a violent husband, drowned his village, creating the magnificent lake in the crater of Mount Ivi and the river Lovo that flows from the crater to the sea. The brothers guided this 'flying' river (*lovo*) as it cascaded out of the caldera through a series of waterfalls, finally slowing in coastal swamps before entering the sea.

In 1983, the Lovo River was designated by government as a site for the generation of hydro-electricity, its flow considered strong enough to eventually power both Kimbe and Rabaul towns. Maututu welcomed the prospect of electricity in the village but the proposal raised quite different issues. The lake and the river have great mythic significance, and the wild environment through which the river courses is home to diverse spirits, most importantly ancestral spirits. These negotiations between government, its agency PNG Power and the indigenous people became the catalyst for a reawakening of Maututu consciousness of their foundational relationship with the forest and its 'wild' forces.

In those early discussions with government, the Baikakea community advised that the river and Lamo Auru caldera were affiliated with nine lineages and, because these lineages had been co-resident in the original hamlets of the caldera, they would partner as one coalition in negotiating the hydro development. But the state-owned electricity supplier PNG Power ignored this community advice in their bid to facilitate the development. The agency determined to deal only with the lineage that was affiliated with the soil on which the turbines would be built, the Lolo lineage. Lolo leaders from the villages of Baikakea and Urumaili formed the Kumo Development

Corporation as an incorporated land group (ILG) to negotiate with PNG Power. The sidelining of the other lineages not only fractured the home communities but also invited the ill will of the ancestral spirits.

The agreement consisted of a small annual payment of K10,000 over a 25-year period (1988–2012) to the Lolo lineage, who would then distribute the money as they determined. Many Maututu were mystified that, while PNG Power had millions of kina, the landowners were only being paid K10,000 a year. The contract provided no guarantee of the supply of electricity to Maututu villages and no transparency of how the annual payment would be distributed, if at all, to the wider community of nine lineages. Villagers later claimed to me that only in the first year of the scheme was the lease money distributed to other lineages. After that, the Kumo Development Corporation kept it all within their own lineage, suggesting that the Kumo leaders had chosen to ignore their relationships with others, in the style of 'big shots'.

Many villagers both in Baikakea and neighbouring villages objected to this secrecy between Kumo and PNG Power. John Ilisi, the former LLG chairman and an Urumaili big man, disputed the Lolo claim. The origin of the Lolo lineage, he claimed, was in Tamoru, a hamlet some distance to the north-east of the Lovo River; therefore, any affiliation they had to soil was limited to the north bank of the river. The waters of the Lovo River, he said, could not be claimed by any one lineage, as these waters and those from tributaries of the Lovo pass through many lineage territories. Villagers were particularly incensed that PNG Power had undermined community relations through preferring one or two individual entrepreneurs over the lineage coalition.

Approaching 2012, the agreement came up for renegotiation and the nine lineages again sought to establish their rights to the area. Four lineages claimed primary rights in the Lovo River area where the turbines were situated, with the other five lineages claiming secondary links by affiliation with the wider catchment area. A senior woman from the Uge clan flew to Port Moresby to put their case to PNG Power, but reportedly was ignored as the government agency again chose to negotiate solely with Kumo. However, in January 2013, a Maututu lawyer representing the nine lineages reportedly reached an agreement with PNG Power for payments to a wider group, recognising affiliations not only to the soil but also to the water used to generate the electricity. However, the Kumo directors countered this with a new offer to PNG Power that retained the existing arrangements for an increased payment. The village magistrate who was telling me the story said that PNG Power executives were surprised at the temerity of the Kumo directors in demanding a much-increased share of electricity revenue, but, once again, they preferred to renew the contract with Kumo. In 2014, a new contract was signed that named a much smaller annual lease than that demanded by the directors, and again with no guarantee of electricity to the villages. It made no mention of Maututu demands for the training and employment of village youth. Instead, there was merely an arrangement for village youth to provide security at its hydro site and town offices. But even this did not continue. For months, PNG Power failed to pay the youths' wages or to make roadworthy the PNG Power vehicle assigned to them for such work. The state-owned company had favoured as its business partner the Kumo 'big shots' who, in their greed, were prepared to ignore wider relationships within the lineage coalition and even within the Lolo lineage.

The hydro development grew in significance without any of its benefits flowing to the community. In 2016, aid funds from the New Zealand Government and an A$1.4 million loan from the Asian Development Bank facilitated the installation of 150 kilometres of high voltage line delivering 1.5 megawatts from Lovo to Kimbe town, the capital of West New Britain. The local regional member of parliament, who opened the refurbished hydro plant, suggested that with two further turbines it had a capacity to produce 10 megawatts of power. But there was still no certainty that Maututu villagers would receive electricity, nor offers of employment, nor an improved distribution of financial benefits. Like the logging and oil palm industries, this development marginalised local indigenous interests in the interests of the national economy.

Over three decades, the frustration of dealing with an unresponsive outside agency had alerted the wider Maututu community to the significance of their forest and its wild rivers, both in terms of the development priorities of government and their existence as a people. The wider community saw not only the greed in the Kumo conduct but also the poor financial results from a relationship with outsiders that was disrespectful of Maututu concerns. Emerging from their frustration, however, was the coalition of nine lineages, a modern transformation of lineage cooperation and an enlightened sense of relationship with the forested hinterland that was rich in beings and sites sacred to them.

Lineage respect for forest resources

The Kumo big shots were undeterred by community hostility to their greed. The Kumo Development Corporation also entered into an agreement in 2003 with a Malaysian company, TSL, to log in their lineage estate north of the Barema River.[1] The agreement was made under a Special Agricultural and Business Lease that gave lessees access to all the timber on a block of primary forest on the understanding that such a lease would then be converted to cash crops such as oil palm.[2] The Kumo Corporation was paid an initial premium of K150,000 and earned royalties on those logs shipped out as recorded by the PNG Forest Authority.[3] These arrangements with TSL disrespected other members of the Lolo lineage, the nine affiliated lineages and the wider village communities. It also brought into prominence the friction between starkly contrasting ontologies, the one based in relationships and the other in profit generated through efficiencies of capital production. Vegter (2005, p. 582), in reviewing the effectiveness of forestry law in PNG, noted that customary leaders become no more than the 'puppets of logging companies' and:

> do not challenge logging companies because the companies continue to offer lucrative profits to the indigenous groups. Thus, their leadership decisions fail to meet the resource and social needs of the communities.

TSL and the Kumo directors ignored any impact their operations might have on the forest environment or community relations in the interests of realising maximum profits from timber exploitation. The directors repeatedly failed to share information or royalties adequately with lineage and *karakara* members.[4]

---

1   The corporation, or rather the lineage, held 14,045 hectares of forest with a project volume of 613,900 cubic metres of timber under a permit titled Maututu (Hargy) 1995–2005. The projected harvest for 1996–2001 was 57,576 cubic metres (Filer, 1997b).

2   In 2013, a government inquiry found systematic violations of laws intended to protect customary land rights and native forests throughout PNG. In August 2016, the PNG Supreme Court found a major log exporting Special Agriculture and Business Lease (SABL) to be illegal, violating the rights of the West New Britain landowners. In 2017 the Globalwitness report *Stained Trade* reported that 6.3 million cubic metres of logs valued at over US$1 billion had been exported (88 per cent to China) under SABL licences since 2009. Under intense political pressure, the prime minister announced the cancellation of all SABLs. Rarely had these leases been converted to cash crops such as oil palm, which was the government's objective, but, rather, were regarded as a timber bounty.

3   An abandoned car in the village indicated where some of these funds were spent. Kumo directors made multiple plane trips to Port Moresby staying in hotels in Kimbe and Port Moresby and spending big on entertainment and food.

4   This may have been used to purchase a car that was used by the ILG chair for several years before it became undriveable.

Though they represented themselves as partners of TSL, the Kumo directors appeared to have little interest in monitoring the activities of the logging company, further inflaming community hostility. On one occasion, TSL began to extract logs from outside the approved ILG area, seemingly with the approval of the Kumo directors who turned a 'white eye' (*mata kea*). In desperation, senior women from lineages other than Lolo raided the loggers' camp, took machinery keys and lodged them with police until the illegal operations were investigated. TSL was subsequently fined. Many villagers condemned the Kumo directors for failing to control the company on 'home' soil, and for failing to extract promises made by TSL to build a classroom at the Baikakea school or to improve the road from Bubuu to Gomu.[5]

In addition, the wider community became increasingly concerned for the forest hinterland, its biodiversity and spirit being. Their unease was confirmed by an incident in 2007. TSL flew the three male Kumo directors to Port Moresby, putting them up in a comfortable hotel. The company had organised passports for the three directors, intending to take them to Malaysia to view the oil palm industry there, thus flagging the intent of TSL to convert the logging lease to oil palm. Just before the directors' departure for Malaysia, they were drinking with the company CEO in Port Moresby when he became violently sick (some say he was victim to sorcery or poison) and later died. TSL abruptly abandoned its operations, leaving the forest area and Bubuu beach strewn with logs. Because these logs were never exported, they earned no royalties for the lineage. The logs still lay on the beach in 2018 as evidence to many of the greed of the Kumo directors and their failure to negotiate a beneficial partnership with the outsiders. For my Maututu interlocutors, the death of the CEO confirmed the amorality of the Kumo entanglements with the Malaysian strangers. This was further confirmed when a Kumo car ran over and killed four pedestrians near Bialla. When the Kumo directors later announced a plan to establish an oil palm estate on the logged land, younger clan members, male and female, and older women, prevented them, intent to preserve the forest and knowing they would see little of the proceeds from oil palm.

---

5   To appease village anger, the logging camp of timber huts on Bubuu beach was later dismantled by the ILG directors and re-erected in Baikakea as two classrooms at the school.

Victoria Stead (2017a) refers to practices of 'intimate exclusion', where neighbours and kin are excluded from recognition in land agreements. She writes:

> power often goes to those able to translate across ontological difference. That is, power goes to those who are best able to position themselves within, and across both modernist and customary systems of land use and governance.
>
> (Stead, 2017a, p. 375)

But the Kumo directors failed to develop, or even pursue, a beneficial partnership with outside companies. The arrangements benefited themselves as individuals but undermined their standing as dividuals. For the wider community, the lack of respectful partnership in the TSL arrangements led to the disasters that befell the company CEO and the fatal accident involving the Kumo car. The ravage of the lineage-affiliated forest visible in wasted logs and stripped foliage, and the piles of logs abandoned on the beach, alerted many in the community to *la iruru* of neglecting relations with the forest beings.

Protecting relations between home and wild

The Roundtable on Sustainable Palm Oil (RSPO), supported by environmental activists and national governments around the world, was established in 2004 to promote the environmental and social sustainability of palm oil production. Although it was not welcomed by the major oil palm producing countries of Indonesia and Malaysia, who recognised it would severely challenge their operating procedures, it became key to the operations of PNG oil producers, as it enabled them to access the European markets that had imposed tariffs on Indonesian and Malaysian oil palm products (Cramb & Curry, 2012). To be accredited under the RSPO, companies were obliged to protect customary land and interests, and to support local populations and improve their living conditions, health and education. They also committed to ensure that no primary forest was felled, and that seas were not polluted by industrial run-off.

The RSPO encouraged companies to work in partnership with indigenous communities, leading to Hargy Oil Palm Ltd (HOPL) working with Maututu in the protection of the Mount Ivi/Lamo Auru caldera. A Gonu entrepreneur obtained a forestry permit over land (Portion 2081) that stretched into the caldera. He then approached HOPL to convert the block to oil palm. Portion 2081 fell under the Special Agriculture and Business Lease (SABL) issued to HOPL, leading villagers to suspect that HOPL was assisting the Gomu man. HOPL staff were adamant that they opposed oil palm on the steep slope of the caldera and could not explain how the man had obtained the permit. The 'big shot' proceeded to register two companies, a sawmill and an oil palm plantation, to develop the block and began processing timber there.

Their recent experiences with Kumo had led Baikakea villagers and other Maututu to a new respect for forest resources and the risk unfettered big men could pose in exploiting—disrespecting—these resources. They were angry that the big shot could do this without consultation with those lineages affiliated to the area. Alerted by HOPL staff, together they raised concerns about the conservation status of the caldera. This led to the registration of the Lamo Auru Community Conservation Association (LACCA) based in Baikakea in 2018. The association formally sought a restraining order from the District Court on the big shot's activities, registering their case through the Division of Forestry and Climate Change. HOPL assisted by engaging lawyers to take him to court. They submitted that forest soils in the caldera could not be issued with private title and opposed expansion of oil palm into the pristine caldera. In the court proceedings, LACCA sought to excise Portion 2081 from the SABL lease and reinstate it as part of the caldera reserve.

The big shot's actions were seen by fellow villagers as amoral in that he did not respect home relationships and affiliations, nor recognise the innate powers of the forest. Their unease was confirmed on 20 November 2018 when his nephew was killed while felling a tree on the site. Baikakea villagers attributed his death to a huge snake, a *taua* spirit called Buabua, that occupied the caldera.[6] Buabua, they said, had been offended by the illegal felling of timber in the caldera and taken revenge on the chainsaw operator. There was sympathy for his widow and three children and two other families who all depended on his income, but this only intensified their hostility towards the big shot for ignoring the court's restraining order. The community demanded he pay full compensation to his nephew's wife and young family.

---

6   Villagers told me that three hunters once encountered it in the caldera and stood motionless while its huge body slithered slowly past.

Rewilding through partnership

The opening up of the island through industrialisation sparked the interest of environmental non-government organisations (NGOs) and scientists in the interior of New Britain. At the same time, the Nakanai Mountains, which lie along the border of West and East New Britain, began to attract adventure tourism, such as kayaking the wild rapids, experiencing its vast biodiversity and exploring its massive cave systems. This was facilitated by some small-scale expatriate tourism operators, but indigenous groups, particularly in East New Britain, also responded to sharing their 'wild' with tourists.[7] In the Bialla area, outside scientific and tourism interest has focused on the caldera of Mount Ivi and its lake Lamo Auru. Such interest grew once the oil palm roads brought access to the rim of the caldera. Indeed, local school and youth groups also began to trek into the lake.

In 1995–96, at the instigation of environmental NGOs, the caldera was proposed as a nature conservation area and potential ecotourism site. But this was largely done without consultation with Maututu and without consideration of the relations they held with forest beings. In their review of such tourist initiatives in New Britain, Gabriel et al. (2017, p. 14) cautioned that, 'too often, local people come to be treated as commodities or objects, or are displaced and dispossessed in the tourism encounter'. Such dispossession occurs through outsiders presuming that their ontological perspective regarding forest and marine resources is the only or the superior one to take.

In anticipation of the proposed nature conservation area, HOPL and the Ewasse school founder Fred Hargesheimer approached Chico University (California State University) to make a comprehensive study of the flora and fauna of the caldera and the lake. HOPL agreed to facilitate the 2007 expedition. The Chico team, on their first visit, stayed at the HOPL executive housing area and HOPL provided a staff member to liaise between them and the Lamo Auru Development Corporation (LADC) representing lineages affiliated with the caldera soil.[8] A group of village young men escorted the university team to explore the caldera and were involved in the collection and documentation of flora and fauna and the mapping of the geographical

---

7   A local villager from Pakia village in the Pomio District is promoting a Trans New Britain Trail that would bring hikers from the south coast near Pomio to the north coast in Meramera territory. Local communities on the south coast have set up the Jacquinot Bay Conservation and Ecotourism Association.
8   The LADC was replaced in 2018 by the Lamo Auru Community Conservation Authority (LACCA).

features of the area. The university team produced a report in July 2008 entitled 'Land Use Recommendations Report for the Management of the Hargy Caldera Phase 1' (Lane, 2008), which proposed:

1. Ecotourism with helicopter landing pad at lake, a small accommodation hut, a rowing boat for travel to interior Nakanai Mountains side of lake, with another helicopter landing pad there. The site would be advertised through Kimbe town tourist venues and HOPL.
2. The charging of bioprospecting fees along the Costa Rican model for those collecting flora and fauna.[9]
3. The accounting of carbon credits.
4. Corporate sponsorship of the project.
5. Expansion of the protected forest as one of the last untouched areas of natural beauty and resources in PNG.
6. The patrol of protected areas.
7. Construction of research facilities.
8. Protection of the area against logging and oil palm incursions.

Under this proposal, the park, including the 930 hectare Lake Hargy (Lamo Auru), would offer hiking, fishing, bird watching, tree climbing, canyoning, caving, kayaking, whitewater rafting, canopy walks and volcano tours to outside adventurers.

The report barely acknowledged people indigenous to the area. It noted local hunting tracks 'that would make excellent hiking trails' (Lane, 2008, p. 7) and suggested that local villagers could be employed as guides, hotel and restaurant staff, drivers, porters and cooks. Further:

> If locals have a vested interest (i.e. are compensated via entrance fees, hired as guides, make handicrafts to sell to tourists, and learn to value their ecosystem for the services it can provide), they will want to watch the park so that the source of their income is not diminished. Community surveillance is the most effective way to patrol a protected area, though it will probably be necessary to have park staff conduct patrols as well.
>
> (Lane, 2008, p. 23)

---

9   According to the report, in Costa Rica a bioprospecting fee was charged for all those seeking pharmaceutical plants, carbon credits were claimed under corporate sponsorship of the parks and international environmental groups were engaged to monitor.

These recommendations reflect the perceptions of this scientific group, which was ontologically primed to objectify the scientific value and tourist potential of the region and to acknowledge local interest only in terms of financial gain. Maututu's deep engagement with the area based on quite different ontological perceptions was not acknowledged.

In her account of change in PNG, Paige West (2016) considered how distinct the ontologies of expatriate and indigene are, and how the knowledges of indigenous and expatriate conservationists could profitably inform one another. By her admission, current exchanges of ideas fall well short of such ideals. As she points out, the solution lies not in the 'development' of the native but, rather, in the enlightenment of the outsider developer or government to the point where they come to accept the value of local engagements with the natural. In the analysis of Neil Smith (2010), this entails the stranger 'developers' recognising that, in their ontological conceptualisation, even specific kinds of natural processes are highly social forms, driven by historic and social needs. Smith shows that these conceptualisations are actually generated by the logics of capitalism rather than the needs of plants, animals or people.

Although the Chico report was ostensibly prepared for the LADC, few if any of the members of that corporation or the wider Maututu people had input into the final recommendations. Instead, a public meeting was held in 2008 at which the Chico University team presented their findings to villagers. The meeting was held at HOPL headquarters quite remote from and inaccessible to most villagers. Only Ben Masori as chairman of LADC with one other director attended. A copy of the report, written in English, was left with the LADC chairman but he did not share it with the wider community. The many proposed actions were designed to be implemented by outsider researchers, sponsors and HOPL without, necessarily, any consultation with local villagers. All the outsiders needed was the agreement of a local Maututu representative to set the proposals in motion, with maximum benefit to researchers, tourists and HOPL. It was another instance of the marginalisation of Maututu villagers as a result of the ontological incompatibility of expatriate and local approaches, and the consequent assumption by expatriates of indigenous incapacity to fully partner with more 'knowledgeable' outsiders.

Altogether Chico University staff and students made three visits to the caldera while Maututu interest in the project turned from cooperation to hostility. On the second Chico research visit, three of the American researchers kayaked alone to the opposite side of the lake where they reportedly explored a deep cave and took away with them something that Maututu claimed looked like a rock or a human skull. They showed villagers photographs of this object but did not return it to the village. Their GPS survey at the lake also aroused Maututu suspicions that the outsiders were looking for something, perhaps gold, some said. Hostility grew when the Maututu former national land commissioner claimed that Chico researchers had not sought permission from the government tourism office in Port Moresby for their visit and did not have permission to do research or take out of the country the photographs, films and material collected at the caldera. Chico provided no report to villagers on this research. On a third visit, in January 2010, Chico personnel stayed in the Bialla town hotel, reportedly because it was too expensive to stay at HOPL.[10] The Chico team had apparently arranged for the HOPL helicopter to drop their kayaks at the lake. However, villagers made their opposition clear, barricading the road with fuel drums to prevent the Chico vehicles gaining access to the track inland. This caused the researchers to cancel this visit.

After the Chico team departed Baikakea, villagers marched on HOPL offices demanding clarity about the Chico–HOPL arrangements. In response, HOPL staff held a meeting in Baikakea that I attended. HOPL was represented by a Maututu university graduate, its indigenous (non-Maututu) sustainability officer and an administrative officer, who emphasised that the company was acting as a facilitator of the project, in accordance with its RSPO responsibility to conserve the environment. The sustainability officer was critical of the Chico team for publishing photographs and findings of their visit without the approval of LADC. He stressed the need for Maututu to be represented by strong leaders and encouraged LADC to maintain their organisational structure and records to ensure the continuity of their government registration. The meeting helped to rebuild a partnership with HOPL but strengthened Maututu frustration with the way outsiders had assumed control over the forest domain.

The Chico recommendations assumed that discussions with one or two representatives of LADC could constitute negotiations with the village community. From the villagers' perspective, however, such big men needed to cultivate relationships within their community. They did not have

---

10 According to California State University records, the Center for Ecosystem Research, including John Lane, received a grant of A$3,000 in 2010 entitled 'Towards designation of the Lake Hargy Caldera, West New Britain, as a special conservation area in Papua New Guinea'.

authority to act alone. A leading woman in the community advised me that discussions with the wider community were essential to air different assumptions and so reach a community consensus. Consensus was possible, but it could not be obtained through the signature of the LADC chairman.[11] The recommendations also assumed that, by attracting outsiders to the unique environs of the caldera, local villagers would benefit from increased economic activities. Maututu were none too confident that they would derive any benefit from this intrusion into their world. For that to happen, they needed to forge a partnership with the outsiders that was respectful of Maututu priorities.

Within the Baikakea community, the failure of LADC leaders to reach a partnership of mutual respect in their dealings with the Chico team led to the demise of LADC. In 2017, Baikakea lineages transferred their support from the LADC to a newly formed association, the LACCA.[12] LACCA was designed as a more inclusive community organisation; it had a new chair and comprised 18 members, two from each of the nine lineages that had fought the Kumo directors over the hydro-electricity development.[13] This new body applied for registration through the Conservation and Environment Protection Authority. Its founding board envisaged it as an active partner in any negotiations to do with Mount Ivi caldera, promoting local perspectives and approaches to 'conservation and environmental protection'.

Significantly, LACCA promoted a greater respect for indigenous cultural and ontological priorities. LACCA advocated not only the beauty and sacredness of the caldera, but also the richness of the local village society, its languages and cultures. It sought the promotion of the whole caldera of Lamo Auru as a conservation area, with bans on hunting and gardening there, under the protection of the nine lineages. The LACCA committee advanced an alternative tourist project that was to include building a number of forest-material guesthouses near the rim of the caldera and from there guiding tourists to the lake. Maututu would offer a range of activities onsite and in the village: canoeing, mountain climbing and bush walking,

---

11 The chairman continued to negotiate with outsiders. In 2014, the HOPL community engagement team helped LADC, with advice from the Provincial Conservation Department, to lodge an application for a US$5,000 grant from the United Nations Development Programme and the Global Environment Facility to initiate a conservation area around the caldera. However, when this application was unsuccessful, village support for the LADC dissolved.

12 See p. 228.

13 The lineages include Giloilouli, Vorega, Kabulu Buleha, Biso, Uge, Gararua and Rosarosa, all recognised by the community as having affiliation with the soils of the caldera, because their ancestors' hamlets were situated within the caldera.

the study of fish, birds and butterflies, and demonstrations of indigenous canoe making, sago processing and cooking. The committee proposed constructing a track to the peak of the volcano, with due respect for the *taua* spirit sites along the way. It intended to train village youth as tour guides and to hold cultural performances that would enhance outsider appreciation of village culture.

The identification of these nine custodian lineages was in itself a highly political event. The village decided that it would not accept any division of the caldera into lineage domains, as had been insisted upon by government in areas outside the caldera. In addition, it did not include the Lolo lineage whose claims over the Lovo River hydro power site had been the cause of so much dissension within the community. The Lolo leaders (Kumo Development Corporation) challenged their exclusion but the LACCA directors insisted that Lolo was simply a lineage within the Gararua clan and was adequately represented by the Gararua leader. The LACCA committee was also ready to recognise the claims of Maututu living in other villages to membership in the nine lineages.

Thirty years of Baikakea engagement with outsiders in respect of the wild hinterland had witnessed consolidation of lineage structures. It also witnessed the acceptance and then rejection of two former ILG associations, Kumo and LADC, in their effort to establish a community organisation registered by government that adequately represented Maututu ontological positions. There was growing recognition of the need for home locals to challenge outsider assumptions about the wild and frustration with the Kumo and LADC leaders who were drawn into acting more like big shots than big men. The partnerships they sought with outsiders through the LACCA proposals would give due respect to the wild, and recognise the interest that outsiders had in the wild, while focusing on partnerships with both the caldera and tourists that would promote home society. I refer to this as 'rewilding' their environment.

Conclusion

> To restore stability to our planet, therefore, we must restore its biodiversity, the very thing we have removed. It is the only way out of this crisis that we ourselves have created. We must *rewild* the world!
>
> (Attenborough, 2020, p. 74)

The term rewilding has become prominent in ecological literature in the last two decades (Monbiot, 2014; Pettorelli et al., 2019). Pettorelli et al. (2019, p. 1) aim to synthesise the literature on 'rewilding as a conservation tool' and see rewilding largely as 'the repair or refurbishment of an ecosystem's functionality'. A key challenge for them is redefining the role of humans in rewilded landscapes. Kim Ward (2019, p. 45) suggests the term 'wildness' as more useful than 'wilderness', as it points to rewilding being relational, between people, and animals, plants and soils, and 'premised on non-human autonomy: the self-willed and self-sustaining qualities of non-human nature'. Butler et al. (2019, p. 387), in their review of rewilding across development contexts, point out the 'predominance of external experts, their knowledge and goals above social considerations and local stakeholders' roles'. They pursue this angle by calling for recognition of 'local actors' ways of knowing … their values … and interests', and advocating for the approaches of 'adaptive co-management' and 'social license to operate' based on trust and transparency (Butler et al., 2019, 396).

While these authors focus on rewilding as restoration of the ecosystem, reflected in Attenborough's quotation above, they acknowledge the social and ontological complexities of restoring wildness, and call for co-learning and co-management. I address these concerns by indicating that Maututu responses to industrialisation have also focused on 'rewilding'. Maututu have recognised that the loss of the wild through industrialisation has impacted 'home' society and, in the last two decades, have endeavoured to restore or recapture that wildness in their relations with the caldera. As in the origin myth, they are asserting that they can revive their lives, their identity and their relationships in a partnership between home and wild agents. Understood as the restoring of partnerships with 'non-human nature', rewilding suggests an awakened consciousness of the richness of the wild in all its 'natural' and spirit forces, and a renewed appreciation of what it can offer to communities when they negotiate productive partnerships with it.

10

Conclusion

The wild and the hunter

When I have been privileged to walk with hunters and healers who know the forest, we have walked in silence. When we have rested to smoke and chew betel nut, we have kept that silence. This silence contrasts so keenly with the noise of hamlet spaces. In silence, the forest explorer is intent on listening and watching, alert to the life of the forest. He observes the passage of birds or the gusts of wind as possible activities of spirit beings, ever alert to what he may learn from them. Similarly, when someone falls sick or has an accident, the elder examines their recent activities for possible dangerous encounters with the wild. To ignore the living world of the forest is to invite misfortune, even disaster.

As Maututu move about the forest or the seas they remain alert to the possibility of encountering spirit entities and other forces with whom they must engage. The surrounding forest zone is dotted with totemic sites, such as mountains, creeks, headlands and reefs at which key encounters with ancestral spirits have occurred and may occur again. As West (2016, 128) notes of Kabe, a Gimi hunter:

> Kabe's hunting is epistemological: it is how he knows the world and how he acquires knowledge. It is how he produces knowledge. It is also a source of his ontology—he understands what exists, what features of objects are essential, what categories things fit into ... and what identifies objects ... One hunts on one's ancestor's lands. With this, one pulls life force of the ancestors into oneself, and into creation and re-creation of self.

Maututu stories reflect such knowledge and inspire villagers' engagement with their local environment. For generations that environment consisted of a vast forest enclosing their scattered hamlets. Out of the forest people carved their gardens and through the forest they hunted game and collected wild fruits. Rather than retreat into the defence of their cleared spaces, Maututu sensed through their narratives that their future lay in exploring partnerships with the beings of the outside world. Mythical heroes formed partnerships with 'natural' species, such as frogs, wallabies, cassowaries, mice, mosquitoes and snakes, based on ancestral, kin or totemic ties. This mythic perspective was, and is, reflected in Maututu openness to partnerships with the outside world; however, it came into tension with the contrasting ontological viewpoints of the outsiders, the colonial administration and industrial corporations.

The following myth suggests the importance of that awareness and the partnership that people must form with the living wild to survive.

> The hunter set up nets in the forest and captured birds, insects and animals. They entreated him not to kill them so he stuffed them alive in his bag. On the way home he was challenged by a *buata* when he climbed the *buata*'s coconut palm. To distract the *buata*, he threw down, one by one, the live beings in his bag. Each time the *buata* caught them and returned to the base of the palm. Finally he threw down the cassowary, which the *buata* chased for some distance. While they were gone, the hunter climbed down and escaped. Next day his older brother went hunting and, despite his brother's warning, killed the birds, insects and animals that he caught in his nets. When accosted by the *buata*, he could only throw him the carcasses, which the *buata* swallowed while remaining at the base of the palm. Finally, the brother himself had to descend and was consumed by the *buata*. His younger brother rescued him by slaying the *buata* and cutting him out of the *buata's* stomach.

The wild is unpredictable and dangerous. The older brother discovers the live birds as partners and survives the wild. The younger brother has no respect for his brother or the live birds and is swallowed by the *buata*. Only the relationship with his brother restores him. This myth reminds us of one narrated in an earlier chapter:

> Orphan fled in shame from his two wives in the village. His grandparent spirit in the forest told Orphan to catch live birds and from these the grandparent constructed a *sapepe* headdress.[1] Orphan emerged triumphantly into the village replete in the headdress of live birds and accompanied by invisible spirits. Trees fell around them. He was thus restored to his two wives.

In this story, Orphan, the social outcast imprisoned by shame, is rescued by the ancestral spirit through the vital energy of the birds. These partnerships help to restore Orphan to his two wives and a respected position in the hamlet.

When Maututu reminisce about the surrounding forest and sea domains it is frequently in terms of the spirits who inhabit the place. The respected storyteller and hunter John Kau explained to me in 2017:

> On the Kabulu Vaa lineage estate there is a huge snake called Olea. It resides in the reef and it resides inland, we can see its mark in both places. It will travel from reef to inland forest. It will chase us on the reef. If it chases us in the forest it will threaten to catch and cook us, singeing our skin. Inland it will take the form of a cassowary. At Buleha there is a huge cassowary that chases any intruder, causing strong winds. It will go onto the mountain or will lie still on the reef, where we see the trail of bubbles. It is associated with the reef called Buleha and with the inland village Buleha, the mountain Paialo and the coastal point of land near Tairobi called Paialo.

His account not only documents the spirit beings sacred to the Kabulu Vaa lineage but also the variety of sites to which the clan and lineage are linked, and the variety of 'natural' events that can be explained 'supernaturally'. Lineage members pass through a domain inhabited by wild beings with whom they expect to engage.

Encounters with the wild have continued despite the disruption that industrialisation has brought. In recent years, I heard stories that I had not encountered before of a tribe of one-legged people who inhabit the mountains beyond Lamo Auru. Some narrators suggested these are the Kol people who live in the mountains above Pomio, others that they are a spirit

---

1 According to one owner of a *sapepe* headdress, Maututu obtained the *sapepe* from Mamusi people. The lower rings of the headdress are sewn with *sasa* vines and *tubeli* shells, and large leaves compose the dome, into which are stuck layers of feathers, the black feathers of the *koau* bird at the bottom, white cockatoo feathers above those, and then red and yellow layers of parrot feathers.

people.[2] One storyteller narrated that a Maututu hunter ventured into these mountains and met and married a one-legged woman. They had a child born with two legs but the hunter was not allowed by his wife's group to take the child to meet his 'home' kin. Finally, in desperation to return to his hamlet, he abandoned his wife and child to return home. He sought a partnership with these strangers in the remote reaches of the forest hinterland, but when this partnership ignored home relations he abandoned it.

Pre-industrial relations with the outside

Maututu myth-tellers referred to their tribal ways as *la masori* (the dark). The term was in no way derogatory but an acknowledgement of the distinctiveness of the ancestral worldview. *La masori* referred to times when small hamlets were scattered through the dark forest, when the violence of *la gata* (spear) and sorcery threatened hamlet residents, and when *suara* (big men) had powerful spirits in their wristbands. It was the time of their ancestors whose spirits continue to partner with their living kin.

My informants contrasted this with *la matagaga* (the light, bright, clear), recognising the transformations brought by colonialism and Christianity. Throughout the twentieth century, outside forces threatened to erase tribal lifeways. Colonial control through *kiap* patrol officers, the aggregation of hamlets into villages, the establishment by pastors of village churches, the alienation of soil, the chaos of the Pacific War and the pressure to pay taxes all challenged tribal ways. However, the 'traditions' (James et al., 2012) of colonialism and Christianity that engaged the Maututu in the twentieth century did not erase their 'tribal' identity; rather, such traditions came to constitute what they recognised as 'the light'. The Maututu perspective passed down through myth, ritual and shared experience advocated partnership with 'wild' outsiders, and, on that basis, they engaged with these foreign ideas and practices while always seeking to articulate those new encounters with the exigencies of home. They actively sought the Christian holy books, invited the pastors, demanded cocoa seedlings and schooling for their children, and spent their new money on consumables from the plantation trade store. The term *la matagaga* reflected their distinct way of viewing the changes of the last century. It refers to the 'clear eye' (*mata*, 'eye'; *gaga*,

---

2   Kol language is reported as a language isolate spoken by 4,000 people, unrelated to the Austronesian languages of the coast.

'without hindrance') enlightenment of beneficial transformation. This is how the Christian era was described, particularly once the revival brought a sense of power to Maututu villages. It was also a term used to describe the other changes associated with modernity, schooling, local government and cocoa. Becoming modern 'they sought ways to draw the outside world into their own and, thereby, gain access to and control over what they perceived as its future possibilities' (Minnegal & Dwyer, 2017, p. 8).

The expatriate strangers, on the other hand, dismissed the 'natives' as lazy and resistant to change. The outside administration dispossessed them of their forests and soil. Failing to build relationships of respect with the expatriates, the villagers denounced them as greedy, arrogant or devious—that is, focused on exploiting rather than partnering with them as hamlet residents. The fundamental distinction between the two perspectives, paradoxically, was that whereas the Maututu were ontologically disposed to engage with and partner the strange and wild, the disposition of the expatriate was to assume that their 'civilised' way was the only way and Maututu were 'stupid' to ignore what was best for them.

Industrialisation's impact

Industrialisation through logging and oil palm has been the major assailant of Maututu life worlds. Industrialisation violated Maututu relations with the forest world. The forest was ransacked, its fauna and flora destroyed and even its spirit sites desecrated. Wild pigs, cassowaries and wallabies were driven deep into inland forests, and the cockatoos and other parrots that could no longer feed on forest fruit trees fed instead on the food gardens, particularly destroying the taro crop, the key prestige food. The sea grass fields with their rich marine life became polluted by mill effluent. All this seemed to run counter to the fourth and fifth goals of the Papua New Guinea (PNG) Constitution, which called for the 'natural resources and environment to be conserved and used for the collective benefit of us all, to be replenished for the benefit of future generations' (Vegter, 2005, p. 557).

Industrialisation introduced a new concept of wildness to Maututu engagements with outside worlds. Like the ogres of the origin myth, the new forces were less open to partnership and were committed to hegemony over the environment and the people. First logging and then oil palm obliterated the forest and the fertility of its soils and marginalised the indigenous populations. In their overview of the oil palm industry in the Asia-Pacific region, Cramb and Curry (2012, p. 225) suggest that 'environmental issues arising from oil palm development have perhaps attracted the most widespread global concern'. In her study of oil palm developments in Papua, Chao (2018b, p. 422) suggests that:

> the oil palm sector is notorious for its destructive environmental impacts. Oil palm plantations reduce biodiversity and destroy the habitat of endangered species. They undermine ecosystem services such as nutrient cycling, water purification, and soil formation and stability, and are major contributors to greenhouse gas emissions.

According to Chao, many Marind characterise oil palm as a murderer. They describe oil palm as 'a destructive, greedy and foreign being … [that] devours the land and drinks up the rivers … [and] even transforms the climate, causing droughts, heat waves and untimely rainfall' (Chao, 2020, p. 11). Maututu also found the oil palm industry threatening, destructive and resistant to partnership, initially confining locals to village limits.

Rist et al. (2010, p. 1022), in their overview of the livelihood impacts of oil palm on smallholders in Indonesia, conclude: 'We must continue to look for alternative production scenarios that allow ecologically and socially sustainable oil palm development.' Such a scenario must start from respect for the smallholders' own ontological perspectives. The Marind viewed oil palm as a wilful actor with whom they sought a relationship and were disappointed when the plant did not 'hug back' (Chao, 2018a). Maututu never spoke to me of oil palm or other plants as actors, but they spoke of the many agentive beings who inhabited the wild. It was with these beings that villagers sought partnerships in building their lineages, their hamlets, their gardens and, ultimately, themselves as dividuals. It was relationships with these beings that were disturbed by the destruction of the forest. Nonetheless, dividuals and groups sought to sustain their world by engaging with the new 'wild' challenges of industrialisation. As with the copra and cocoa that preceded it, oil palm as a cash crop offered opportunities for beneficial transformation of Maututu worlds through respectful partnerships with outsiders.

Unlike the oil palm industry in Indonesia, the Australian administration envisaged that the development of oil palm in West New Britain would be centred on settler and village smallholders. After independence, the PNG Government built on that foundation in its Constitution by stressing the cultural and social dignity of all peoples. But the extent of oil palm plantings raised a further spectre for Maututu: namely, that in the process of replacing the forest, oil palm had also sucked the life out of 'home' lifeways. The spirits and non-human actors of the forest whom they sought as partners were threatened. The abundant area of forest, gardens and streams was reduced so far that Maututu found themselves in dispute over access to soil. With the forests now so distant they were unable to furnish village needs, and with the streams too polluted to drink or even wash in, they were forced to walk inland to natural springs. In the place of the forest, ordered lines of the oil palm monocrop extended up the slopes of the hinterland. The trucks that brought the fresh fruit bunches to the mill rumbled through their hamlets, scattering the dogs and posing a safety risk to children.

Friction was unavoidable as the demands of industrialisation cut across village ways of knowing and being. Initially marginalised by the industry, Maututu responded actively by applying for settler blocks, and some years later planting oil palm on their own soils. However, efficiencies of production were driven by the industrial emphasis on individual responsibility. The individual grower was saddled with a large debt that could only be paid back through optimum harvesting of the crop. The individualism of oil palm production was in tension with the Maututu stress on the dividual formed through mutual respect among kin and hamlet neighbours and exchange relations with more distant partners. This ontological friction only added to other ontological clashes: either land or soil, either lineages and clans as flexible or as exclusive memberships, either hamlets centred on the big man or the big shot, either gender relations that inspired or devalued women's role in transformation, and inheritance of oil palm blocks either through paternal or maternal lines.

Alternative production scenarios

Alternative production scenarios practised by the Maututu anticipated such mutual respect between the distinct ontological perspectives of the global and local, outside industry and home. When more arrogant 'enterprising' villagers assumed the stance of 'big shots' by adopting the values of outsiders they were condemned for their greedy neglect of home relationships. In the Maututu ontoepistemic frame, relational ways of knowing and acting are central to villagers' interactions with the world beyond their hamlet, extending in the industrial era to peoples from mainland PNG and beyond PNG and to a powerful company that guides the local economy and government. In the face of such challenges, Maututu hold to ontologies crafted in their engagement with both *la masori* and *la matagaga* and transformed in their struggles with industrialisation.

This account is therefore premised on the necessity of understanding something of the ontology and epistemology of Maututu villagers expressed in the 'dark' and the 'light' as they focused their interaction with outsiders. How then can we imagine this articulation between such distinct ontologies? Curry and Koczberski (2013, p. 336) indicated that in Oceania:

> indigenous economic and social structures have shown remarkable resilience and a capacity to accommodate change while retaining and even enhancing indigenous socioeconomic practices and values that people hold dear to them.

According to Curry (2003, p. 406):

> smallholders' relationships with each other and with a large, ostensibly capitalist development can be transformed or recast by place-based practices to create an alternative modernity that in practice bears little resemblance to the idealised notions of market economic relationships and the economically rational, utility-maximizing individual.

The account presented here suggests that, even as the outsiders' ontology focused on categorically defining the village or the clan, the precise block of land, the individual bank account, or the authority of the bishop and *talatala*, Maututu instead have prioritised relationships and reciprocity that remain flexible and processual. Maututu have sought to discover in those outside interventions a basis for mutual respect in partnership, a working with sympathetic outside forces to revitalise indigenous community, identity and capacity, just as mythic heroes found allies in the 'wild' species of the forest.

This suggests an articulation of distinct ontological approaches. In West New Britain, Curry (2005, pp. 127, 130) observed the 'inflection of capitalist development to serve non-capitalist ends' and that 'other logics associated with kinship, gift exchange and identity override market economic considerations in what are ostensibly enterprises of the market economy'. Is it possible, Curry (2005, p. 130) asks, 'to imagine futures in which indigenous communities are able to shape how capitalist development is to be embedded in their communities to accord with indigenous sociocultural values and practices?'

This account has attempted to explore such an approach, to imagine through their ontology how Maututu engage with the outside world. Maututu have never shied away from the challenges of partnering with the wild. The theme of praising the hero who engages with the wild to wrest benefit for villagers at home is constant in their mythology. Maututu leaders brought cocoa into the village economy and pioneered its processing in fermentary and drier, as they had done previously with copra. They enthusiastically embraced the new crop of oil palm, moulding it into an alternate modernity that continues to stress the values of exchange and reciprocity. In doing so, 'home' has been transformed. Lineages have become more compact, even corporate as incorporated land groups, and the *posalagu* arrangement allows fathers to pass on their blocks to their first child. Oil palm revenue is subject to communal needs, such that in harvesting routines, households respond less to the demands of debt repayments and more to the social demands of exchange, school fees, house construction and the like. The wild of the oil palm has, in these ways, become absorbed in new engagements with the 'home', and village life has benefited in ways not foreseen by government and company planners. In this context, Maututu endeavour to maintain a balance in livelihood strategies between food gardens and cash crops, and to educate their children for roles beyond the village, while preserving their sense of pride in their group identity and in their relations with the spiritual world.

Viveiros de Castro (2015, p. 10), citing Jensen and Morita (2012), suggested that 'ontologies are never hermetically sealed but always part of multiple engagements'. Chao (2022) refers to multiple ontologies 'rubbing against each other'. In a similar approach, Minnegal and Dwyer (2017, p. 15) suggested that 'people slide in and out of multiple frames of reference', what Viveiros de Castro (2015, p. 9) termed the 'war of worlds', or de la Cadena and Blaser (2018) referred to as political ontology or 'a world of many worlds'. Paige West (2016, p. 27) suggests that what emerges is a new symbolic order and, connected to it, new modes of being and knowing. This then is *la matagaga* that Maututu set alongside *la masori*, seeking to embrace multiple worlds within their new world. Building partnerships with the outside has led to radical transformations. I have stressed that, in their affirmation of *la matagaga*, Maututu resisted and protested the imposition of worlds that negate their own. We see this in their many attempts to regain lost soil and assert their identification with the forest world, their demands for cocoa and oil palm seedlings earlier denied to them, their demand for 'tribal' educational material, their protests against illegal logging and industrial pollution of waterways and seas, and their rejection of 'big shots'. Women played a lead role in these protests, just as they did in the revival and the rewilding movements, and in the myths.

Minnegal and Dwyer (2017, p. 268) noted among the Kubo that once 'outsiders departed, as they usually did, people returned to conventional ways of living', but this account of the Maututu suggests otherwise. Instead, they forged partnerships that not only enriched community life but also transformed it. They recognised that entanglement with the strange outside necessitated engagement, leading to transformation in their own social relationships of 'home'.

Ontological delegation

My initial understanding of this Maututu perspective was derived from their mythology but it became clear that this was mirrored in language, ritual and dance, and hamlet relations. I charted it in responses to colonial and industrial worlds. The centrality of myth in framing local ontology was stressed by West (2016, p. 216) with regards to another PNG people, the Gimi of the Eastern Highlands Province:

> Gimi philosophy, as articulated in narratives of past events, crafts both ontology, or a set of propositions about what is in the world, and epistemology, as the story is then used by Gimi women (and men) to understand what is happening in the present. A tale some might have discounted as a 'myth' is actually a clear set of propositions that help people understand and be in the worlds they create and in the worlds that they are cast into with outside interventions of all kinds.

Stella (2007, p. 39) states that myth in PNG narrates the meaning of existence, and that PNG oral traditions draw attention to the importance of land and place as the partner of people in reciprocal relations.[3] Viveiros de Castro (2015, p. 6) suggests that, as we all face the ecological catastrophe, we will increasingly look to 'people whose world has already ended' to provide guidance to survival. This recognition of Maututu ontological positions seeks to do that.

I am conscious of the risk of misrepresenting indigenous thought. Writing can be an act of colonisation, a technology of knowledge and (dis)possession (Stella, 2007, pp. 58, 82). Ontological delegation demands 'that the anthropologist is forced to take his/her own ontological assumptions out of the strongbox and risk their robustness and transportability by letting

---

3 Halvacsz (2020, p. 55) confirms this for the Biangai people of PNG: 'Land is alive and enters directly into constitution of persons.'

them be counter-analysed by indigenous knowledge practices' (Viveiros de Castro, 2015, p. 7). As Strathern (1987, p. 257) noted, anthropology's problem is 'how to create an awareness of different social worlds when all at one's disposal is terms which belong to one's own'. Chao (2020, p. 514) recommends 'careful translation work across ontoepistemic divides that are certainly consequential but not necessarily insurmountable'. She warns both of 'the reification of difference across distinct cultural groups, particularly in the context of indigenous lifeworlds', and of 'ontological anthropology's indifference to the power dynamics that crosscut and reconfigure situated lifeworlds' (Chao, 2020, p. 515; cf Turner, 2009).

I have attempted in this account to represent something of the distinct Maututu ontology, while indicating a diversity of interpretations of that in daily lives. Such an account will always be a caricature. To take the ontology of others seriously, according to Viveiros de Castro (2015, p.14), is 'to learn to be able to speak well to the people you study … to speak about them to them in ways they do not find offensive or ridiculous'. I was always an outsider, but one who sought a relationship with Maututu long before I glimpsed their distinctive perspective. For their part, Maututu sought a partnership with me. They had specifically asked for help to integrate *la masori* into the school classroom. They accepted me into kinship relationships and later recruited me to assist their cocoa cooperative and their dealings with the outside.

What does it take to bring distinct parties and ontologies together in a way that is mutually beneficial? The answer has to be in challenging hegemonic conceptions of development and progress, profit and the future, and in sensing and respecting indigenous ontological frames. This process can, perhaps, most hopefully be entertained in a country with a constitution that respects 'traditional' ways and cosmologies, and in which politicians still live lives interwoven with village kin and *wantok*. The pluriverse approach pursued in this analysis has allowed us to imagine the world through others' eyes and ways, and to question the dogmatic one-world world in which we assume that, apart from some insubstantial cultural variance, we are all looking through the same glasses. The analysis has clearly shown that land, sea, forest, natural species, cash crops and money assume very different meanings for the different protagonists in this story, because they view them from the perspective of different ontologies.

In 2008, on my return to Bialla after a 33-year absence, I was accompanied by Lydia Gah, who was at school in Uase when I taught there and is now living in Australia. Together we participated in *e rae* dances in the village. Afterwards she exhorted the crowd to continue to perform such dances as an important element of Maututu culture, and asked me to make a similar appeal. It struck me that, whereas for the two of us, dance might be conceived as keeping alive tribal *kastom*, for those who danced this was confirmation and celebration of a distinct relational ontology. It was not *kastom* as a 'thing' in terms of static display but a process of re-formation of dividuals and groups. As such, it has thrived through all the transformations of modernity. In 2024, *e rae* accompanied the ordination of three Maututu United Church ministers. Maututu engage with Christianity and *tavulovulo* (culture, tradition), with *la masori* and *la matagaga*, with subsistence gardens and cash crops, with cooperatives and industrial corporations, with village meetings and district courts, and with the wild forest and the domestic hamlet *karakara* to forge who they want to be and what goals they seek. In seeking fruitful exchange with outside actors, people articulate outside ideas and practices with local 'home' patterns of community. In the 'rewilding' venture of ecotourism, Maututu see their *tavulovulo* of lineage and hamlet communities and their respect for the wild forest as something valuable to be shared with outsiders. As they look to the future, many of my Maututu friends dream not of more oil palm or cocoa, but of regaining their lost soils and protecting the forests and seas. They also seek a revived sense of identity built around a revitalised Maututu culture, strengthened relationships, and a steady stream of young people engaging with the 'wild' by gaining an education and employment beyond the village. They anticipate that, with that knowledge and those relationships, the youth will return to reinvigorate community life, like the mythic heroes. This is not a return to the past but a negotiation of new ways and a transformation of community through partnering the wild.

Glossary

Note: Tok Pisin origin terms are marked TP. Kuanua origin terms marked K. All other terms are Maututu.

ata	above on the mountain slopes
bali	foreign, outside
baramana (K)	young men, youth, youth group
big het (TP)	big head, arrogant people, troublemakers, big shot
bili	overwhelm, kill
bua	betel nut, *buai* (TP)
buata	grotesque giant spirits, wild spirit being
didiman (TP)	agricultural field officer
e rae	type of traditional dance
gala	outside, foreign, strange
galamo	slit-gong
gata	spear
gavman (TP)	government
gilogo	compassion
go	go (in a certain direction, as in *goale*, *gomuli*)
-ale	-southwards along the coast
-gala	-outside, into the strange
-ilo	-inland
-lau	-seawards
-muli	-northwards along the coast
-rai	-inland
-rivo	-to the gardens
-talo	-down the coast
gogo	care for, fond of, generous to
gris (TP)	bribe

halulu	shadow, ghost
hitu (Bileki)	spirit
hoihoi	forest
hulumu	men's house
isa-gu	my aunt
Jesu Karisto	Jesus Christ
kadere (TP)	my friend
kalulu	spirit
kaluvuti	finished, died out
kampani (TP)	company, communal plot
kansil (TP)	ward councillor
kapti (TP)	food fairs
karakara	hamlet groups
kastom (TP)	culture, traditions
kiap (TP)	patrol officer
kilisi (TP)	police cell
koi	wild betel nut
koimu	type of tree (*Octomeles sumatrana*)
komiti (TP)	government village leader
la	(article) prefixed to the majority of nouns
La (A)uru	Mighty (God)
la iruru	being lost, error, sin
La Kalou	God (term adopted from Kuanua)
lagu	forward, in front
lain (TP)	group
lain ologala	outside groups
lapu la valua	attract people
latula gola	orphan
lotorobo	protect by purchase
lovo	fly, flying
luluai	village headman
luma	home, house
lus frut (TP)	loose fruit

magasa	soil
mage	major feast
malo	laplap cloth, wrapped around body
mapa	price, value
mapa la magasa	price of soil, value of soil
mapa la vuluti	an instalment of bridewealth passed from the husband's group to the wife's group
maratatila	matrilineage, clan
mari	wisdom
markim mun (TP)	monthly rotation
maroto	type of dance, partner in dance of that name
masori	dark, traditional times
masta (TP)	expatriate white people
masta mak (TP)	Surveyor
mata kea	white eye, blind eye
matagaga	bright, clear, the light
mautu (maut?utu)	hamlet, village (villages)
moimosi (sing. mosi)	hostile agents, strangers, enemies
no gut tok (TP)	bad talk
o-	at, as in compounds above under *go-*
olu	sacred locations, sacred site
Papa God (TP)	Father God
pigo halaba	new born
polisboi (TP)	native police
posolagu	first child, first born
pupu	my grandparent
raskol (TP)	hoodlum, criminal
raunwara (TP)	lake
ruvu	totem
saiogi	strangler fig
sapepe	headdress of bird feathers
savei (pl. saveivei)	human-like spirit
sibitala halaba	appear in fresh form

siloa	type of dance
so-	towards, as in compounds above under *go-*
tabaragu	my brother
tabu (TP)	my in-law
tagu la ivula	adorn one's hair
tahalo	man, person
tahalo auru	big man
tahalo la igototolola	angry man, aggressive, impetuous
tahalo la vuluti	men of wealth
tahaloa	personify, take it into one's person
tailagu	my cross-cousin
talatala (K)	ordained minister, reverend
tama-la	father of
tambu	nassarius/nassa shells
tao la pou makovula	person of shame/silence/sitting in secret, introvert
tao la tulugala	person of anger/talk/movement/hyper-sexual activity, assertiveness and mobility
taogu	my namesake
taua	type of wild spirit
tautauoilo	store inside, believe
tavulovulo	ways, culture, traditions
tavulovulo halaba	fresh ways
tila (pl. tatila)	mother
tilogo	respect
tuali	gold-lip shells
tubeli	nassarius/nassa shell
tultul (TP)	government hamlet leader
tulugala	restlessness
uele	almond nuts and tree
ulu	breadfruit tree and fruit
uma	my father, dad
vai-karakara	speaking together
vaipalahia	revealed/brought into existence

vakakuala	ritual beating of male dancers by women
vauta	deaf, foolish, forgetful, mad
visigolo	lie, deceive
vogari	difficult, strong
vogari te la igogolu	hardworker
vuluti	exchange valuables
vunatarai (K)	matrilineal descent groups, clan/lineage group
wantok (TP)	own ethnic group
wok bung wantaim (TP)	cooperative labour
wokakea	white people
wokman blong gavman	government labourers
wokurukuru	black people

Appendix

Table A.1: Population of Bialla area, July 1973

Village	Child		Adult		Absent		Total
	Male	Female	Male	Female	Male	Female	
Gigipuna	15	24	18	16	2	1	76
Bubuu	33	34	36	29	10	0	142
Baikakea	39	45	33	24	2	0	143
Apupulu	43	35	34	32	3	1	148
Gomu	42	62	67	49	9	11	240
Uase	55	50	65	58	16	8	252
Matililiu	46	44	56	40	4	2	192
Mataruru	13	11	16	12	1	0	53
Kiava	10	8	17	9	0	0	44
Total	296	313	342	269	47	23	1,290

Source: Author's research based on government patrol reports.

Table A.2: Airmen's Memorial School admissions of commencing students

Village	1964	1965	1966	1967	1968	1969	Total
Mataruru/Kiava	2	0	0	0	0	8	10
Matililiu	28	3	1	7	8	5	52
Uase	53	5	0	16	17	2	93
Gomu	7	7	35	9	11	1	70
Apupulu	2	6	16	7	6	2	39
Baikakea	0	3	12	6	5	3	29
Bubuu	0	2	15	3	3	5	28
Meramera	1	4	8	0	1	0	14
Uasilau/Silanga	2	11	0	0	0	14	27
Kaiamo/Tairobi	1	6	8	0	5	6	26

Village	1964	1965	1966	1967	1968	1969	Total
New admissions	96	47	95	48	56	46	388

Source: Author's research based on school reports.

Table A.3: Profit (loss) accounts of Maututu Cooperative Society ($)

Year	Trade store	Copra	Cocoa
1963/64	146	336	–
1964/65	636	216	(–352)
1965/66	716	(–73)	987
1966/67	(–2,000)	(–2,000)	1,000
1967/68	(–1,200)	0	(–600)

Source: Author's research based on business development field records.

References

Allen, M & Monson, R. (2014). Land and conflict in Papua New Guinea: The role of land mediation. *Security Challenges, 10*(2), 1–14.

Anderson, T. (2006). *Oil palm and small farmers in Papua New Guinea.* Centre of Environmental Law and Community Rights.

Attenborough, D. (2020). *A life on our planet: My witness statement and a vision for the future.* Witness Books.

Badiou, A. (2003). *Saint Paul: The foundation of universalism.* Stanford University Press.

Bank, W. (1965). *The economic development of the Territory of Papua New Guinea: Report of a mission organized by the IBRD.* Johns Hopkins University Press.

Bariasi, A. (2020, 14 August). Revival preacher remembered. *The National.*

Barry, M. (1933). *Bialla [virgin land, New Britain District].* Plan of Property Bialla District of New Britain, scale 1:20,000—subitem. Canberra.

Bolyanatz, A. (2000). *Mortuary feasting on New Ireland: The activation of matriliny among the Sursurunga.* Praeger. doi.org/10.5040/9798216978619.

Butler, JRA, Young, JC & Marzano, M. (2019). Adaptive co-management and conflict resolution for rewilding across development contexts. In N Pettorelli, SM Durant & JT du Toit (Eds.), *Rewilding* (pp. 386–412). Cambridge University Press. doi.org/10.1017/9781108560962.019.

Chao, S. (2018a). In the shadow of the palm: Dispersed ontologies among Marind, West Papua. *Cultural Anthropology, 33*(4), 621–49. doi.org/10.14506/ca33.4.08.

Chao, S. (2018b). Seed care in the palm oil sector. *Environmental Humanities, 10*(2), 421–46. doi.org/10.1215/22011919-7156816.

Chao, S. (2020). A tree of many lives: Vegetal teleontologies in West Papua. *Hau: Journal of Ethnographic Theory, 10*(2), 514–29. doi.org/10.1086/709505.

Chao, S. (2022). *In the shadow of the palms: More-than-human becomings in West Papua*. Duke University Press. doi.org/10.1515/9781478022855.

Chowning, A. (1969). Recent acculturation between tribes in Papua-New Guinea. *The Journal of Pacific History*, *4*(1), 27–40. doi.org/10.1080/00223346908572144.

Chowning, A. (1978). Changes in West New Britain trading systems in the twentieth century. *Mankind*, *11*(3), 296–307. doi.org/10.1111/j.1835-9310.1978.tb00660.x.

Chowning, A. (1989). Sex, shit and shame: Changing gender relations among the Lakalai. In M Marshall & JL Caughey (Eds.), *Culture, kin and cognition in Oceania: Essays in honour of Ward Goodenough* (pp. 17–32). American Anthropological Association.

Clifford, J. (2001). Indigenous articulations. *The Contemporary Pacific*, *13*(2), 468–90. doi.org/10.1353/cp.2001.0046.

Colchester, M, Jiwan, N, Andiko, SM, Firdaus, AY, Surambo, A & Pane, H. (2006). *Promised land. Palm oil and land acquisition in Indonesia: Implications for local communities and indigenous peoples*. Forest Peoples Programme/Perkumpulan Sawit Watch.

Cooter, RD. (1991). Kin groups and the common law process. In P Larmour (Ed.), *Customary land tenure: Registration and decentralisation in Papua New Guinea* (pp. 33–50). Institute of Applied Social and Economic Research.

Cramb, R & Curry, G. (2012). Oil palm and rural livelihoods in the Asia-Pacific Region. *Asia Pacific Viewpoint*, *53*(3), 223–39. doi.org/10.1111/j.1467-8373.2012.01495.x.

Curry, G. (1999). Markets, social embeddedness and precapitalist societies: The case of village tradestores in Papua New Guinea. *Geoforum*, *30*(3), 285–98. doi.org/10.1016/S0016-7185(99)00020-2.

Curry, G. (2003). Moving beyond postdevelopment: Facilitating indigenous alternatives for 'development'. *Economic Geography*, *79*(4), 405–23. doi.org/10.1111/j.1944-8287.2003.tb00221.x.

Curry, G. (2005). Reluctant subjects or passive resistance? A commentary on JK Gibson-Graham's 'Surplus possibilities: Postdevelopment and community economies'. *Singapore Journal of Tropical Geography*, *26*(2), 127–31. doi.org/10.1111/j.0129-7619.2005.00209.x.

Curry, G & Koczberski, G. (2007). *Social assessment report for the Smalholder Agriculture Development Project (SADP) Papua New Guinea*. Curtin University of Technology.

Curry, G & Koczberski, G. (2009). Finding common ground: relational concepts of land tenure and economy in the oil palm frontier of Papua New Guinea. *The Geographical Journal, 175*(2), 98–111. doi.org/10.1111/j.1475-4959.2008. 00319.x.

Curry, G & Koczberski, G. (2012). Relational economies, social embeddedness and valuing labour in agrarian change: An example from the developing world. *Geographical Research, 50*(4), 377–92. doi.org/10.1111/j.1745-5871.2011.00 733.x.

Curry, G & Koczberski, G. (2013). Development implications of the engagement with capitalism: Improving the social returns of development. In F McCormack & K Barclay (Eds.), *Research in Economic Anthropology* (pp. 335–52). Emerald Group Publishing Limited. doi.org/10.1108/S0190-1281(2013)0000033015.

Curry, G, Koczberski, G & Inu, SM. (2019). Women's and men's work: The production and marketing of fresh food and export crops in Papua New Guinea. *Oceania, 89*(2), 237–54. doi.org/10.1002/ocea.5222.

Curry, G, Nake, S, Koczberski, G, Oswald, M, Rafflegeau, S, Lummani, J, Peter, E & Nailina, R. (2021). Disruptive innovation in agriculture: Socio-cultural factors in technology adoption in the developing world. *Journal of Rural Studies, 88*, 422–31. doi.org/10.1016/j.jrurstud.2021.07.022.

de la Cadena, M. (2010). Indigenous cosmopolitics in the Andes: Conceptual reflections beyond 'politics'. *Cultural Anthropology, 25*(2), 334–70. doi.org/ 10.1111/j.1548-1360.2010.01061.x.

de la Cadena, M & Blaser, M (Eds.). (2018). *A world of many worlds*. Duke University Press. doi.org/10.1215/9781478004318.

Department of External Territories. (1968). *TPNG patrol reports*. Australian Government.

Department of the Senate. (1973). *Palm oil industry (South Pacific Oil Palm Development Pty Ltd Agreement) Ordinance 1972*. Australian Government.

Dove, MR. (1983). Theories of swidden agriculture, and the political economy of ignorance. *Agroforestry Systems, 1*, 85–99. doi.org/10.1007/BF00596351.

Elahi, KQ-I & Michael, PS. (2017). Oil palm plantation, smallholders and land settlement schemes in Papua New Guinea. *Contemporary PNG Studies: DWU Research Journal, 26*, 15–29.

Emmery, P. (1970). *Increasing economic efficiency from plantation tree crops* [Paper presentation]. 42nd ANZAAS Congress, Port Moresby.

Epstein, AL. (1969). *Matupit: Land, politics and change among the Tolai of New Britain*. Australian National University Press.

Epstein, TS. (1968). *Capitalism, primitive and modern: Some aspects of Tolai economic growth*. Australian National University Press.

Escobar, A. (2016). Thinking-feeling with the earth: Territorial struggles and the ontological dimension of the epistemologies of the South. *Revista de Antropologia Iberoamericana, 11*(1), 11–32.

Eves, R. (1998). *The magical body: Power, fame and meaning in a Melanesian society*. Harwood Academic Publishers.

Filer, C. (1997a). Introduction. In C Filer (Ed.), *Political economy of forest management in Papua New Guinea*. National Research Institute.

Filer, C. (1997b). A statistical profile of Papua New Guinea's log export industry. In C Filer (Ed.), *The political economy of forest management in Papua New Guinea*. National Research Institute.

Filer, C. (2007). Local custom and the art of land group boundary maintenance in Papua New Guinea. In J Weiner & K Glaskin (Eds), *Customary land tenure and registration* (pp. 135–73). ANU E Press. doi.org/10.22459/CLTRAPNG. 06.2007.08.

Filer, C. (2014). The double movement of immovable property rights in Papua New Guinea. *The Journal of Pacific History, 49*(1), 76–94. doi.org/10.1080/00 223344.2013.876158.

Filer, C & Lowe, M. (2011). One hundred years of land reform on the Gazelle Peninsula: A Baining point of view. In V Strang & M Busse (Eds.), *Ownership and appropriation* (pp. 149–70). Routledge. doi.org/10.4324/9781003086239-10.

Filer, C & Sekhran, N. (1998). *Loggers, donors and resource owners: Policy that works for forests and people*. International Institute for Environment and Development.

Fingleton, J. (2007). A legal regime for issuing group titles to customary land: Lessons from the East Sepik. In J Weiner & K Glaskin (Eds.), *Customary land tenure and registration in Australia and Papua New Guinea: Anthropological perspectives* (pp. 15–38). ANU E Press. doi.org/10.22459/CLTRAPNG.06.2007.02.

Fleming, T. (1972). The company view. In JP Longayroux, T Fleming, A Ploeg, RT Shand, WF Straatmans & W Jona (Eds.), *Hoskins development: The Role of oil palm and timber*, New Guinea Research Bulletin.

Foster, RJ. (2005). Afterword: Frustrating modernity in Melanesia. In J Robbins & H Wardlow (Eds.), *The making of global and local modernities in Melanesia* (pp. 207–216). Ashgate.

Foucault, M. (1980). *Power/knowledge.* Harvester Press.

Gabriel, J, Filer, C, Wood, M & Foale, S. (2017). Tourist initiatives and extreme wilderness in the Nakanai mountains of New Britain. *Shima, 11*(1). doi.org/10.21463/shima.11.1.11.

Gah, L. (2020). *Survive and thrive: My courageous journey out of domestic violence.* Ultimate World Publishing.

Gewertz, D & Errington, F. (2016). Retelling Chambri lives: Ontological bricolage. *The Contemporary Pacific, 28*(2), 347–81. doi.org/10.1353/cp.2016.0031.

Globalwitness. (2017). *Stained trade: How US imports of exotic floring from China risk driving the theft of indigenous land and deforestation in Papua New Guinea.* globalwitness.org/en/campaigns/forests/stained-trade.

Golub, A. (2007). Ironies of organization: Landowners, land registration, and Papua New Guinea's mining and petroleum industry. *Human Organization, 66*(1), 38–48. doi.org/10.17730/humo.66.1.157563342241q348.

Goodenough, W. (1962). Kindred and hamlet in Lakalai, New Britain. *Ethnology, 1*(1), 5–12. doi.org/10.2307/3772925.

Gregory, C. (1982). *Gifts and commodities.* Academic Press.

Grieve, RB. (1986). The oil palm industry of Papua New Guinea. *Australian Geographer, 17*(1), 72–76. doi.org/10.1080/00049188608702902.

Guinness, P. (1973). *Bush and village: An analysis of Maututu Nakanai mythology* [Unpublished MA thesis]. University of Sydney.

Guinness, P. (1982). Transmigrants in South Kalimantan and South Sulawesi. In GW Jones & HV Richter (Eds.), *Population resettlement programs in Southeast Asia.* Development Studies Centre.

Hahl, A. (1980). *Governor in New Guinea.* Australian National University Press.

Halvacsz, JA. (2020). *Gardens of gold: Place-making in Papua New Guinea.* University of Washington Press. doi.org/10.1515/9780295747613.

Hargesheimer, F. (2005). *The school that fell from sky.* eBookstand Books.

Holznecht, H. (1997). Problems of articulation and representation in resource development: The case of forestry in Papua New Guinea. *Anthropological Forum, 7*(4), 549–73. doi.org/10.1080/00664677.1997.9967474.

Houghton, E. (2017). *Courting disputes: The materialisation and flexibility of a dispute forum network in West New Britain, Papua New Guinea* [Unpublished PhD thesis]. University of Kent.

Hulme, D. (1984). *Land settlement schemes and rural development in Papua New Guinea* [Unpublished PhD thesis]. James Cook University.

Independent State of Papua New Guinea. (1975). *Constitution.* paclii.org/pg/legis/consol_act/cotisopng534.pdf.

Ingold, T. (1994). Humanity and animality. In T Ingold (Ed.), *Companion encyclopedia of anthropology: Humanity, culture and social life* (pp. 14–32). Routledge.

James, P, Nadarajah, Y, Haive, K & Stead, V. (2012). *Sustainable communities, sustainable development: Other paths for Papua New Guinea.* University of Hawai'i Press. doi.org/10.21313/hawaii/9780824835880.001.0001.

Jebens, H. (2000). Signs of the Second Coming: On eschatological expectation and disappointment in Highland and Seaboard Papua Guinea. *Ethnohistory, 47*(1), 171–204. doi.org/10.1215/00141801-47-1-171.

Jebens, H. (2004). 'Vali did that too': On Western and Indigenous cargo discourses in West New Britain (Papua New Guinea). *Anthropological Forum, 14*(2), 117–39. doi.org/10.1080/0066467042000238958.

Jebens, H. (2010). *After the cult: Perception of other and self in West New Britain (Papua New Guinea).* Berghahn Books.

Jensen, CB & Morita, A. (2012). Anthropology as a critique of reality: A Japanese turn. *Hau: Journal of Ethnographic Theory, 2*(2), 358–70. doi.org/10.14318/hau2.2.018.

Jones, G & Wale, J. (1999). Diversification strategies of British trading companies: Harrisons & Crosfield, c.1900 – c.1980. *Business History, 41*(2), 69–101. doi.org/10.1080/00076799900000258.

Kapia-Mendano, S. (2012). *The effectiveness of extension services provided by OPIC for the production of oil palm to smallholder growers in Hoskins, West New Britain Province* [Unpublished MPhil thesis]. Curtin University of Technology.

Kean, P. (2000). Economic development in the Siki settlement scheme, West New Britain. *Critique of Anthropology, 20*(2), 153–72. doi.org/10.1177/0308275X0002000204.

Koczberski, G. (2007). Loose fruit mamas: Creating incentives for smallholder women in oil palm production in Papua New Guinea. *World Development, 35*(7), 1172–85. doi.org/10.1016/j.worlddev.2006.10.010.

Koczberski, G & Curry, GN. (2005). Making a living: Land pressures and changing livelihood strategies among oil palm settlers in Papua New Guinea. *Agricultural Systems*, *85*(3), 324–39. doi.org/10.1016/j.agsy.2005.06.014.

Koczberski, G, Curry, G & Anjen, J. (2012). Changing land tenure and informal land markets in the oil palm frontier regions of Papua New Guinea: The challenge for land reform. *Australian Geographer*, *43*(2), 181–96. doi.org/10.1080/00049182.2012.682295.

Koczberski, G, Curry, G & Bue, V. (2012). Oil palm, food security and adaptation among smallholder households in Papua New Guinea. *Asia Pacific Viewpoint*, *53*(3), 288–99. doi.org/10.1111/j.1467-8373.2012.01491.x.

Koczberski, G, Curry, GN & Imbun, B. (2009). Property rights for social inclusion: Migrant strategies for securing land and livelihoods in Papua New Guinea. *Asia Pacific Viewpoint*, *50*(1), 29–42. doi.org/10.1111/j.1467-8373.2009.01379.x.

Koczberski, G, Numbasa, G, Germis, E & Curry, GN. (2017). Informal land markets in Papua New Guinea. In S McDonnell, MG Allen & C Filer (Eds.), *Kastom, property and ideology* (pp. 145–68). ANU Press. doi.org/10.22459/KPI.03.2017.05.

Lane, J. (2008). *Land use recommendation report for management of the Hargy Caldera*. California State University.

Lattas, A. (1998). *Cultures of secrecy: Reinventing race in Bush Kaliai cargo cults*, University of Wisconsin Press, Madison.

Lattas, A. (2011). Logging, violence and pleasure: Neoliberalism, civil society and corporate governance in West New Britain. *Oceania*, *81*(1), 88–107. doi.org/10.1002/j.1834-4461.2011.tb00095.x.

Li, T. (2015). *Social impacts of oil palm in Indonesia: A gendered perspective from West Kalimantan*. Center for International Forestry Research.

Li, T. (2016). *Land's end: Capitalist relations on an indigenous frontier*. Duke University Press.

LiPuma, E. (2001). *Encompassing others: The magic of modernity in Melanesia*. University of Michigan Press. doi.org/10.3998/mpub.15532.

Long, G. (1963). Operations on New Guinea. In *The final campaigns: Australia in the war of 1939–1945* (pp. 241–70). Australian War Memorial.

Martin, K. (2006). *After the volcano: Land, kastom and conflict in East New Britain* [Unpublished PhD thesis]. University of Manchester.

Martin, K. (2007). Land, customary and non-customary, in East New Britain. In K Glaskin & J Weiner (Eds.), *Customary land tenure and registration in Australia and PNG* (pp. 39–56). ANU E Press. doi.org/10.22459/CLTRAPNG.06.2007.03.

McCarthy, J. (2010). Processes of inclusion and adverse incorporation: Oil palm and agrarian change in Sumatra, Indonesia. *Journal of Peasant Studies*, *37*(4), 821–50. doi.org/10.1080/03066150.2010.512460.

McCarthy, J & Cramb, R. (2009). Policy narratives, landholder engagement, and oil palm expansion on the Malaysian and Indonesian frontiers. *The Geographical Journal*, *175*(2), 112–23. doi.org/10.1111/j.1475-4959.2009.00322.x.

McKillop, B & Pearson, M. (1997). *History of railways in Papua New Guinea*. UPNG Press.

Minnegal, M & Dwyer, P. (2017). *Navigating the future: An ethnography of change in Papua New Guinea*. ANU Press. doi.org/10.22459/NTF.06.2017.

Monbiot, G. (2014). *Feral: Rewilding the land, the sea, and human life*. University of Chicago Press. doi.org/10.7208/chicago/9780226205694.001.0001.

Mortimer, R. (1979). The colonial state: Paternalism and mystification. In A Amarshi, K Good & R Mortimer (Eds.), *Development and dependency: The political economy of Papua New Guinea*. Oxford University Press.

Mumu, R. (2019, 13 September). Gospel reaches Galilo in 1918. *The National (Weekender)*.

National Archives of Australia (NAA). (1946–48). Australian New Guinea Production Control Board ANGPCB, 'Plantation owners and employees'. A518, JU813/1/12.

NAA. (1947–63). McInnis, D E [Macinnis, Douglas Evan] – Director of Lands Survey and Mines – Papua and New Guinea. A452, 1962/638.

Nelson, HN. (2000). John Keith McCarthy (1905–1976). In *Australian Dictionary of Biography*. National Centre of Biography. adb.anu.edu.au/biography/mccarthy-john-keith-10910/text19375.

Nelson, PN, Webb, MJ, Orrell, I, van Rees, H & Banabas, M. (2010). *Environmental sustainability of oil palm cultivation in Papua New Guinea*. ACIAR.

Olivier de Sardan, J-P. (2005). *Anthropology and development: Understanding contemporary change*. Zed Books.

Panoff, M. (1976). Patrifiliation as ideology and practice in a matrilineal society. *Ethnology*, *15*(2), 175–88. doi.org/10.2307/3773328.

Pettorelli, N, Durant, SM & du Toit, A. (2019). Rewilding: A captivating, controversial, twenty-first-century concept to address ecological degradation in a changing world. In N Pettorelli, SM Durant & JT du Toit (Eds.), *Rewilding* (1–11). Cambridge University Press. doi.org/10.1017/9781108560962.001.

Post Courier. (1970, 3 July). 11 elected to council. *Post Courier*, 12.

Power, T. (2008). Incorporated land groups in Papua New Guinea. In DFAT (Ed.), *Reconciling customary ownership and development*. DFAT.

Rist, L, Feintrenie, L & Levaung, P. (2010). The livelihood impacts of oil palm: smallholders in Indonesia. *Biodiversity and Conservation, 19*, 1009–24. doi.org/10.1007/s10531-010-9815-z.

Robbins, J. (2004). *Becoming sinners: Christianity and moral torment in a Papua New Guinea Society*. University of California Press.

Robbins, J. (2005). The humiliation of sin: Christianity and the modernization of the subject among the Urapmin. In J Robbins & H Wardlow (Eds.), *The making of global and local modernities in Melanesia* (pp. 43–56). Ashgate.

Robbins, J. (2008). On not knowing other minds: Confession, intention, and linguistic exchange in a Papua New Guinea community. *Anthropological Quarterly, 81*(2), 421–29. doi.org/10.1353/anq.0.0007.

Robbins, J. (2010). Anthropology, Pentecostalism and the New Paul: Conversion, event, and social transformation. *South Atlantic Quarterly, 109*(4), 633–52.

Roberts, M. (2013). Ways of seeing: Whakapapa. *Sites, 10*(1), 93–120. doi.org/10.11157/sites-vol10iss1id236.

Rowley, CD. (1972). *The New Guinea villager: A retrospect from 1964*. Cheshire.

Roundtable on Sustainable Palm Oil (RSPO). (2019). *Reflecting on a decade of growth: Impact report 2019*.

Rumsey, A. (2004). Christianity, culture change, and the anthropology of ethics. *Anthropological Quarterly, 77*(3), 581–93. doi.org/10.1353/anq.2004.0032.

Rumsey, A. (2006). The articulation of indigenous and exogenous orders in Highland New Guinea and beyond. *The Australian Journal of Anthropology, 17*(1), 47–69. doi.org/10.1111/j.1835-9310.2006.tb00047.x.

Rumsey, A. (2008). Confession, anger and cross-cultural articulation in Papua New Guinea. *Anthropological Quarterly, 81*(2), 455–72. doi.org/10.1353/anq.0.0013.

Sack, P. (1971). The future of land titles in Papua and New Guinea. *Australian External Territories, 11*(1).

Sahlins, M. (1981). *Historical metaphors and mythical realities: Structure in the early history of the Sandwich Islands Kingdom*. University of Michigan Press. doi.org/10.3998/mpub.6773.

Sahlins, M. (1992). The economics of develop-man in the Pacific. *Anthropology and Aesthetics, 21*. doi.org/10.1086/RESv21n1ms20166839.

Sahlins, M. (2005). On the anthropology of modernity, or, some triumphs of culture over despondency theory. In A Hooper (Ed.), *Culture and sustainable development*. ANU E Press. doi.org/10.22459/CSDP.04.2005.

Salisbury, R. (1970). *Vunamami: Economic transformation in a traditional society*. Melbourne University Press. doi.org/10.1525/9780520378827.

Saulei, S. (1997). Forest exploitation in Papua New Guinea. *The Contemporary Pacific, 9*(1), 23–38.

Simet, J. (1991). *Tabu: Analysis of a Tolai ritual object* [Unpublished PhD thesis]. The Australian National University.

SIPEF. (n.d.). *About Hargy Oil Palms Ltd*. sipef.com/sipef-papua-new-guinea/about-hargy-oil-palms-ltd/.

Slattery, D, Dornan, M & Lee, J. (2018). *Road maintenance in Papua New Guinea: An evaluation of a decade of Australian Support 2007–2017*. Australian Government.

Smith, N. (2010). *Uneven development: Nature, capital and the production of space*. University of Georgia Press.

Stead, V. (2013). Greeting the state: Entanglements of custom and modernity on Papua New Guinea's Rai Coast. *Anthropological Forum, 23*(1), 16–35. doi.org/10.1080/00664677.2012.724008.

Stead, V. (2017a). *Becoming landowners: Entanglements of custom and modernity in Papua New Guinea and Timor-Leste*. University of Hawai'i Press. doi.org/10.1515/9780824856694.

Stead, V. (2017b). Landownership as exclusion. In S McDonnell, M Allen & C Filer (Eds), *Kastom, property and ideology: Land transformations in Melanesia* (pp. 357–81). ANU Press. doi.org/10.22459/KPI.03.2017.12.

Stella, RT. (2007). *Imagining the other: The representation of the Papua New Guinean subject*. University of Hawai'i Press.

Strathern, M. (1980). No nature, no culture: The Hagen case. In C MacCormack & M Strathern (Eds.), *Nature, culture and gender* (pp. 174–222). Cambridge University Press.

Strathern, M. (1987). Out of context: The persuasive fictions of anthropology. *Current Anthropology, 28*(3), 251–81. doi.org/10.1086/203527.

Strathern, M. (1988). *The gender of the gift: Problems with women and problems with society in Melanesia.* University of California Press.

Suratman & Guinness, P. (1977). The changing focus of transmigration. *Bulletin of Indonesian Economic Studies, 13*(2), 78–101. doi.org/10.1080/0007491771 2331333124.

Thomas, A. (2013). *RSPO 4th annual surveillance assessment: Hargy Oil Palm Limited.* BSI.

Threlfold, N. (1975). *One hundred years in the islands: The Methodist/United Church in the New Guinea islands region 1875–1975.* Toksavo Na Buk, United Church, New Guinea Islands Region.

Tsing, AL. (2005). *Friction: An ethnography of global connection.* Princeton University Press. doi.org/10.1515/9780691263526.

Turner, T. (2009). The crisis of late structuralism. Perspectivism and animism: Rethinking culture, nature, spirit, and bodiliness. *Tipiti: Journal of the Society for the Anthropology of Lowland South America, 7*(1). doi.org/10.70845/2572-3626.1098.

Valentine, CA. (1958). *An introduction to the history of changing ways of life on the island of New Britain* [Unpublished PhD thesis]. Pennsylvania.

Valentine, CA. (1961). *Masks and men in Melanesian society.* Lawrence.

Valentine, CA. (1963). Men of anger and men of shame: Lakali ethnopsychology and its implications for socio-psychological theory. *Ethnology, 2*(4), 441–77. doi.org/10.2307/3772956.

Valentine, CA. (1965). The Lakalai of New Britain. In P Lawrence & MJ Meggitt (Eds.), *Gods, ghosts and men in Melanesia* (pp. 162–197). Oxford University Press.

Valentine, CA & Valentine, B. (1979). Nakanai: Villagers, settlers, workers and the Hoskins oil palm project. In CA Valentine & B Valentine (Eds.), *Going through changes: Villagers, settlers and development in Papua New Guinea* (pp. 48–71). New Guinea Research Unit, The Australian National University.

van Rijswijck, O. (1966). *The Silanga resettlement project* (vol. 10). New Guinea Research Unit, The Australian National University.

Vegter, A. (2005). Forsaking the forests for the trees: Forestry law in Papua New Guinea inhibits indigenous customary ownership. *Pacific Rim Law and Policy Journal, 14*(2), 545–74.

Viveiros de Castro, E. (2004). Perspectival anthropology and the method of controlled equivocation. *Tipiti: Journal of the Society for the Anthropology of Lowland South America, 2*(1), 3–22. doi.org/10.70845/2572-3626.1010.

Viveiros de Castro, E. (2012). *Cosmological perspectivism in Amazonia and elsewhere.* HAU.

Viveiros de Castro, E. (2015). Who is afraid of the ontological wolf? Some comments on an ongoing anthropological debate. *The Cambridge Journal of Anthropology, 33*(1), 2–17. doi.org/10.3167/ca.2015.330102.

Ward, K. (2019). For wilderness or wildness? Decolonising rewilding. In N Pettorelli, SM Durant & JT du Toit (Eds.), *Rewilding* (pp. 34–54). Cambridge University Press. doi.org/10.1017/9781108560962.003.

Weiner, J. (2002). *The Foi incorporated land group: Land and custom in group definition and collective action in the Kutubu oil project, PNG.* State, Society and Governance in Melanesia Project, RSPAS, The Australian National University.

Weiner, J. (2013). The incorporated what group? Ethnographic, economic and ideological perspectives on customary land ownership in contemporary Papua New Guinea. *Anthropological Forum, 23*(1), 94–106. doi.org/10.1080/00664677.2012.736858.

West, P. (2016). *Dispossession and the environment: Rhetoric and inequality in Papua New Guinea.* Colombia University Press. doi.org/10.7312/west17878.

World Bank. (2023). *Not just a water system: How a small remote town is flourishing from access to clean running water at their doorsteps.* World Bank Group. www.worldbank.org/en/news/feature/2023/03/21/not-just-a-water-system-how-a-small-remote-town-is-flourishing-from-access-to-clean-running-water-at-their-doorsteps.

Yang, M. (2000). Putting global capitalism in Its place: Economic hybridity, Bataille, and ritual expenditure. *Current Anthropology, 41*(4), 477–509. doi.org/10.1086/317380.

Zelenietz, M & Grant, J. (1986). The problem with *pisins*: An alternative view of social organization in West New Britain. *Oceania, 56*(3), 199–214. doi.org/10.1002/j.1834-4461.1986.tb02133.x.

9 781760 467159